Public Policy and Politics

Se~~ries Editors~~ ~~Joan Pugh and Robin Hambleton~~

Public policy-making in Western democracies is confronted by new pressures. Central values relating to the role of the state, the role of markets and the role of citizenship are now all contested and the consensus built up around the Keynesian welfare state is under challenge. New social movements are entering the political arena; electronic technologies are transforming the nature of employment; changes in demographic structure are creating heightened demands for public services; unforeseen social and health problems are emerging; and, most disturbing, social and economic inequalities are increasing in many countries.

How governments – at international, national and local levels – respond to this developing agenda is the central focus of the *Public Policy and Politics* series. Aimed at a student, professional, practitioner and academic readership, it aims to provide up-to-date, comprehensive and authoritative analyses of public policy-making in practice.

The series is international and interdisciplinary in scope and bridges theory and practice by relating the substance of policy to the politics of the policy-making process.

Public Policy and Politics

Series Editors: Colin Fudge and Robin Hambleton

PUBLISHED

Kate Ascher, *The Politics of Privatisation: Contracting Out Public Services*

Rob Atkinson and Graham Moon, *Urban Policy in Britain: The City, the State and the Market*

Jacqueline Barron, Gerald Crawley and Tony Wood, *Councillors in Crisis: The Public and Private Worlds of Local Councillors*

Danny Burns, Robin Hambleton and Paul Hoggett, *The Politics of Decentralisation: Revitalizing Local Democracy*

Aram Eisenschitz and Jamie Gough, *The Politics of Local Economic Policy: The Problems and Possibilities of Local Initiative*

Christopher Ham, *Health Policy in Britain: The Politics and Organisation of the National Health Service* (third edition)

Ian Henry, *The Politics of Leisure Policy*

Peter Malpass and Alan Murie, *Housing Policy and Practice* (fourth edition)

Robin Means and Randall Smith, *Community Care: Policy and Practice*

Gerry Stoker, *The Politics of Local Government* (2nd edition)

FORTHCOMING

Robin Hambleton, *An Introduction to Local Policy-Making*

Clive Harris, Michael Keith and John Solomos, *Racial Inequality and Public Policy*

Patsy Healey, *Places We Could Make: The Future of Environmental Planning*

Kieron Walsh, *Public Services and Market Mechanisms*

The Politics of Decentralisation

Revitalising Local Democracy

Danny Burns
Robin Hambleton
Paul Hoggett

MACMILLAN

First published 1994 by
THE MACMILLAN PRESS LTD
Houndmills, Basingstoke, Hampshire RG21 2XS
and London
Companies and representatives
throughout the world

ISBN 0–333–52163–3 hardcover
ISBN 0–333–52164–1 paperback

A catalogue record for this book is available from the British Library.

Copy-edited and typeset by Povey–Edmondson
Okehampton and Rochdale, England

Printed in Hong Kong

Series Standing Order   **(Public Policy and Politics)**

If you would like to receive future titles in this series as they are published, you can make use of our standing order facility. To place a standing order please contact your bookseller or, in case of difficulty, write to us at the address below with your name and address and the name of the series. Please state with which title you wish to begin your standing order. (If you live outside the UK we may not have the rights for your area, in which case we will forward your order to the publisher concerned.)

Customer Services Department, Macmillan Distribution Ltd, Houndmills, Basingstoke, Hampshire, RG21 2XS, England

For our parents

Contents

List of Tables and Figures   xi

Acknowledgements   xii

Guide to Reading the Book   xiv

PART I   THE CONTEXT OF CHANGE

1   The Crisis in Local Government   3
    Introduction   3
    Decentralisation versus markets   5
    Local government and economic restructuring   7
    The political space for local government   10
    Big is beautiful – local government in the 1970s   13
    The local government battles of the 1980s   16
    Driving forces for change: exit, voice and self-
        improvement   21
    Conclusion   27

2   Rethinking Local Democracy   30
    Introduction   30
    Empowerment strategies   31
    Developing the voice option   34
    The four Cs: clients, customers, consumers, citizens   38
    Treating people as clients   39
    The customer revolution   41
    Consumer power   43
    Strengthening citizenship   46
    Conclusion   50

3   The Character of Local Political Innovation   52
    Introduction   52
    Two inner-city areas – Islington and Tower Hamlets   53
    The political origins of decentralisation in Islington   56
    The decentralisation strategy in Islington   60
    The political origins of decentralisation in Tower
        Hamlets   64

The decentralisation strategy in Tower Hamlets   67
Constructions of 'community'   71
The nature of political innovation   73

PART II   DECENTRALISED MANAGEMENT

4 Neighbourhood Decentralisation and the New Public
   Management   81
   Introduction   81
   New forms of organisation and management   81
   The new public management   83
   Neighbourhood management   85
   Localisation   89
   Flexibility   94
   Devolved management   101
   Cultural change   104
   Linking the components of decentralisation   107

5 Shaking up the Bureaucracies   111
   Introduction   111
   The organisation and political structures in Islington
     and Tower Hamlets   112
   Localisation – getting closer to the public   114
   The impact of localisation on service priorities   121
   Restructuring for flexibility   124
   Devolved management   132
   Central control and local autonomy   136
   Devolved management and service efficiency   140
   Paying for local democracy?   142
   Cultural change   143
   Conclusion   146

   Decentralised Management: Lessons from Experience   149

PART III   DECENTRALISED DEMOCRACY

6 Citizen Participation: Theory and Practice   153
   Introduction   153
   Participation, choice and control   153
   Spheres of citizen power   158
   A ladder of citizen empowerment   160

Citizen non-participation 164
Citizen participation 166
Citizen control 174
Rethinking the boundaries of citizen control 177

7 Enhancing Participatory Democracy: Islington **180**
Introduction 180
The development of proposals for neighbourhood
  participation 180
The neighbourhood forums: scope and purpose 182
The neighbourhood forums: membership and
  organisation 186
The composition of the forums 189
The operation of the forums 192
Forums and organisational responsiveness 194
Forums and political education 196
Forums and empowerment 198
Conclusion 200

8 Extending Representative Democracy: Tower Hamlets **202**
Introduction 202
Giving power back to local representatives 202
The neighbourhood committees 204
Participation: whose voices are heard? 206
The politicisation of community 210
Old wine in new bottles 213
Liberalism and racism in Tower Hamlets 216

Decentralised Democracy: Lessons from Experience **219**

PART IV   BEYOND DECENTRALISATION

**9 Fragmented Communities and the Challenge to
  Democracy** **223**
Introduction 223
Concepts of community 224
Reflections on a public meeting 234
Imagined communities 236
Communities of interest 240
The idea of civil society: a plea for realism 242
The democracy project 245

The opportunistic state   246
A funny thing happened on the way to the forum   249

10 Local Democracy beyond the Local State   **252**
Introduction   252
Rolling back the frontiers of local government   253
Re-empowering local government   256
Varieties of democracy   262
Consuming politics?   266
Empowering who?   269
Democracy without bureaucracy   270
A pluralistic public service   273
A new vision for the public sphere   277
The 'general good'   280

Bibliography   283
Index   296

List of Tables and Figures

Tables

5.1 Borough-wide housing capital expenditure and allocation in Tower Hamlets, 1982/3–1990/1   136
5.2 Rent arrears: Islington, Tower Hamlets, all London boroughs   140
5.3 'Central' staffing levels in Tower Hamlets   143
8.1 Voter turnout in London Borough elections, 1982–90   211

Figures

1.1 Public service reform strategies   22
2.1 Ways of strengthening voice in local government   35
2.2 Relationships between people and the council   51
3.1 The neighbourhoods in Islington and Tower Hamlets   54
3.2 Typical structure of a neighbourhood office in Islington (1985–91)   63
4.1 Typical complaints about public service bureaucracies   86
4.2 Possible objectives of decentralisation   88
4.3 Neighbourhood decentralisation: an ideal-type model   88
4.4 Levels of devolved resource control   102
5.1 Basic features of decentralisation in Islington and Tower Hamlets   113
5.2 Typical structure of a neighbourhood office in Islington (1992)   115
5.3 The neighbourhood office structure in Globe Town, Tower Hamlets   116
6.1 Arnstein's ladder of citizen participation   157
6.2 Spheres of citizen power   158
6.3 A ladder of citizen empowerment   162
8.1 Tower Hamlets: percentage increase in voter turnout by ward, 1982–90   213
10.1 Varieties of democracy   264

Acknowledgements

A large number of people have helped us to develop the ideas set out in this book and to produce the finished volume. First, we would like to record our thanks to colleagues and friends at the School for Advanced Urban Studies, University of Bristol. We were all involved with the Decentralisation Research and Information Centre when it was based at the School in the late 1980s and early 1990s. Numerous staff worked in or with the Centre and we learnt a great deal from them. These included: Lorraine Cantle, Cynthia Galliers, Lucy Gaster, Syd Jeffers, Lyn Harrison, Murray Stewart and Marilyn Taylor. Our wider debt to the academic community both here in the United Kingdom and elsewhere is recorded in the Bibliography.

Another large group of people who have contributed significantly to the development of the thinking in this book are the hundreds of councillors, officers and activists we have worked with in training, consultancy and research activities. The insights they have provided have been invaluable.

Although this book draws on the research and consultancy we have been engaged in for over ten years, the detailed case study of developments in the London Boroughs of Islington and Tower Hamlets was made possible by a grant from the Economic and Social Research Council (ESRC) covering a two-year period (1989–90). We enjoyed an enormous amount of help and support, not only from members and officers in the two authorities, but also from people living in our case-study neighbourhoods. Our findings are based on a range of research methods, including documentary research, some 300 interviews, and a small number of group interviews. We also attended numerous council meetings, committee meetings, party political meetings, chief officer meetings, neighbourhood management team meetings, service delivery team meetings, neighbourhood forums, neighbourhood forum sub-committees and meetings of tenants' associations.

Among the many people who have helped, we would, however, like to single out a few because of the special support they have given us: Liz du Parcq for her many detailed comments on the Islington case study; Terry Rich for his help throughout the research and for his work on the survey of neighourhood forums drawn on in Chapter 7; Adrian Franklin, who worked extensively with Robin Hambleton and Paul Hoggett during the second year of the ESRC research and who provided many of the ideas concerning the construction of community which are developed in Chapter 3; Frank Tolan, who worked with us during much of the first year of research and who was particularly helpful to us in developing frameworks for considering the impact of decentralisation on service delivery; and Colin Fudge and our publisher Steven Kennedy, whose feedback helped considerably as we put together the final drafts of this book. And finally thanks to Jenny Capstick and Margaret Criddle who provided secretarial support both during the research and the ensuing period when the book was written, and, in particular, special thanks to Lorraine Cantle for typing the final manuscript.

DANNY BURNS
ROBIN HAMBLETON
PAUL HOGGETT

Guide to Reading the Book

Local government in the United Kingdom is having to change and adapt as never before. The driving forces for change are many and varied – they include new public expectations about the role of local government in a changing society, a constant flow of interventions from central government restricting local initiative, and new ideas about the nature of good management in public service organisations. In this book we suggest that neighbourhood decentralisation – that is, decentralisation below the level of the local authority – offers a promising way forward for public service reform.

A sound local government system needs to combine good management with democratic accountability. Decentralisation offers an attractive alternative to market models because it has the potential not only to provide responsive, high-quality services, but also a range of possibilities for strengthening citizen involvement in the governing process.

The book is in four parts. Part I explains the context within which neighbourhood decentralisation has shifted from the periphery to the centre of debates about local government and local democracy. Part II concentrates on the management dimensions of decentralisation while Part III considers the way that decentralisation can be used to democratise public services. Part IV moves the debate beyond decentralisation to examine the notion of community and to put forward a range of suggestions for revitalising local democracy.

Chapter 1 sketches the outlines of the current crisis in local government. It suggests that change in local government cannot be divorced from wider national and international socioeconomic forces which shape the context for local political action. Three major reform strategies for public services – the extension of markets, new managerialism and the extension of democracy – are considered.

Chapter 2 stresses the importance of thinking more deeply about the nature of local democracy. It explores alternative ways of empowering people in relation to the organisations that are intended to serve them. It suggests that, in a public service context, the 'exit' mechanism is, on the whole, flawed and that the alternative strategy of developing 'voice' deserves much more attention. The analysis of four key words used to describe the public – clients, customers, consumers and citizens – suggests that future strategies relating to the strengthening of local democracy should concentrate on the development of citizenship.

Chapter 3 grounds the discussion by focusing on the nature of local political innovation in the inner London boroughs of Islington and Tower Hamlets. These two local authorities have gone further in developing multi-service neighbourhood offices than any other councils in the country. The chapter shows how political activists in the two boroughs were, notwithstanding the suffocating controls imposed by central government, able to use various forms of decentralisation to drive forward significant innovation at local level.

Chapter 4 sets out a new framework for understanding decen-tralised management. It shows how moves towards neighbourhood decentralisation can be situated within broader shifts in the private and the public sectors towards new forms of organisation and management – a shift which seeks to create 'freedom within boundaries'. Following a discussion of the possible objectives of decentralisation an ideal-type model of neighbourhood decentrali-sation is put forward. This suggests that there are four interlocking dimensions of decentralisation: (i) localisation; (ii) flexibility; (iii) devolved management; and (iv) organisational culture change. These dimensions are discussed and illustrated with practical examples drawn mainly from UK local government.

Chapter 5 uses the framework developed in Chapter 4 to conduct an evaluation of decentralised management in Islington and Tower Hamlets. The organisational structures for decentralisation in the two boroughs are described and then each of the four dimensions of decentralisation is discussed in turn. It is hoped that the framework and its application will be useful to local authorities and other organisations wanting to reflect on and develop their own approach to decentralised management.

Chapter 6 examines the concept of citizen participation. It reviews existing concepts and puts forward a new ladder of citizen participation. This has twelve rungs, ranging from civic hype at the bottom to interdependent control at the top. The new framework identifies three main zones on the ladder: citizen non-participation; citizen participation; and citizen control, and illustrates the discussion with examples drawn mainly from UK local government.

Chapter 7 appraises Islington's efforts to develop public participation in local government through a system of twenty-four neighbourhood forums. This imaginative reform has increased public involvement in the borough and helped local people identify shared concerns and priorities for action.

Chapter 8 examines the system of neighbourhood committees in Tower Hamlets and shows how these have strengthened councillor power in the borough and almost certainly increased voter turnout in local elections. While Islington and Tower Hamlets are to be praised for the boldness of their initiatives, the limitations of both models are also considered.

Chapter 9 revisits long-standing debates about the notion of 'community'. It distinguishes various concepts – communities of interest, imagined communities and communities of place – and suggests that the word 'community' is used far too loosely in ongoing policy debates. Using a cameo of a public meeting in east London the chapter shows how local communities are often fragmented and in conflict, and that this poses a major challenge to local political leadership.

Chapter 10 sets out a new vision for local democracy in the UK – one in which local authorities have far more power and develop an outward-looking role designed to shape the local social, economic and cultural environment, as well as extending public accountability into a wide range of public and private institutions which have an impact on the lives of local people. The chapter outlines ways in which local democracy can be reinvigorated by developing the democratic capacity of civil society.

PART I
THE CONTEXT OF CHANGE

1 The Crisis in Local Government

Introduction

Local government in the United Kingdom is currently undergoing a profound shift in the way it organises its activities and the way it relates to the public it serves. The changes of the 1980s and the 1990s have catapulted local government from relative obscurity into a highly visible role at the centre of national political debates. Indeed, it is possible to argue that the public services in general and local government in particular have become the most consistently contentious sphere of politics in Britain in the period since 1979. Driven by pressures from consumers and citizens at local level, by a maelstrom of legislation emanating from Whitehall, and by new thinking within the political parties, local authorities are being forced to change as never before.

In the past the political parties tended to neglect issues relating to local government and local service delivery. Indeed, some politicians looked down on what they saw as the 'low politics' of dropped street kerbs and refuse collection. Not any more. Now all the political parties are at least talking about strategies for improving the quality of public services, strengthening the accountability of councils to their electorates and challenging the inward-looking cultures found in so many town halls.

Despite huge cuts in central government grants, growing numbers of councils are striving to make public services more welcoming, responsive and accountable. As a result, a string of new slogans and catch-phrases has entered the vocabulary of those concerned with local government – for example, 'getting closer to the consumer', 'going local', and 'caring for customers'. Many of these initiatives may turn out to be cosmetic, but enough change is now underway to suggest that numerous councils are undergoing something of a

3

cultural revolution. Central to many of these initiatives is the idea of decentralisation.

In an earlier book, written in the mid-1980s, we argued that decentralisation should not be regarded as a passing fad (Hoggett and Hambleton, 1987). We outlined various political and managerial trends which suggested that support for decentralisation would grow, and explained how decentralisation offered possibilities not only for improving the quality of local public service delivery, but also new opportunities for enhancing the quality of local democracy. In recent years large numbers of councils have opened neighbourhood offices and local service delivery points, devolved power to local managers and experimented with new forms of community consultation and public involvement. It was not obvious that this would happen. Indeed, in the early 1980s, decentralisation was viewed as a radical form of organisation which represented 'a fundamental challenge to established ways of organising and running public services' (Hambleton and Hoggett, 1984, p. 1). Many authorities avoided the idea altogether; others examined the notion only to back quickly away.

Times have changed. Now decentralisation is seen as sensible, mainstream practice in local government. For example, decentralisation figures boldly in discussions about the reorganisation of local government. Many councils, in their bids to the Local Government Commission for unitary authority status, claim that they will introduce decentralised models. Central government has endorsed advice on internal management which invites local authorities to address the 'decentralisation of the decision-making process to the lowest possible level' (Department of the Environment, 1993, p. 29). Few in local government would now doubt that decentralisation is here to stay. It follows that the experiences of the authorities which have pioneered decentralisation are potentially very significant for the future of local government. Despite this, the efforts of these authorities have received comparatively little scrutiny. This book is an attempt to fill that gap.

In the 1980s much of the thrust for change in public services came from the political right. The government of Margaret Thatcher, elected in 1979, embarked on a series of measures designed to weaken the power of local authorities, to reduce central government financial support to local government and to introduce market principles into the process of public service management. Cost reduction, deregulation and, above all, privatisation were catch words of the Thatcher years. Through a stream of interventions emanating from Whitehall the right launched a massive ideological attack not only on the provision of public services, but also on the institutions of local democracy.

Somewhat late in the day, the Conservative Party realised that their onslaught on public services might have gone too far. In July 1991, in a blaze of publicity, John Major launched the government's Citizen's Charter in a bid both to distance himself from the Thatcherite dogma of 'public bad, private good', and to present the Conservatives as a party with a positive agenda for public services (HM Government, 1991). The Labour Party and the Liberal Democrats had published their citizens' charters somewhat earlier and the argument about how to improve the quality of public services has since become a dominant theme in public debates. But we will argue that the Citizens' Charter, while it is a small step in the right direction, does not go nearly far enough in empowering consumers and citizens.

Decentralisation versus markets

Developments at national level have tended to obscure the fact that politicians and managers in local government have been actively pursuing a wide range of local initiatives designed to close the gap between the institutions of local government and the people they are intended to serve. In the last ten years or so media attention has tended to focus on the battle between central and local government over spending cuts and the privatisation of public services and, in the late 1980s, on the struggle over the poll tax. By contrast, there has been comparatively little discussion or coverage of the efforts to decentralise and democratise local government that have been pursued by a large number of local authorities.

There are, of course, many kinds of decentralisation. Some are neighbourhood-based, some focus on projects and some include the devolution of power to voluntary groups. Some approaches are purely managerial, others seek to widen public involvement in council decision-making. Those on the right even argue that the introduction of market mechanisms into public services is the ultimate form of decentralisation, on the grounds that power, in theory at least, is 'decentralised' to the individual service user who can exercise choice between competing service providers. Decentralisation is, then, a slippery term.

It is helpful, in discussions about local government, to distinguish two meanings of decentralisation. On the one hand it is used to refer to the physical dispersal of operations to local offices. In a second sense it is used to refer to the delegation, or devolution, of a greater degree of decision making authority to lower levels of administration or government. In common usage, these meanings are sometimes combined. In this book we are concerned with both definitions – in Chapter 4 we explore these meanings in more depth and identify four dimensions of decentralisation. Here, however, we would simply highlight the potential of decentralisation as a vehicle for 'empowering the people in the neighbourhoods'.

By 'empowering' we mean enhancing the degree of decision-making authority. By 'neighbourhoods' we refer to sub-areas within the geographical area of the authority – these could, in practice, be small districts within a city or villages/small towns within a county. By 'the people' we include the local authority staff working in the neighbourhood, the locally elected councillors, and the people living in the area. Because there are many ways of defining the geographical units and a diversity of possibilities and models for devolving power to the localities, this clarification still leaves scope for a huge variety of forms of decentralisation. It does, however, distinguish decentralisation sharply from the alternative strategy of introducing markets into public services.

For reasons which will become clearer as the argument unfolds, we believe that market models are likely to damage local democracy because, in essence, they promote ways of behaving which are selfish. They tend to accentuate an individualistic perspective. This works against collective concerns and action. Can decentralisation provide, or at least pave the way towards, an alternative to the market model which is not a regression to the bureaucratic local government models of the past? We address this broad question by concentrating mainly on neighbourhood decentralisation. This is not because other forms of decentralisation are unimportant or lack potential for making local authorities more responsive and accountable. Rather it is because the neighbourhood approach provides a promising route towards democratisation which, because it has been tried out in practice, can generate a number of useful insights on the potential for non-market approaches to public service reform.

In many authorities, neighbourhood decentralisation is helping to redefine the relationships between members, officers and citizens – new ways of working are being tried out. In order to lend weight to our claim about the significance of decentralisation we can note that large numbers of local authorities are decentralising their services to neighbourhood level. The magazine of the Decentralisation Research and Information Centre, at the School for Advanced Urban Studies, *Going Local*, has documented since 1984 how these decentralisation initiatives have emerged in a wide variety of settings – inner city areas, peripheral housing estates, small towns and rural areas. Moreover, there is evidence from experience with public policy in several other countries that neighbourhood-based programmes are experiencing something of a resurgence (Carmon, 1990). As we argue further below, there are sound reasons for believing that decentralisation will continue to be a significant trend in local government in the coming years.

Indeed, it is possible to view these shifts as part of a wider movement towards decentralised working which cuts across both public and private sectors. It is certainly the case that, aided by new information technology, decentralised forms of organisation are rapidly developing within private-sector companies across the world, as both management consultants (Peters, 1988; Handy, 1990) and academics (Scott, 1988; Clegg, 1990) have noted. These innovations are, in various ways, being imported into the public sector and we explore this trend further in Chapter 4.

Local government and economic restructuring

While the focus of attention in this book is on neighbourhood decentralisation it is important to locate the discussion within the context of wider debates about the politics of place, the relative autonomy of local government *vis-à-vis* central government, and the polarisation of social and economic conditions within cities. Most academic texts, when they discuss decentralisation, refer to the amount of autonomy local authorities can exercise within the context of national and international political and economic forces. While this is clearly very important, we hope to show that attention also needs to be given to the operation of democracy below the level of the local authority.

Our starting point is that the national and international economy is being restructured and that this has profound implications for local authorities. Theories of economic restructuring are comparatively new and there is no agreed interpretation of the events of the last twenty years or so. However, following Logan and Swanstrom (1990) we can identify some common themes. A fundamental crisis struck the capitalist world economy in the 1970s – not least because of the impact of the first oil cartel of 1973. The so called 'Fordist' regime of mass production and mass consumption of goods, which had dominated many industries for around forty years, ran into serious problems of profitability, with heightened international competition placing new pressures on the organisation of production. The so called 'new' regime of flexible accumulation represents an attempt to resolve the crisis. It requires more flexible labour, short production runs, and high quality production for increasingly specialised markets.

Some commentators dispute the view that Western economies are in the midst of a total transformation from mass production to flexible specialisation. They argue that the shift is less cataclysmic. Few, however, contest the fact that economic restructuring is bringing about significant shifts in the geographical location of production, consumption and residence, and that this has profound implications for local government. City economies have reflected a global change from a goods-producing to a service-producing economy. Faster increases in labour productivity in the goods-producing sector have meant that progressively higher portions of total employment are in services. A consequence is that many cities have changed from being centres of manufacturing to becoming centres of advanced services: from metal benders to paper pushers. Innovations in transportation and communication technology have made industrial capital much more mobile. The result is intense competition for industry, with much routine manufacturing moving from developed to less developed regions, principally in search of lower wages. Some go so far as to argue that the globalisation of production has rendered older, compact, industrial cities obsolete.

In any event, it is crucial to grasp the fact that economic restructuring is having an increasingly uneven impact on city regions, on parts of cities and on different groups within cities – not least because of the emergence of dual labour markets. Thus, major commercial developments in city centre areas often create new jobs with reasonable career prospects for professional workers within the service sector. However, educational and social barriers prevent many potential workers – women, ethnic minorities, young people, poor people – from competing in this primary labour market. These disadvantaged groups find themselves, if they have a job at all, confined to a secondary market which consists of low-paid, insecure and undesirable jobs characterised by frequent lay-offs, no prospect of advancement and few worker rights.

In many cities the jobs which used to exist between these two realms – historically the reasonably stable, skilled, blue-collar jobs – have been decimated by the collapse of major manufacturing industries. Unless steps are taken to close the gap between the two labour markets the routes out of the despair of unemployment and/or the inferior labour market are almost impossible to find. The increasing social polarisation of the population within cities is an established trend in cities in the UK, the USA and elsewhere – and it is a trend not only in declining cities but also in cities which, in terms of overall economic indicators, appear to be prospering. The urban riots in Los Angeles in April 1992 and, on a smaller scale, the periodic disturbances which have taken place in the years since 1980 in disadvantaged areas around the UK, can only be understood in this broader socioeconomic context.

The characteristics of the areas that have experienced urban unrest share a common sense of frustration and powerlessness in the face of often mutually reinforcing problems such as fear of crime, unsatisfactory housing, high levels of unemployment, low incomes and poor health. Residents are confronted by a bewildering array of local authority departments and public agencies, each dealing with only a part of the overall problem. As we shall see, many of the decentralisation initiatives being pursued by city councils are an attempt to respond to the day-to-day frustrations experienced by people living in disadvantaged areas by offering improved corporate working at street level. However, these initiatives also need to be seen as part of the municipal response to problems which have their roots in a world-wide process of economic and urban restructuring.

The political space for local government

What autonomy do local authorities have to address the challenges raised by economic restructuring? Have they the power to do anything useful? Reference has already been made to the measures taken by central government to weaken the power of local authorities and we refer in more detail below to the legal constraints on local action. At this point, however, we want to refer briefly to the international debate about the autonomy of local government or, as some prefer, the 'local state.' Some writers argue that, because of the drastic economic restructuring which is taking place, local people and local politicians are virtually helpless in the face of wider social and economic forces. Interestingly, there are scholars on both the right and the left who, while they disagree on prescription, agree that local authorities are extremely limited in their policy options.

Thus, arguing from a position on the political right, some American political scientists suggest that, because cities need to generate revenue to fund services, they must limit their activities to courting capital – they must attract outside investment and promote economic growth as this is the only way to avoid a fiscal crisis (Peterson, 1981). This, it is argued, is why cities engage in 'civic boosterism' – that is, the aggressive marketing of the city and the promotion of economic growth at all costs. Various writers have argued that Peterson's argument only makes sense if growth does, indeed, benefit cities and most of their citizens. The evidence from the USA suggests that this is not the case (Logan and Molotch, 1987; Hambleton, 1990). It is more plausible to argue that cities pursued growth not because they had to, but because those who controlled their politics stood to benefit from using their cities as 'growth machines'.

A second critique suggesting that cities have little or no scope for autonomous political action comes from the political left. Writers such as Cockburn (1977) in the UK and Gottdiener (1987) in the USA argue that local politics is hemmed in by the power of corporations, finance capital and higher levels of government. Cockburn applied a neo-Marxist analysis to the London Borough of Lambeth in the mid-1970s and concluded that the scope for using local government to pursue progressive policies was strictly limited. Gottdiener is, if anything, even more pessimistic about the possibilities for local political initiative. He believes that expanding the involvement of formerly disenfranchised groups in US cities is fruitless because there really is no system of democratic self-realisation left. Indeed, he offers a counsel of despair, for he claims that efforts to mobilise people towards new political demands merely makes the present system stronger.

These prognostications have been challenged by both political practice in numerous UK and some US cities and by more recent academic studies of the nature and operation of city politics. Thus, in the 1980s, as part of a campaign against oppressive Whitehall controls, a large number of UK urban authorities embarked on progressive policies relating to, for example, equal opportunities, employment planning and decentralisation (Boddy and Fudge, 1984; Blunkett and Jackson, 1987). As we shall see, some of the radical decentralisation initiatives in urban areas have been pursued as part of a strategy of opposition to the national trend towards centralised control of local authorities.

Even Cockburn recognised that there is 'play within the structure of the state'. She suggested that there are divisions within the dominant class and that the state is not tightly in control of circumstance because it is continually having to cope with a changing balance of power: 'Though capital and the state structure the situation of struggle, they by no means always have the initiative' (Cockburn, 1977, p. 51). In recent years there has been a renewal of academic interest in the operation of city governance and the politics of urban restructuring and this is beginning to throw new light on the notion of 'play within the state'. While it is difficult to generalise we can note that this literature suggests there is more scope for local political action and leadership than previous writers had suggested (Judd and Parkinson, 1990; Logan and Swanstrom, 1990; Pickvance and Preteceille, 1991; Keating, 1991).

In various ways these writers challenge the notion that markets are natural forces which can be separated from public policies and that restructuring follows a global economic logic. Contrary to this, recent international comparative research suggests that markets are always embedded in specific social and political relations. Different countries, regions and cities have different regimes of governance reflecting different histories and cultures. The space for local political initiative will therefore vary from place to place, although it has to be said that central governments play a crucial role in shaping and delimiting that space. *It is also the case that local governments can choose to ignore the space that may be available to them.* Certainly, it can be argued that the lack of forceful council opposition to the poll tax, given the degree of community support for such resistance, had more to do with councillors' fears of ignoring the boundaries imposed on them than the external constraints themselves.

In the UK in recent years social scientists have shown considerable interest in the idea that different localities have different degrees of local autonomy in responding to social and economic processes (Gyford, 1991a; Duncan and Goodwin, 1988). Some theorising about industrial modernity has suggested that local differences in society are disappearing, eroded by powerful forces – such as the 'nationalisation' of local politics and the mass media – making for homogeneity and uniformity. The authors of various locality studies contest this view, arguing that the idea of locality developed as a reaction to these over-abstract accounts of social forces which seemed to leave no place for variation with space and time, or for human agency in creating this variation.

Not surprisingly, there are differences of view within the 'locality debate'. There are scholars who argue that some localities have specific class, social and gender relations which create virtually autonomous social systems with their own political cultures. Others believe that this is to take the argument too far and prefer to suggest that these factors contribute to the creation of local political cultures which are best viewed as distinct variations in a wider political culture. *There is agreement, however, that place does matter* – that it is a source of human identity, that it is a resource that can be 'commodified' and marketed, and that it can provide a basis for the creation of 'spatial coalitions' which can be mobilised politically to defend local interests. It is clear that:

> locality now looms large, both as the context and the substantive focus of much activity in civil society. For that reason local government now stands potentially at the frontiers of civil society and the state, and perhaps therefore on the threshold of a new conception of its role. (Gyford, 1991a, p. 27)

As we shall see, some of the decentralising authorities view it as a key part of their strategy to enliven civil society – that is, life outside the world of work and state. This idea of using decentralisation to reach out to and empower different interests within civil society is a theme we will return to in subsequent chapters. In the remainder of this first chapter we examine the evolution of UK local government and identify the alternative strategies for transforming local government that have emerged in recent years.

Big is beautiful – local government in the 1970s

Between 1960 and 1975 a great deal of effort went into various reviews of local government in different parts of the UK. At risk of some over-simplification we can record that the main outcome of these reviews was the formation of much larger units of local government than hitherto. Thus the Herbert Commission on the government of London led to the London Government Act 1963 (Herbert, 1960). This created the Greater London Council covering the whole London conurbation and replaced the existing patchwork quilt of local authorities with thirty-two much larger London Boroughs. The Royal Commission on Local Government in England, which sat from 1966 to 1969, recommended the creation of much bigger all-purpose (or unitary) authorities for virtually the whole of the country (Redcliffe-Maud, 1969). Meanwhile the Royal Commission on Local Government in Scotland recommended a two-tier structure based on the concept of the enlarged city region (Wheatley, 1969).

While there were important variations in emphasis the underlying analysis put forward in all these reviews was that local government needed to be reorganised into larger units because of changes in the socioeconomic geography of the country:

> The growth of suburbia and the use of the motor car, it was argued, were making the old boundaries irrelevant for planning purposes and a cause of friction between existing local authorities. In addition, many of the authorities were considered too small for existing or possible future purposes. (Hampton, 1987, p. 22)

The incoming Conservative government of 1970 rejected the Redcliffe-Maud proposals for unitary authorities in England and proposed instead the two-tier structure which, following the Local Government Act 1972, was implemented in England and Wales in

1974. The government did agree, however, with the Commission in believing that there were too many authorities and that many of them were too small. It took the view that the population size of the new major authorities should be within the range 250 000 to 1 million. The Local Government (Scotland) Act 1973 broadly followed the Wheatley proposals and created the system of regions and districts which exists in Scotland at present – again, the total number of local authorities was slashed.

These various changes in England, Wales and Scotland not only increased the size of local authority areas, they also reduced dramatically the number of councillors. Not surprisingly, there were fears in some quarters that while the larger local authorities might command more resources and be able to develop a more strategic role, they were in danger of becoming remote from, and inaccessible to, the local population. Several of the new councils recognised this drawback and attempted to develop organisational arrangements for strengthening local accountability. For example, the innovations with area management which took place in the 1970s were a reaction to the perceived problems of the 'big is beautiful' approach which had come to dominate thinking about local authority management at this time. These innovations had both a managerial and a political dimension.

First, in relation to management thinking, even as the new larger authorities were coming off the drawing board, ideas about how to avoid the inflexibilities associated with large-scale bureaucracies were already being developed and debated. The work of E. F. Schumacher, and particularly his book *Small is Beautiful*, was particularly influential. He argued convincingly that the fundamental task in organisational design is to achieve smallness within large organisations (Schumacher, 1974). These ideas were given expression in the local government context by various writers who argued that the new movement to corporate management required innovation at the neighbourhood level as well as at the centre of the authority (Stewart, 1974; Hambleton, 1978).

Stockport was the first authority in the UK to experiment with an area committee system designed to move towards a corporate approach at local level, and it was the first to introduce a formal area organisation into its management structure at both the member and the officer level in 1974. The council appointed area co-ordinators, opened a network of information offices, invested in community development, and even tried to build community views directly into the central policy making and resource-allocating process (Hambleton, 1975).

The Department of the Environment took an interest in these innovations, which chimed in with ideas emerging from the Department's own research on urban management (Department of the Environment, 1973a and 1973b). A series of area management trials was launched and, by 1977–8, various reports appeared outlining the potential of area management for tackling departmentalism and improving service responsiveness (Davis *et al.*, 1977; Harrop *et al.*, 1978; Hambleton, 1978). The main conclusion that can be drawn from the area management initiatives of the 1970s is that while a wide range of specific (and mainly modest) improvements in local government effectiveness can be identified, the lasting outcome was that *the practice of local authority management remained substantially unchanged.* This is mainly because the initiatives were seen as add-ons to the established, usually highly centralised, decision-making structures.

Turning to political innovations in the 1970s, we can note that there was a surge of innovation with public participation and community development in the period from 1968. There were new initiatives in neighbourhood participation which cut across service responsibilities involving, for example, the creation of neighbourhood or community councils (Rowe, 1975). New arrangements for public involvement were introduced in relation to land-use planning, road planning, housing management and housing renewal and, to a lesser extent, in relation to the management of education, health and social services (Boaden *et al.*, 1982). These developments can be interpreted as a major shift from the idea of viewing local authorities as guardians of the common good to an approach in which authorities accord greater recognition to sectional interests (Gyford, 1986). Efforts to introduce new forms of participation were encouraged in the early 1970s by a swift expansion of community work in many local authorities. A key book on community work enthused: 'new ideas and approaches are being generated . . . much faster than the rate at which they are being written down, digested and analysed' (Jones and Mayo, 1974, p. xiii). It was a heady time.

For a variety of reasons the late 1970s witnessed a retreat from the ambitions of the late 1960s and the early 1970s. The participatory democracy which some believed to be just around the corner did not materialise. The reasons are complex, but we can point to two features. First, the work of many of the twelve Home Office-funded Community Development Projects pointed to the limitations of localised community development strategies when not coupled with wider policies to combat inequality (Loney, 1983). Second, public expenditure restraint from 1974–5 (following on from the oil/ economic crisis of 1973–4) reduced funds available for innovation, and many local authority departments became inward-looking and cautious. The 'urban' professions were able to reassert their resistance to both 'political' control and public 'participation' in decision-making (Dunleavy, 1980, pp. 112–19). Professionals and politicans were not prepared to widen public access and local groups lacked the resources to take power.

In summary, we can say that the dominant trend in local government in the 1970s was towards larger local authorities with increasingly centralised internal management structures. By the late 1970s many of these new authorities found themselves wrestling with unexpected resource constraints and this diminished the scope for innovation. In the early 1970s there was a good deal of experiment with initiatives designed to improve the responsiveness and accountability of local authorities. But these reforms were fairly ineffective – they left the big bureaucracies and centralised patterns of decision-making largely undisturbed. Arguably the most significant link from the community initiatives of the early 1970s to the decentralisation movement of the 1980s was that many community activists later became local authority councillors and/or officers. They brought into the town halls considerable hostility towards the conventional workings of local authorities and became crucial agents of change.

The local government battles of the 1980s

The election of a Conservative government in 1979 was, to put it mildly, something of a turning point for local government. While central government had always had the formal power to change the policies of local authorities, it would only be likely to do this after consultation. All the political parties claimed that they supported a vigorous local democracy. While bargaining and negotiation would constantly take place between central and local government, there was a fairly clear consensus about the 'rules of the game'. Thus policy planning systems linking the two levels of government mushroomed in the 1970s and it was possible to view central–local relations as a pattern of interaction between organisations trading resources within a framework of interdependence (Hambleton, 1986, pp. 20–34). There would be 'ups and downs' but the structure of the relationship was not considered to be under threat. One text written at the end of the 1970s suggested that:

> Our system of government means that the centre has to carry the localities with it in relation to policy development, which helps to explain the gradualism and caution inherent in many areas of policy. (Boaden *et al.*, 1982, p. 178)

Margaret Thatcher changed all that! Within a short space of time the government had launched a sustained attack not only on local spending but also on the institutions of local democracy. The detailed twists and turns of the unfolding central–local conflict need not concern us here as they are well documented elsewhere (Blunkett and Jackson, 1987; Lansley *et al.*, 1989; Stoker, 1991; Burns, 1992). However, four key trends need to be drawn out from the struggles over local government in the Thatcher era because they have shaped the context within which all post-1979 decentralisation initiatives have taken place.

First, there have been *staggering cuts in central government financial support to local government*. At constant prices the revenue support grant to local government in England was slashed from £14.6 billion in 1980–1 to £9.5 billion in 1989-90 (Willmott and Hutchinson, 1992, p. 67). In addition, the government sought to reduce the amount of revenue raised locally – first through a system of penalties for so-called 'overspending', then by rate capping, and then, following Margaret Thatcher's election for a third term in 1987, by introducing the poll tax and poll tax capping. In the 1990s we have seen a continuation of this policy as the council tax, which replaced the poll tax in 1993, also operates within a capping regime – that is, the government can limit, or cap, the level of local taxation regardless of the wishes of local voters. Time and again local authorities have developed ways of getting round the spending restrictions imposed, but slowly the loopholes have been closed off. A consequence of these bitter struggles over local spending is that many of the decentralisation initiatives of the 1980s had to be pursued, particularly after 1987, in an extremely unfavourable resource climate – some of the more ambitious strategies had to be ruthlessly cut back and some virtually collapsed.

A second key trend has been the *politicisation of local government*. Before 1980 local government politics was relatively non-ideological in form. The coming to power of the new urban left in many city councils in the 1980s was, in part, a reaction to the lurch to the right which took place at national level. Many on the left felt local government offered exciting possibilities for developing new forms of local socialism (Boddy and Fudge, 1984; Gyford, 1985). For example, the Walsall Labour Party, which pursued a radical programme of decentralisation in the early 1980s, developed their strategy in the belief that 'socialism is most likely to be achieved in this country through participative democracy' (Walsall Labour Party, 1980). The formation of the Social Democratic Party in 1981 and its alliance with the Liberal Party introduced a 'third force' into party politics – a force that secured 25 per cent of the popular vote at the 1983 general election. A consequence of these political shifts was that the controlling party on many local authorities changed more frequently, and councils without a clear majority became more common (Gyford *et al.*, 1989).

Many of the new generation of councillors – whether from the right, left or centre – were more determined in their political beliefs than their predecessors and, to the consternation of many local government officers, introduced bold and assertive styles of operation into the local corridors of power. Local government came to be seen by all the political parties as 'political space' that could be used to pursue ideological objectives. More than that, all the parties came to see local authorities as test beds for new forms of politics that might generate workable approaches which could be applied in other settings. Those outside the ranks of local government became increasingly interested in what was happening in and around the town hall:

> Particular policies or practices have been widely publicised by the media and by national politicians either as bold experiments or as evidence of political depravity. Those with national influence or power have sought to elevate the experiences of a Westminster or a Lambeth as object lessons – good or bad – for us all. (Gyford *et al.*, 1989, p. 321)

use as
intro.

This idea of local authorities providing a fertile ground for imaginative political innovation was new and it had a profound impact on the development of decentralisation strategies at the local level. The general point we would wish to stress is that, although party politics in local government was established well before 1979, the 1980s witnessed a sharp increase in the intensity and polarisation of political activity. Different forms of decentralisation came to be used by all the political parties to pursue particular ideological objectives.

So far the focus has been on the changing relationship between party politics and local government. The third strand of change we want to highlight from the 1980s relates to broader *shifts in the politics of local communities*. Gyford (1986) has provided a helpful overview of these developments in which he argues that the traditionally dominant representative form of local democracy, which adheres to the notion of the public interest, is now challenged by three variants. First is ratepayer democracy, which is concerned with the rights of individual rate (or local tax) payers. Second is delegate democracy operating on a class-based model of politics – an approach which was only tried in a small number of 'hard left' councils in the early 1980s. Third is participatory democracy which facilitates the promotion of a range of sectional interests. Gyford is careful to point out that these are variations of ideal types that may shade into one another. His overriding point is, however, that local politics has become much more sectional and that this reflects a general trend towards a more assertive society. It also stems from the trend towards increasing social polarisation in cities, referred to earlier in the chapter. As we discuss in more detail in Chapter 9, this fracturing of communities has profound implications for decentralisation strategies.

The origins of the shift towards more assertive behaviour in local politics can be traced to the rise of community action groups in the early 1970s. Many of those involved saw community action as part of a search for radical change different from that posed by the traditionalists, whether in the ranks of the established parties or in the splinter-left groups (Hain, 1976). Building on these experiences, and strongly influenced by the feminist struggles of the 1970s, the 1980s witnessed an expansion of interest in 'new forms of democracy' (Held and Pollitt, 1986). These shifts began to redefine politics as a process which stretches from the mundane, day-to-day

Key point

experiences of ordinary life through to major policy decisions about resource allocation. Community politics:

> implicitly challenges the notion that certain areas can be defined out of political discussion and that other areas of decision-making, namely government, have to be left to political experts, whether bureaucrats or party politicians. (Cochrane, 1986, p. 53)

These ideas suggest that it is difficult, if not impossible, to separate 'civil society' and 'the state'. This suggestion that everyday life is unavoidably enmeshed with the activities of the state, particularly at the neighbourhood level, is crucial to the development of an understanding of those decentralisation initiatives which have attempted to democratise local government. As we shall see, such initiatives aim to do far more than enhance service responsiveness to consumers – they aim to alter the power relationships between those providing and those using local services, by strengthening the voice of local citizens.

   A fourth key trend of the 1980s which has lasting implications for the future direction of change relates to the *emergence of new ideas about the nature of 'good management' in local government* (Clarke and Stewart, 1990; Hambleton and Hoggett, 1990) and more broadly within the public services (Hood, 1991). We explore these ideas in more detail below. Here we would highlight the following changes in emphasis:

- From an emphasis on hierarchical decision making to an approach stressing delegation and personal responsibility;
- From a stress on the quantity of service provided to a concern for issues of quality;
- From a preoccupation with the service provider to a user orientation;
- From a tendency to dwell on internal procedures to a concern for outcomes;
- From an emphasis on professional judgement to an approach emphasising the management of contracts and trading relationships within an internal market; and
- From a culture that values stability and uniformity to one that cherishes innovation and diversity.

All these shifts in local authority management are taking place within the context of the centralisation of power to Whitehall, referred to earlier. There has been a tendency for central government to impose particular forms of management on local government – for example, models based on competition rather than trust – and this has constrained, although not determined, the nature of managerial innovation at local level. In the remainder of this chapter we put forward a conceptual framework which attempts to make sense of the major trends in local authority management covering the period from the 1950s through to the 1990s.

Driving forces for change: exit, voice and self-improvement

The framework in Figure 1.1, which represents a drastic simplification of a far more complex reality, identifies three main phases in the evolution of local authority management. The first phase, described as unresponsive public service bureaucracies, refers to the build-up of large, highly professionalised departments structured to mass-produce services in the period from the 1950s to the 1970s. These were the years when local authority services expanded dramatically and we have already referred to the 'big is beautiful' current of change which swirled through local government towards the end of this era. The dominant organisational form was bureaucratic. For each service there emerged a defined department or division; an administrative hierarchy of control; a set of procedures designed to ensure uniformity of treatment; and groups of professionals or specialists to perform the tasks. While, at their best, such departments provided an impartial and fair service to the population, they were often inflexible, insensitive and displayed a paternalistic, 'we know best' attitude in their dealings with the public.

During the late 1960s and the 1970s public dissatisfaction with this form of service management and delivery increased. This discontent rolled together concern about the remoteness of centralised decision-making, irritation with the insensitivity and lack of accountability of at least some officers, and frustration with the blinkered approach often associated with highly departmenta-lised organisations. The 1980s, the second phase in Figure 1.1,

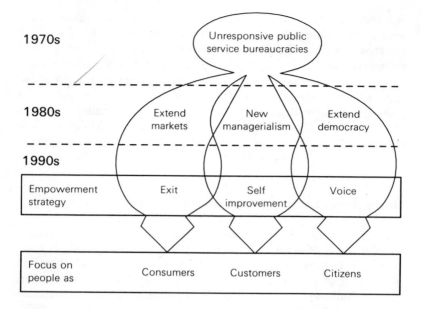

FIGURE 1.1   Public service reform strategies

witnessed a crisis in these old solutions and the emergence of three sets of reactions.

The first broad alternative, usually associated with the radical right, seeks to challenge the very notion of collective and non-market provision for public need. Centring on the notion of privatisation it seeks to replace public provision with private. A central theme in the Conservative government's policies for local government has been 'enabling, not providing'. The argument runs that the role of the local authority should no longer be that of universal provider. Rather, its role should be to encourage a diversity of alternatives, with elements of competition between the different providers (Ridley, 1988).

The key aim underlying a number of recent central government policy shifts is to create a 'market', that is, replace monolithic state services with numerous competing providers. In the period since 1979 central government's preferred approach to public service reform has been to attempt to introduce competitive models of behaviour. The Education Reform Act 1988 attempts to create a market for schools, the Housing Act 1988 applies the idea to housing, and the Local Government Acts of 1980 and 1988 insist on compulsory competitive tendering for a range of council services. The Conservative Government's consultation paper, *Competing for Quality*, proposed the extension of compulsory competitive tendering to central white-collar services such as legal and finance departments (HM Treasury, 1991). As mentioned earlier, these major changes in the legal framework have, together with the huge cuts in central government financial support, done much to unsettle established approaches to management in local government.

The second alternative, shown on the right of Figure 1.1, aims to preserve the notion of public provision, but seeks a radical reform of the manner in which this provision is undertaken. Thus it seeks to replace the old bureaucratic paternalistic model with a much more democratic model. Advocates of the extension of local democracy are, for a variety of reasons, wary of the market models admired by exponents of the first alternative. They question whether the market model does, in fact, offer real choices to most people. For example, because levels of disposable income and personal mobility are crucial factors, the actual choices open to consumers who are unemployed, infirm or disabled are few and may even be non-existent. They also dispute the view that a system which relies on a myriad of privately-made decisions will create an effective and accountable means of producing and allocating needed goods and services. Indeed, the research which has so far been undertaken on privatisation, deregulation and commercialisation of public services has found that the market model has only delivered a few of the benefits that have been claimed for it (Whitfield, 1992; Stewart, 1993).

Interestingly, advocates of both the major change strategies of the 1980s agreed in many ways on what they saw as being wrong with the organisational forms of the 1970s. The shared perception was that the big bureaucracies had become remote and unaccountable – they needed shaking up, they needed to be stimulated into developing more cost-effective and responsive approaches and, above all, they needed to be exposed to countervailing pressures *from outside* the organisation. Both the right and the left took the view that public service bureaucracies, whatever their stated intentions, were incapable of transforming themselves. New

mechanisms needed to be created which would force the bureaucracies to become responsive to external pressures.

But, having agreed upon the nature of the problem, the solutions
then prescribed differ dramatically. Whereas the new right offers
markets, competition and individual choice, the new left offers
strengthened democracy, participation and collective control.
Whereas the right champions the individual consumer, the left
advocates a new form of democratic collectivism built upon
concepts of citizenship, consumer groups and communities.

We have found the concepts of exit and voice developed by
Hirschman to be most helpful in clarifying these distinctions. He
argues that when the quality of the product or service provided by a
private firm or other organisation deteriorates, management finds
out about its failings via two alternative routes:

1. Some customers stop buying the firm's products or some
members leave the organisation: this is the *exit option*. As a result,
revenues drop, membership declines, and management is impelled
to search for ways and means to correct whatever faults have led
to exit.

2. The firm's customers or the organisation's members express
their dissatisfaction directly to management or to some other
authority to which management is subordinate or through general
protest addressed to anyone who cares to listen: this is the *voice
option*. As a result, management once again engages in a search
for the causes and possible cures of customers' and members'
dissatisfaction. (Hirschman, 1970, p. 4)

Hirschman is at pains to point out that while these two mechanisms
are strongly contrasting, they are not mutually exclusive. Indeed, a
central thrust of his book is to search for the elusive optimal mix of
exit and voice. Hirschman argues, however, that there is a
fundamental schism because exit belongs to the realm of economics
while voice is rooted in politics.

In the UK local government context we can now see clearly that
the Thatcherite reforms of the 1980s were largely built around the
exit option. As Figure 1.1 shows, the preferred approach of central
government was to attempt to extend markets. In this model the
customer, dissatisfied with the product of one supplier of a service,

can shift to that of another. In theory this switch sets in motion market forces which may induce recovery on the part of the service provider that has declined in comparative performance. This theory – that competition drives improvements – underlies the various moves not only towards competitive tendering for a range of council services, but also the introduction of quasi-markets into the welfare state (Le Grand, 1990). These are 'markets' because they replace monolithic state providers with competitive, independent ones. They are 'quasi' because they differ from conventional markets in a variety of ways. Some of the organisations competing for public contracts are likely to be non-profit organisations; consumer purchasing power may be in the form of an earmarked budget or vouchers rather than cash; and, in some cases, the 'consumer' is represented in the 'market' by an agent instead of acting for themselves (as in the area of health and social care, where a GP or a case manager can be the purchaser of services for the consumer).

A substantial number of criticisms have been levelled at the competitive model and we touch on some of them here. First, in many public service situations there is nowhere else to exit to. For example, how can the individual consumer change his or her electricity supplier, refuse collector, water provider or gas supplier? Second, the approach is widely criticised for creating 'two tier' systems of service – with reasonably high-quality services for the wealthy and articulate mirrored by declining services for the poor and less well off. Third, from a management point of view, the need to specify requirements in detail in advance of the contract leads to a highly centralised form of control which works against innovation and local learning. Fourth, the market mechanism can be viewed as an attack on the local polity in that, by fostering a self-interested and individualistic approach to decision-making, it works against debate and discussion about collective concerns and needs. A fifth argument, developed at some length by Hirschman in his discussion of the value of loyalty, is that ready and widespread use of exit can lead to the unnecessary demise of otherwise salvageable enterprises.

The ascendancy of the competitive model in government thinking probably peaked even before the Conservative Party leadership contest in late 1990 which unseated Margaret Thatcher as Prime Minister. Certainly, some of the strongest advocates of privatisation and the virtues of market mechanisms were expressing dismay at what they saw as government dilution of competitive solutions. For example, Graham Mather, when Director of the Institute of Economic Affairs, was warning that excessive institutional conservatism was working against the exposure of important services to competition in the market (Mather, 1990).

Figure 1.1 suggests that an alternative to competitive models is the extension of democracy. In Hirschman's terminology this alternative is concerned with strengthening voice. Although it represents more than this because the democratic model is not just about creating the conditions under which management can rectify its own mistakes, but is also about direct control by communities. The democratic approach starts from the position that many services cannot be individualised – they relate to groups of consumers and citizens or society at large. Such collective interests can only be protected through appropriate forms of political accountability. Hence councils pursuing this strategy put their primary emphasis on the democratisation of local government service provision. This approach highlights the importance of local government as a vital element of the representative state. The focus is not so much on the individual recipient of services, rather it is on the interaction between representative institutions and the communities they serve.

In particular there is a concern to address the perceived failing in the accountability of public-sector institutions to those communities who, while being under-represented at national and local government levels of the state, are also often the most dependent on government services – poor families, ethnic minorities, tenants, women and so on. Such strategies therefore focus on community development, the creation of sub-municipal forms of political decision-making (for example, area and neighbourhood committees), user-group control and non-spatially-based forms of political devolution (for example, race committees). The model initially strives to give local people a voice in decision-making and ultimately real power over the decisions which affect their lives. We discuss this model further in the next chapter.

Figure 1.1 suggests that there is a third broad strategy for public service reform which we have labelled 'new managerialism'. The politically-led innovations based upon market or democratic-empowerment models were launched in the early 1980s and it was some time before a managerial response emerged. The response borrowed from the competing political models in a way which sought to imitate or simulate such radical methods but in a form which preserved existing power relations between producers and consumers of services. In place of the sometimes violent and unpredictable signals of exit and voice a panapoly of techniques (market research, user satisfaction surveys, complaints procedures, customer care programmes, etc.) was developed to provide more gentle and manageable 'feedback'. The key point about 'feedback' as opposed to 'pressure' is that it doesn't force the organisation to respond. Rather, if a consensus for change can be engineered from within the organisation, it provides the informational basis for self-improvement. This model has become extremely popular in local government – it is difficult now to find any local authority that does not claim to be trying to get closer to its consumers (Local Government Training Board, 1987; Local Government Management Board 1988).

Some councils are pursuing approaches to decentralisation which combine strategies for managerial self-improvement with the extension of voice for local citizens. For them the challenge is enormous. Not only are they rethinking their managerial values, form and structure, they are also striving to widen public involvement in the governing process. Such attempts to extend local democracy inevitably encounter more opposition than radical managerial changes because they offer a more fundamental challenge to the dominant culture of representative local government (Hambleton, 1988). Nevertheless, significant innovations in this direction are taking place and we explore many of them in subsequent chapters.

Conclusion

In this opening chapter we have suggested that local government in the UK is being transformed, not just by central government interventions but also by a strong movement towards the decentralisation of services to neighbourhood level. This important current of change, which affects all local authorities and a wide range of services, has not been studied in any depth despite the fact that it is potentially very significant for the future of local government. Much discussion of 'decentralisation' tends to focus on central–local relations – on the amount of decentralisation from central to local government. This debate is extremely important and few would deny the worrying trend towards centralisation of power in Whitehall which has been a feature of the local government scene for more than a decade. However, in this book we want to draw attention to decentralisation below the level of the local authority. Decentralisation offers glimpses of a new vision for local government which is rather different from the current obsession with markets and quasi-markets.

The chapter has set the discussion of sub-local authority decentralisation in context by examining the changing role of local authorities in the national and international economy; assessing the uneven impact of economic restructuring on cities and parts of cities; and considering the growing polarisation of the population within cities. While these trends are international in scope, national governments can do much to shape the amount of autonomy exercised by local authorities. The central controls now exercised over local government are so overbearing that they limit significantly the scope for local initiative. Even so, the evidence from various locality studies suggests that local political culture matters – that the central state cannot extinguish local innovation.

The chapter has also explored the historical context to the current moves towards decentralisation. In the 1970s there was a lurch towards bigger local authorities with bigger budgets, bigger areas and bigger departments. The experiments with area management soon after local government reorganisation can be seen as a reaction to this enthusiasm for 'big is beautiful' and the associated concentration of authority in chief officer management teams and central committees of councillors. However, the area management trials and associated innovations with community development and public participation, while they paved the way for new patterns of working, left the big bureaucracies and centralised approaches to decision-making largely undisturbed.

The 1980s witnessed a series of battles between central and local government with the centre constantly striving to impose its will on the elected local authorities – particularly the urban areas. Central government financial support to local government was slashed, local government became highly politicised, community activism increased, and new ideas about the nature of 'good management' in local government were introduced.

In an effort to impose some sense of order on these turbulent times, the chapter has set out a conceptual framework which maps the major trends in local authority management. While it is a drastic simplification of a more complex reality we have found, through a large number of seminars and workshops with councillors, officers and others, that the strategies outlined in Figure 1.1 resonate well with the experience of many in local government. Bureaucratic paternalism, we argue, was challenged by, on the one hand, the extension of markets and, on the other, the extension of democracy. Later in the 1980s a new managerialism emerged, emphasising caring for the customer. Together, they symbolise a radical change in emphasis, and a starting point on which to build a new conception of local government.

2 Rethinking Local Democracy

Introduction

Recent debates about the role, form and function of local government have tended to focus on local authorities as mechanisms for delivering services. Yet we have argued for some years that while local government does offer a range of ways of providing good quality service, it is about much *more* than service delivery (Hambleton, 1988; Hambleton and Hoggett, 1990). If local government stands for a notion of community, if it is concerned to foster a vigorous civic culture and to improve the quality of life in the broadest sense, then attention must focus on the welfare of the local polity. Councillors and officers need to devote energy, time and resources to strategies designed to improve the quality of government, as well as the quality of service.

This is because local government has a crucial role to play in protecting political liberties. By supporting political diversity it is able to moderate a tendency towards autocracy which is itself destructive of good government. Moreover, local government contributes to political education – it is a setting in which democratic habits are acquired, practised and advanced. It is a central means by which collective goals are set and, if it works well, it enables the views and concerns of citizens and communities to be injected into the process of local policy-making. For all these reasons the quality of government is just as important as the quality of service. This is an argument that extends well beyond the local level because local democracy contributes directly to the health of the national polity. It follows that any valid theory of local government cannot be built on management theory, it must be a *political* theory.

During the 1980s numerous councils pursued decentralisation strategies in the belief that they could help to bring about a democratisation of council decision-making – either by extending representative democracy to the neighbourhood level and/or by developing new local forms of participatory democracy (Hoggett and Hambleton, 1987). Two London boroughs – Labour-controlled Islington and Liberal-controlled Tower Hamlets – have led the way nationally in this area and we explore their experience with democratisation in some detail in Chapters 7 and 8. In this chapter we offer a fresh examination of debates about local democracy and an exploration of alternative ways of empowering citizens. We compare and contrast market models with ways of strengthening public involvement in local government. We then analyse four key terms which have become common currency in local government – client, customer, consumer and citizen. These words are used far too loosely in ongoing debates. We hope that the discussion in this chapter will help to sharpen thinking about the nature of the options now being considered for local democracy in the UK.

Empowerment strategies

There are different ways of empowering people in relation to the organisations that are intended to serve them. Not surprisingly, different mechanisms have grown up in the private, public and non-profit sectors. As mentioned in Chapter 1, we have found the concepts of exit and voice developed by Hirschman (1970) to be very helpful in understanding the power relationships between people and organisations. Stated simply, the market model, in theory at least, gives individuals the power of exit – dissatisfied customers can take their business elsewhere. The democratic process, again in theory at least, relies on individuals or groups having the power of voice – dissatisfied citizens obtain a response by taking political action.

It is, of course, possible for an organisation to have both sets of reaction mechanisms – thus many voluntary organisations are responsive both to the views expressed by their members and to shifts in membership and participation rates. Hirschman argues that there is no implication that organisations which are equipped with both feedback mechanisms are necessarily more advanced than those which rely primarily on one alone. Everything depends on the responsiveness of the organisation whichever mechanism or combination of mechanisms it is equipped with.

While Hirschman is concerned to explore ways of mixing exit and voice mechanisms he is at pains to point out how different they are. This is because exit belongs to the realm of economics and voice to the realm of politics:

> Exit is the sort of mechanism economics thrives on. It is neat – one either exits or one does not; it is impersonal – any face-to-face confrontation between customer and firm with its imponderable and unpredictable elements is avoided and success and failure of the organisation are communicated to it by statistics; and it is indirect – any recovery on the part of the declining firm comes by courtesy of the Invisible Hand, as an unintended by-product of the customer's decision to shift.
>
> In all these respects voice is just the opposite of exit. It is a far more 'messy' concept because it can be graduated, all the way from faint grumbling to violent protest; it implies articulation of one's critical opinions rather than a private, 'secret' vote in the anonymity of a supermarket; and finally, it is direct and straightforward rather than roundabout. Voice is political action par excellence. (Hirschman, 1970, pp. 15–16)

As explained in Chapter 1, the consensus which appeared to dominate much of the post-Second World War period broke down in the 1980s. Under the leadership of Margaret Thatcher the Conservative Party discarded the 'one nation' Conservatism of earlier years and set about 'rolling back the frontiers of the state'. Instead of commitment to welfare services and to government intervention in the economy the 'new right' stressed the pre-eminence of market forces and sought to restrain state spending on social services (Loney *et al.*, 1987).

There are, as Green (1987) observes, numerous strands within new-right thinking – from the minimal statism of Robert Nozick, through Milton Friedman's views on economics as the science of wealth creation, to Friedrich Hayek's claim that the role of government is to create conditions 'favourable' to progress rather than to 'plan' progress. A common strand in new-right thinking, however, is that individuals should be able to direct their own lives to a far greater extent than is normally the case. The mainstream new liberals, Friedman, Hayek and the public choice school believe that the main role of government is to maintain liberty and to provide a framework within which competitive markets can operate: 'As far as possible competition should prevail, or at least, every supplier should be open to competition' (Green, 1987, p. 211).

In relation to local government, Chapter 1 has already shown how the Thatcherite approach to reform attempted to introduce competitive models into the public sector. This approach was taken forward with particular vigour after the 1987 General Election, with 'quasi-markets' being introduced into housing, education, health services and elsewhere:

> In each case, the intention is for the state to stop being both the funder and the provider of services. Instead it is to become primarily a funder, with services being provided by a variety of private, voluntary and public suppliers, all operating in competition with one another. (Le Grand, 1990, p. 2)

In terms of the Hirschman model the empowerment strategy underlying these government policies depends almost entirely on the exit mechanism. As mentioned in Chapter 1, this mechanism has serious drawbacks in the public service context. In particular, power and choice become illusions when there is nowhere else to exit to. Even where there is an element of choice, for example in education, the evidence suggests that, as with conventional markets, quasi-markets create inequalities and foster social injustice. Thus critics of the government's education policy argue that some schools will cream off the most able pupils and leave the rest to struggle in 'sink' schools. Suffice it to say that, despite the enthusiasm of some of its advocates (Ridley, 1988), the fact remains that there are few, if any, success stories demonstrating how the competitive model has created high-quality, cost-effective services which meet the needs of all citizens.

Hirschman's alternative strategy for empowering people by giving them voice is, of course, much more familiar to those concerned with local government. Indeed, a central justification for local authorities is that they can at least give local people an indirect voice because they are democratically elected and are accountable to their citizens. Following a basic distinction made in political theory it can be suggested that, in relation to local government, citizens can exercise voice in two main ways – through the ballot box and through direct participation in local affairs. In theory we have a system which combines elements of representative democracy and participatory democracy.

Developing the voice option

The voting avenue for expressing voice has a hundred-year history. The first elections for county councils were held in 1889 and since that date the principle of representative local democracy has taken root in the British political system. Large numbers of councillors continue to give dedicated service despite the erosion of local government powers in recent years. The system of ward-based elections is a major advantage over the at-large elections found in some other countries because it ensures reasonably good geographical representation on the council. Contrary to the government's expectations, the major research study of the conduct of local authority business carried out by the Widdicombe Committee in the mid-1980s provided 'a forthright endorsement of the value of local government, of its place in the political system, and of its present institutional structure' (Gyford *et al.*, 1989, p. 295). Notwithstanding these arguments it would be wrong to imply that local representative arrangements in the UK provide anything like a perfect mechanism through which citizens can express voice. Some of the criticisms of the status quo are as follows.

First, the voter turnout at local elections which, in recent years, has averaged between 39 per cent and 53 per cent (Byrne, 1992, pp. 106–7). While this is higher than in many American cities, it gives no room for complacency. Second, the strain on many local councillors of carrying out the representative and associated roles has become intolerable – the costs for many councillors in terms of damaged family life, eroded social and leisure time and stress-related illness suggest that current arrangements are not viable (Barron, Crawley and Wood, 1991). A third point is that the characteristics of councillors rarely reflect the social composition of the populations they represent – for example, research for the Widdicombe Committee produced national figures showing that, in 1986, only 19 per cent of councillors were women (Gyford *et al.*, 1989, p. 49). Moreover, the lack of a political culture of participation coupled with centralised forms of decision-making mean that most people do not even know who their local councillor is.

Partly because established arrangements have been perceived as unsatisfactory the thirst for new forms of democracy among the public at large has grown considerably. Gyford (1991b) has shown how an increasingly diverse and assertive society is making a wide range of new demands on the traditional representative system. A consequence is that a string of new ideas have developed which seek to increase the scope and/or transform the methods of democratic decision-making (Held and Pollitt, 1986).

In the period since the late 1960s a wide range of methods of involving the public directly in council decision-making have been developed and tried out. Gyford (1991b) provides a helpful overview and various guides to good practice are available (Smith, 1985; Local Government Management Board, 1988). We examine some of the boldest initiatives in subsequent chapters. At this point it is useful to distinguish four broad approaches to strengthening voice and these are summarised in Figure 2.1.

First, there is a range of steps which can be taken to improve the existing mechanisms of local representative democracy. Rhodes suggests that the local authority should take steps to increase the turnout at local elections by advertising, carrying out voter registration drives and providing transport to the polling stations

1 *Improving representative democracy*
  e.g. voter registration drives, open government, citizens' rights at meetings, better support to councillors.

2 *Extending representative democracy*
  e.g. area committees of councillors based on wards or groups of wards, strengthen parish councils.

3 *Infusing representative with participatory democracy*
  e.g. co-option on to committees, neighbourhood committees of councillors and representatives from community and disadvantaged groups.

4 *Extending participatory democracy*
  e.g. funding of non-statutory groups, community development, user-group participation, valuing grass-roots movements.

FIGURE 2.1 **Ways of strengthening voice in local government**

(Rhodes, 1987). Other ways of strengthening accountability include: giving citizens the right to ask questions at council meetings, making key reports available earlier, and improving the support services to councillors so that they can be more effective in dealing with the concerns of constituents.

A second strategy is to extend representative democracy by creating new, more local settings within which ward councillors can decide on local issues. A number of councils have experimented with different kinds of area committee – including Stockport, Birmingham, Newcastle, Middlesbrough and South Somerset District Council. A recent study of the changing roles of councillors gives support to the idea of area committees. It found that, as councils introduce stronger forms of executive leadership, there is an urgent need to balance such a concentration of powers: 'One way of doing this would be through locally-based area management committees with decentralised decision-making to ward councillors' (Rao, 1993, p. 70). We examine the Tower Hamlets experience with this model in Chapter 8. Another approach is to establish separate democratically elected councils at the very local level – by creating urban parish (or community) councils (Perrin, 1986).

A third way of strengthening voice is to infuse representative democracy with participatory democracy. Again a variety of routes is available. One method, which has been used extensively in the fields of social services, leisure, personnel and housing, is to co-opt community representatives on to council committees. The provisions of the Local Government and Housing Act 1989 reduced the scope for co-option. It rules that no one who is not an elected member may be a voting member of a decision-making committee or sub-committee (as distinct from a purely advisory committee). However, this restriction does not apply to certain kinds of local committee – co-opted members can still vote on committees or sub-committees appointed solely for the purpose of managing land or buildings owned by the authority. These must constitute a single site, or lie sufficiently close to each other that they can be conveniently managed as if they were a single site. This leaves the door open for a variety of local management arrangements (Hambleton, 1989).

A related way of enlivening representative structures is to create 'hybrid' neighbourhood committees bringing together local councillors and local people. The strategy for decentralisation developed by Rochdale in the late 1980s provides an interesting example of this model. In 1987 the council created a community development division within a reorganised chief executive's department and, building on earlier initiatives, committed itself to 'a community development driven approach to neighbourhood service delivery'. Several kinds of local democratic forum were developed by the council, including estate committees, community-based action area committees, and community school councils. Another good example of a council injecting public participation into council decision-making is provided by Islington. The council has probably gone further than any other council in developing neighbourhood forums and we examine the performance of this participatory mechanism in Chapter 7.

A fourth strategy is to switch the focus from representative to participatory democracy and community action. Thus some councils use local government resources to underpin a wide variety of non-statutory organisations. The central idea is to break with the notion that local government should always be the vehicle through which local needs are met. It involves devolving influence and power to groups rather than areas. There is evidence to suggest that measures of this kind have been successful, particularly in inner city areas, in building the self-confidence of groups who have previously found it difficult to engage in the local political process (Stewart and Whitting, 1983).

The experience of the Greater London Council in the five or six years before it was abolished in March 1986 deserves to be mentioned in this context. The council pursued an imaginative approach to grant-giving, believing that sharing power means getting resources – funds, primarily, but also research and information – out of County Hall to those groups who could use them. Grants were given to support a wide range of innovative activities such as health campaigning, local initiatives in the Docklands, and organising against multinational management (Mackintosh and Wainwright, 1987). Other local authorities such as the London boroughs of Camden and Islington pursued strategies of this kind in the 1980s, believing that voluntary organisations, both formal and informal, could play a vital developmental role – creating new links, releasing new energies and experimenting with untried approaches (Gyford, 1991b, pp. 125–41). Unfortunately, these kinds of outgoing strategies are now being threatened. Faced with severe budgetary constraints, many local authorities are being forced to cut their support to voluntary and community organisations, sometimes by an across-the-board percentage reduction, sometimes selectively (Chanan, 1991).

Another way of extending participatory democracy involves a new approach to community development, which attempts to make it part of the mainstream, day-to-day practice of local government (Association of Metropolitan Authorities, 1989; Taylor, 1992). There are signs that a community development approach can be built into professional practice – for example, in areas such as community social work (Beresford and Croft, 1986) and community architecture (Woolley, 1986). A third approach – one tied closely to community development – relates to the creation, support and involvement of user groups. Tenants' associations, estate manage-ment boards and tenant management corporations are examples drawn from housing, but the approach is also being tried in other areas – for example, transport users' groups, parks users' groups and so on (Gyford, 1991b, pp. 59–72; Holmes, 1992). Progress with user-group involvement is also gaining momentum in social services and social care (Hadley and Young, 1990; Milner *et al.*, 1991).

The various ways of extending participatory democracy discussed here have identified avenues for change which are being pursued by many local authorities. In concentrating on the local authority agenda we run the risk of understating the importance of popular initiatives and grass-roots activism. Community groups often present a fundamental challenge to established power structures and it can be argued that some of the most inventive and successful examples of participatory democracy have involved direct action against the state. The extraordinary success of the Anti-Poll Tax Unions in organising at neighbourhood level, as well as campaign-ing effectively nationally, provides striking evidence to support this claim (Burns, 1992). We return to explore further the realms of participatory democracy in Parts III and IV of this book.

The four Cs: clients, customers, consumers, citizens

So far we have concentrated on sketching out some of the main approaches to empowerment by drawing on Hirschman's concepts of exit and voice. The options we have referred to do not provide a comprehensive picture – this would be difficult at the best of times in a field of rapidly-developing innovation. Rather, we have attempted to map the broad contours of the debate about empowerment. We have raised serious doubts about the possibilities for developing effective exit mechanisms in a public service context. We have also suggested that putting a cross on a piece of paper once every few years hardly amounts to an effective strategy for giving people an adequate voice in local affairs, especially when very few people have an input to the development of the choices which are presented. The various ways of strengthening voice, which we have outlined, start to identify some possible ways forward but, before we can get much further with the empowerment theme, we need to discuss some of the language, or at least some of the key words, which have become common currency in local government.

This is important because the language which is used by politicians and officers symbolises how they perceive the public, and this perception goes some way to explaining the nature of the different democratic initiatives that they adopt. In our experience different ways of referring to the public are often used rather loosely and in an effort to clarify thinking we now examine the commonly used terms of client, customer, consumer and citizen. These words are sometimes used interchangeably and this has the effect of confusing discussion and masking power relationships.

Treating people as clients

In Chapter 1 we referred to the era of bureaucratic paternalism. In those days the traditional, professional model dominated the server–served relationship. Local authority officers and members would commonly refer to service users or potential service users as *clients* or, on occasion, 'client groups' (Stewart, 1971, p. 122). While there were important exceptions it was often the case that the authority had a 'we know best' attitude to the public. The elected councillors and their professional officers often shared a strong attachment to the 'public interest'. Clearly, at times, this could be a force for good, but too often the public interest was defined without reference to the views of the clients.

In an early study of the impact of professional power on inner city communities, in this case the power of town planners and environmental health officers, Gower Davies provided the following biting contrast between the concepts of client and customer:

> The *customer* is always right: he can choose, criticise and reject. The *client*, on the other hand, gives up these privileges and accepts the superior judgement of the professional. It is one of the aims of the would-be professions to convert its customers into clients and in so doing stake out an exclusive area of discourse in which those persons trained in the skills and inducted into the 'mysteries' of the trade can claim a monopoly of wisdom and proficiency. (Gower Davies, 1974, p. 220; emphasis in original)

The key characteristic of the client relationship is that the client is, on the whole, dependent on the professional. In this model, then, virtually all the power lies with the professional. This can create in people a feeling of impotence in relation to the particular service being provided. Not surprisingly, the term 'client', because of its connotations with closed and often paternalistic decision-making, is now used much less frequently in local government circles than it was – even in social services circles where it was well-established. We can now see that the bureaucratic paternalistic model tended to treat people as clients and that, in terms of Hirschman's framework, the model is doomed because it has extremely poor feedback mechanisms – both the exit and the voice routes are largely blocked.

None of this is to suggest that professional ideologies are no longer significant in local government. The 'urban' professions have had a strong influence on the processes of both policy formulation and policy implementation for many years. While there has always been inter-professional rivalry, local government professionalism has many common elements – for example, all the professions strive to control information gathering and fight to defend bureaucratic autonomy (Dunleavy, 1980). While it is possible to argue that the power of the 'urban' professions has been weakened by the growth of general management in local government, the amalgamation of departments, and the development of stronger forms of political leadership, these shifts have done little or nothing to empower clients. On the contrary, new kinds of professional dominance are emerging. There is a risk that the traditional professions will decline in influence only to be replaced by, for example, a new cadre of so-called experts in quality control who will also claim to know what is best for people.

The customer revolution

Many of those striving to reform town hall bureaucracies have dropped terms such as 'client' and 'recipient', preferring instead to talk of the *customer*. Indeed, it is now possible to suggest that customer care is becoming the dominant public service management ideology, not only in the UK but also in the USA. For example, the International City Management Association (ICMA) has recently produced a package of training materials for American local authorities around the theme of 'providing quality customer service' (International City Management Association, 1989). Developments within private sector management thinking have clearly been influential – for example, popular management books stress the link between quality and the customers' experience of an organisation (Peters, 1988). These ideas have been picked up by those concerned to improve public service management and there is widespread enthusiasm for the idea of customer-driven government – an approach which strives to meet the needs of the customer rather than the bureaucracy (Osborne and Gaebler, 1992, pp. 166–94).

Although customer care programmes were developed by many private companies during the 1980s it would be a distortion to suggest that public service managers have merely picked up on the latest private sector management wheeze. Considerable effort is being made to adapt customer service models to the public service context. The concept of the public service orientation, which sets service for the public as the key organisational value for local authorities and their staff, is a good example (Stewart and Clarke, 1987).

Customer care programmes vary considerably but most focus on the interaction between members of the public and service providers. Front line staff are trained to listen more attentively, to understand the policies and procedures of the organisation, to project a positive attitude and to provide resourceful assistance. It can be argued that the 'service encounters' people experience when they visit a council office can be decisive in shaping the quality of service (Gaster, 1991). In line with this thinking, authorities taking a serious approach to customer care invest in improved information technology support to the front line, substantial staff training to develop good interpersonal skills, and organisational development designed to create a 'customers first' culture in the whole authority (Baddeley and Dawes, 1986; Baddeley and Dawes, 1987).

There is considerable confusion in current debates about customer care, mainly because there are two dimensions to the provider–customer relationship. On the one hand it can be argued that a customer is one who buys and that, for there to be a customer, there has to be a commercial transaction. While local authorities do charge for some of their services – for example, use of a swimming pool – most public service encounters are not like this at all. Even though central government is moving to undermine the public service ethos of local government by encouraging the introduction of new charges it is still the case that, on the whole, citizens do not have to pay a charge at the point of service delivery. On this analysis it can be suggested that the use of the word 'customer' in a public service context is entirely inappropriate.

Indeed, we have ourselves criticised customer care programmes for being dominated by the 'charm school' approach. In the absence of the power of exit, which purchasers usually have in the market place, customer care has often become an aerosol solution. Spraying on a coat of customer care may improve appearances but if the underlying power relationship is untouched, this strategy cannot have a lasting impact on service responsiveness (Hambleton and Hoggett, 1990).

A second dimension of the provider–customer relationship concerns the positive feelings the customer may have towards the providing organisation as a result of their experiences in using the service. Consider for a moment the attitudes many customers have to their local pub or newsagents. Many value visiting the place and interacting with the staff. This is almost certainly different from the large supermarket where consumers concentrate on finding their preferred products – their interest in the place and the staff is likely to be minimal. Hirschman (1970), as well as developing the concepts of exit and voice, also stressed the importance of loyalty. He argued not only that the presence of loyalty to a product or organisation makes exit less likely, it also increases the likelihood of voice. This is because a person with a considerable attachment to a service will often search for ways of trying to influence the organisation if it begins to move in what s/he believes to be the wrong direction. It is certainly the case that neighbourhood offices in many local authorities have developed a strong sense of loyalty among local people. For example, local authorities, like Walsall in 1982, have found it extremely difficult to close neighbourhood offices because local people have come to look upon the offices as 'theirs' (Seabrook, 1984).

The use of the word 'customer' is, then, a mixed blessing. On the one hand it implies that, by renaming clients as customers, they will enjoy the power exercised by purchasers in the market place. This is nonsense, because the seller–buyer relationship rarely exists in the public sector. On the other hand, an inventive approach to customer relations can win loyalty and, in certain situations, strong public support for council services. On balance, however, we take the view that the power relations implied by the customer care model resemble those of the discredited client model. At root the customer care approach does not tip the balance of power strongly in favour of the user. As a result, customer care may turn out to be a form of organisational sleight of hand in which bureaucratic paternalism disappears only to be replaced by a new, more subtle form of managerial paternalism.

Consumer power

It can be argued that the concepts of 'consumer' and 'citizen' have more to offer public service reformers than 'client' and 'customer'. This is mainly because, in very different ways, they focus more sharply on empowering people. First, let us examine consumerism, a cause which has advanced steadily over some thirty years. Consumer theorists argued long ago that there is an imbalance of power between those who provide goods and services and those for whom they are provided. To shift the balance of power in favour of consumers, those representing their interests have built their arguments around five principles: access, choice, information, redress, and representation.

> People must first of all have access to the benefits offered by a product or service (without access, they cannot 'get in'). Their choice of products and services must be as wide as possible to

establish some measure of consumer sovereignty, and they need as much information as possible, both to enable them to make sensible choices, and to make the fullest possible use of what they are seeking. They will also need some means of communicating their grievances when things go wrong, and receiving adequate redress. Finally, they need some means of making sure that their interests are adequately represented to those who take decisions affecting their welfare. (Potter, 1988)

These first four principles were first developed in relation to goods and services sold in the market place – increasingly they have been applied to services in the public sector. The fifth principle has never been adequately developed, either by private firms or the consumer movement – consumers do not have seats in the board room.

The word 'consumer' describes the relationship of a person to a product or service. In terms of Hirschman's framework, then, consumerism, which is grounded in economic theory, draws on the power of exit. If consumers do not like what they are receiving from one service provider they can take their business elsewhere – they can, in theory at least, exercise choice between competing providers. Clearly, this is very much an individualistic model. Consumers are not that interested in taking account of the preferences of other consumers; rather, they seek to maximise their own advantage.

Consumerism can clearly be a powerful force in the market place and the myriad decisions of individuals can, within limits, force companies to respond to consumer preferences. However, there are three main sets of reasons why the model has serious limitations in a public service context. First, if the consumer is to exercise power by virtue of personal choice, there has to be a market place within which a wide range of choice is available. In relation to public services, this is rarely, if ever, the case. Even when services are privatised, individual consumer choice is not enhanced – thus individuals cannot switch their refuse collector, their fire service, their water company, their electricity board and so on. For these services, which are effectively monopolies, the consumer derives power, if s/he has any at all, through the power of voice, and *not* from the ability to exercise choice within the market place.

Experimentation with public service or quasi-markets might be able to create some choices for some consumers at the margins but, when examined closely, these innovations turn out to offer very little choice indeed. How much choice do parents have if there is only one school in their area? How much choice do patients have if there is only one GP? How much choice do residents have over which park they use if there is only one park in their area?

Such no-exit situations are not just the product of spatial location. For example, if you are an elderly person living in a residential home, whether it is run by the local authority, the voluntary sector or the private sector, how easy is it to uproot and move? The fact is that the human and social costs of the upheaval would be formidable. Increasing the power of the voice of residents in running the home is clearly a much more effective and economic approach to service improvement. Not surprisingly, this is increasingly seen as a desirable strategy by public service professionals.

The second major limitation of the consumerist model is that it fails to recognise that the server–served relationship in the public sector is often very different from the private sector. For example, many public services are concerned with social control. If a service is compulsory it is clear that the consumer cannot go (as it were) to the next supermarket, bank or garage. As Pollitt (1990) points out, the public 'service' may be supplied directly against the will of the recipient and enforced coercively. Such situations are not confined to the work of the police and prison services. Professionals from a range of local authority departments have powers to regulate the behaviour of the local population – for example, social workers, environmental health officers and town planners.

Equally there are situations where the public may want to use a particular service, but is not allowed to. For much of the time council officers have the difficult task of rationing limited public services to disappointed citizens – take, for example, the rationing of access to council housing, to community care services, and to nursery school places

> Where this happens in the private sector (waiting lists for the latest Mercedes) the message goes back to the production units. 'Increase output'. In the public services such messages usually fall on deaf ears, especially when they belong to the politicians of the new right. (Pollitt, 1990, p. 128)

The third major problem with the consumerist model is that it has great difficulty coping with the needs of *groups* of consumers. Many public services provide a collective rather than an individual benefit. Clean air, roads, street lighting, environmental quality and schooling are just some of the services provided and consumed on a collective basis. In a democracy, collective needs of this kind need to be addressed collectively. Conflicts of view need to be expressed, and choices which take account of other people's preferences have to be made. This is not to imply that existing arrangements for democratic control of public service organisations are adequate. Indeed, earlier in the chapter we referred to a variety of ways in which local democracy needs to be strengthened. Rather, it is to emphasise that the consumer concept is rooted in the individualistic, even selfish, behaviour of the market system. It can, therefore, contribute little to debates about the concerns of whole communities and issues relating to social justice. It is in these areas where the altogether different concept of citizenship has great promise.

Strengthening citizenship

Citizenship has been a contested concept for centuries. Aristotle observed: 'The nature of citizenship . . . is a question which is often disputed: there is certainly no general agreement on a single definition' (quoted in Heater, 1990, p. vii). Despite the differences of view, the terms 'citizen' and 'citizenship' are in constant use in everyday political discourse and, indeed, they have come to the fore in current public policy debates both in the UK and abroad. In his wide-ranging and illuminating analysis of the concept, Heater stresses the importance of education in developing citizenship: 'much needs to be learned if civic rights are to be exercised, civic duties are to be performed and a life of civic virtue is to be pursued' (Heater, 1990, p. vii). While he argues that citizenship is the foundation of human dignity and secular morality, Heater recognises that the search for an agreed, all-embracing and permanent definition of citizenship is likely to prove futile. This is mainly because the theory and practice of citizenship are continually changing in response to particular economic, social and political circumstances.

   This idea that citizenship is an unfolding concept is the central theme of a seminal series of lectures given by T. H. Marshall and published in 1950 under the title *Citizenship and Social Class*. While it is a simplification we can say that Marshall argues that there has been an historical progression in the development of citizenship through three main phases:

1. The fight for *civil* rights in the seventeenth and eighteenth centuries created a limited amount of legal equality.
2. The growth of *political* rights in the nineteenth and early twentieth centuries involved conflict with capitalist interests because these struggles gained citizens' rights to participate in the exercise of political power without limitation by economic status or gender.
3. *Social* rights – the right to the prevailing standard of life and the social heritage of the society – were advanced through developments in the social services and the education system in the twentieth century.

The egalitarian thrust of social citizenship presents a more powerful challenge to the status quo than the earlier extensions of civil and political rights. Indeed, Marshall argues that this third phase of citizenship, because it is predicated upon the principle of equality, represents a direct challenge to the hierarchical class structure of British society: 'it is clear that in the 20th century, citizenship and the capitalist system have been at war' (Marshall, 1950, p. 29). The limited progress which has been made in securing social rights in the UK is revealed by the fact that many in our society still do not feel themselves to be citizens. There remains an inextricable link between economic and political exclusion and, as society becomes progressively polarised, an increasing number of young people, women and black people sense the concept of citizenship to be alien and inappropriate to their own lived reality.

Barbalet (1988) explores the concept of social citizenship in some detail and notes that the rise of social rights must lead to the decline of or at least the shrinking of, the market and market relations. He points out how Marshall drew attention to the unstable relationship that has developed between the principle of citizenship and the principle of the market (Barbalet, 1988, pp. 72–9). However, Marshall suggested that this tension is not necessarily destructive of the balance between the different components of the mixed economy. What is particularly interesting about Marshall's analysis is the way it encourages exploration of future possibilities for citizenship. Given that citizenship is not a fixed concept it follows that future years could see an erosion of citizenship – for example, further damage to social rights; or a further expansion of citizenship – for example, into the economic and political spheres. We include the latter deliberately because, as we argue in detail in Chapter 10, there never has been extensive political democracy in the UK – the development of the welfare state strengthened social citizenship but it did little to extend the boundaries of political citizenship.

How can we relate these ideas about citizenship to our discussion of empowerment? One way is to suggest that the citizen and the consumer can be regarded as political and economic creatures respectively:

> the citizen debating public issues in the agora of ancient Greece could be seen as the historical symbol of political democracy. The consumer making judgements on price and quality in the shopping centre would be the contemporary symbol of economic democracy. (Gyford, 1991b, p. 18)

Such an image suggests that citizens engage in public debates about shared concerns which lead to collective political decisions, whereas consumers engage in comparison shopping which leads to individual economic decisions. Gyford indicates that, on this basis, it is possible to see citizenship, issuing in political collectivism, as a left-wing concept, with consumerism, issuing in individualism, as a right-wing concept. However, he goes further and suggests that they could also be seen as representing wholly contrasting concepts of humanity. It is possible to argue that the citizen is able, at least some of the time, to put aside immediate and personal interests and consider the wider impact of decisions on other people. On this argument the citizen is concerned with the welfare of the community as a whole and accepts the primacy of the common good. In contrast the concept of the consumer can be viewed as:

> the last in a long train of models that depict man as a greedy, self-interested, acquisitive survivor . . . a creature of great reason devoted to small ends . . . [in] a world of carrots and sticks. (Barber quoted in Gyford, 1991b, p. 19)

The Thatcherite image of the citizen as consumer attempts to resist such an unfavourable analysis by arguing that the strength of citizenship is that it enables each person to engage as an independent unit in the competitive market place. The general availability of civil rights is praised because it means that people can look after themselves – it is the individual that matters, not society. In her now infamous statement Margaret Thatcher said:

> too many people have been given to understand that if they have a problem it's the government's job to cope with it . . . They're casting their problem on society. And, you know, there's no such thing as society. There are individual men and women, and there are families. And no government can do anything except through people, and people must look to themselves first. (Thatcher, 1987)

The opposite view argues that citizenship cannot be based only on a legal–political definition as many citizens, because of social and economic circumstances, are so disadvantaged that they cannot participate effectively in the society in which they have legal membership: 'In the absence of the educational and economic resources required to exercise civil or legal and political rights citizenship remains empty for all practical purposes' (Barbalet, 1988, p. 69). This formulation has the general support of political parties on the centre and left in the UK. For example, Ashdown stresses the importance of society:

> Most of the things that give our lives meaning and purpose, our rights, our roles and our relationships, stem from membership of society. Citizenship defines this membership, giving us opportunities to participate in, contribute to and benefit from our association with each other and the State. (Ashdown, 1989, p. 33)

On this analysis, social entitlements, such as access to housing, education, health and welfare, are essential if the political and civil rights of citizenship are to be exercised. Ultimately the development of social citizenship requires the reversal of the forms of social inequality and polarisation which have gathered pace in most Western-type economies since the mid-1970s. It is also the case that power needs to be as decentralised as possible if the citizen is to be able to express opinions, learn about other views, engage in decision-making and organise politically.

Conclusion

In this chapter we have attempted to provide footholds which can support a deep and thoughtful debate about the nature of local democracy in the UK. At a time when the wholesale reorganisation of local government is taking place, it is vitally important that attention focuses much more sharply on the nature of the local democracy we wish to create. Arguments about boundaries, structures and finance, important as they are, should not be allowed to displace more fundamental rethinking. We are suggesting that empowering people to take action in the public sphere should be the key theme for local government in the 1990s. Following Hirschman's distinction we are arguing that, at root, there are only two ways of empowering people in relationship to public institutions – by creating either exit or voice mechanisms. Organisations, including local authorities, can develop one or both. But they cannot ignore the empowerment agenda. If authorities take the view that the status quo is acceptable they merely pave the way for growing dissatisfaction and, ultimately, the demise of local government. In the absence of widespread innovation with a variety of empowerment strategies we foresee an increasingly weakened local government ripe for takeover by the central state.

We have raised serious doubts about the possibilities for developing effective exit mechanisms in a public service context. Indeed, the introduction of market forces may weaken rather than empower the majority, not least because it will create 'two-tier' systems of service provision. The well-off will either exit altogether or use all the advantages they possess to ensure high-quality services in their areas. The less-well-off will be given the illusion of choice when, in the majority of situations, there really is not any choice at all. The alternative strategy is to develop a wide range of new voice mechanisms to help people achieve what they want to do. In Figure 2.1 on page 35 we provided some suggestions on possible routes to empowerment. We examine these ideas further later in the book.

Description of member of the public	The relationship is strongly shaped by:
Client	The dominance of the client by the *professional*
Customer	The experience of the customer in using the *organisation*
Consumer	The interest of the consumer in the *product* or service provided
Citizen	The concern of the citizen to influence *public decisions* which affect the local quality of life

FIGURE 2.2   Relationships between people and the council

Our discussion of the language used to describe members of the public has attempted to tease out how different terms send out different messages about the nature of the relationships between people and the council. Figure 2.2 attempts to crystallise some of the distinctions we have been making.

This figure is a simplification of a more complex reality and it needs to be examined in conjunction with the text above. We hope it is persuasive. We would wish to highlight the importance for empowerment strategies of keeping the focus on the citizen. Customer care programmes have their place but, when they focus on the citizen as customer they are in danger of missing the point. We need to focus on the citizen as *citizen*. If local government is to have meaning in future any consumerist emphasis on individual and material needs must be balanced by measures which foster attitudes that go beyond self-interest.

3 The Character of Local Political Innovation

Introduction

In this book we seek to outline a vision of a responsive, flexible and above all democratic approach to organising public, and specifically local government, services. As we explained in Chapter 1, decentralisation may assume a variety of forms, but in the context of local government the dominant form will tend to be one which gives emphasis to spatially-based forms of decentralisation – ones built upon the catchment areas of particular facilities such as schools and leisure centres, or upon the spatial distribution of subjectively defined neighbourhoods, or upon political boundaries such as electoral wards.

When developing strategies for public service reform it is essential to go beyond the level of abstract generalisation and prescription to test ideas against particular examples which exemplify some of the claims made and some of the problems. In subsequent chapters we therefore present a fairly detailed evaluation of the implementation of neighbourhood decentralisation in the London boroughs of Islington and Tower Hamlets. These two local authorities – Labour-controlled Islington and Liberal-controlled Tower Hamlets – have gone further in developing multi-service decentralisation than any other councils in the UK. We have chosen these two case studies not because they present an ideal which we seek to advocate (indeed, there are significant aspects of both councils' policies with which we disagree), but because the boldness of the initiatives provides us with a way of grounding our discussion, of testing theory against practice.

This chapter introduces the two boroughs. It considers their recent political history and situates the decentralisation initiatives within this context. It examines the original political objectives for reform in Islington and Tower Hamlets and considers how these may have changed over time. Finally, we reflect upon the nature of political innovation in these two boroughs – how it was possible for such distinctive and ambitious models of reform to have been developed in such an unconducive environment, one in which the space for change at the local level was constantly being eroded by successive national Conservative administrations. The point of this chapter, therefore, is not just to describe the context within which political and administrative innovation occurred in each borough, but to provide a dynamic political analysis of the process of change itself.

Two inner-city areas – Islington and Tower Hamlets

Islington and Tower Hamlets are two inner-city London boroughs, the former lying just to the north of the City and the latter immediately to the east – see map in Figure 3.1. Both boroughs are among the most densely populated in London – Islington's population at 113 persons per hectare being the highest in the capital. According to the 1991 Census the population of Islington was 165 000 and that of Tower Hamlets 161 000. But whereas current estimates suggest that the population of Islington is falling slightly, Tower Hamlets' population is estimated to be growing at a rate faster than any other London borough. This growth can be attributed to two factors. The first, inward migration, attributable to the high rate of private-house-building in the Docklands redevelopment area along the Thames in the south of the borough, has been considerable, particularly since 1985. Secondly, the rapid growth of the Bangladeshi community within Tower Hamlets, a growth not attributable to immigration, which since 1981/2 has undergone a net decrease rather than increase, but to its high birth-rate.

Both Islington and Tower Hamlets are socially and economically deprived inner city areas. According to the Department of the Environment's standardised score analysis based upon 1981 Census data, Islington was the seventh and Tower Hamlets the third most deprived local authority in the UK. At the time of our research in 1989/90, unemployment in both boroughs was approaching 20 per cent. The public housing sector in both boroughs was considerable – 52 per cent of Islington residents rented council accommodation;

54

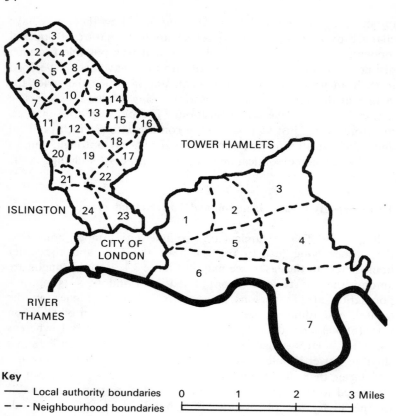

Key
—— Local authority boundaries
— — · Neighbourhood boundaries

0   1   2   3 Miles

ISLINGTON

1	Archway	13	Drayton Park
2	St John's	14	Quadrant
3	Beaumont Rise	15	Highbury
4	Hanley	16	Julie Curtin
5	Irene Watson	17	Canonbury East
6	St George's	18	Canonbury West
7	Tufnell Park	19	Upper Street
8	Durham Road	20	Cally
9	Gillespie	21	Calshot
10	Sobell	22	St Peter's
11	Clocktower	23	Finsbury
12	Rosedale	24	Clerkenwell

TOWER HAMLETS

1	Bethnal Green
2	Globe Town
3	Bow
4	Poplar
5	Stepney
6	Wapping
7	Isle of Dogs

FIGURE 3.1 The neighbourhoods in Islington and Tower Hamlets

just over 70 per cent did so in Tower Hamlets. In common with most other inner London boroughs the housing crisis in the late 1980s was acute – Tower Hamlets had the highest level of overcrowding in England.

The spatial distribution of deprivation varied within each of the two boroughs. In Islington the most deprived wards were concentrated in the north-east and the south-west. In Tower Hamlets deprivation had a more distinctive spatial distribution. Six wards were within the fifty most deprived in the whole of London. They form a continuous band from the fringes of the City through the old docklands to the east. Spitalfields, by this analysis, had the highest deprivation score in London.

The two boroughs have sizeable ethnic minority populations. According to the 1991 census, a large number of different non-European ethnic minority communities resided in Islington, accounting for 19 per cent of the total population. However, although there were sizeable Afro-Caribbean (10.6 per cent) and Asian (5.8 per cent) communities, no single group dominated in population terms. Islington also contains two sizeable European ethnic minority communities – the Irish and Cypriots. All Islington's ethnic minorities tend to be concentrated in the centre and north of the borough. In the south, a traditional white working-class community is concentrated particularly in the Finsbury and Clerkenwell areas immediately to the north of the City. Islington has also provided a home for a number of comparatively large middle-class communities, particularly those based upon the professions.

Whereas Islington could be described as a multiracial area, Tower Hamlets more closely resembles a biracial community in which a rapidly growing Bangladeshi community lives alongside a traditional white working-class population. According to the 1991 census, the total Bangladeshi population in Tower Hamlets was estimated to be 36 955 – that is, 22.9 per cent of the population. The community is concentrated at the western end of the borough in the wards with the highest levels of deprivation. There is also a small Afro-Caribbean population in the borough (7.1 per cent), the most distinctive element of which is the Somali community. The white population is strongly working-class. Until the recent redevelopment of the southern part of the borough by the London Docklands Development Corporation, the middle classes were noticeably

absent from the borough except for small pockets around Victoria
Park in the north.

The overall picture therefore is of two deprived inner city areas,
one marked by its cultural diversity, the other divided into a few
culturally distinctive territories: Bangladeshis to the west, white
'East Enders' to the east, the new, rich City workers to the south
along the River Thames. What is also striking is the lack of social
and geographical mobility, particularly among some of the large
poor white and ethnic minority communities concentrated on the
big housing estates.

In Chapter 1 we discussed in general terms the processes of
economic restructuring which are taking place in cities around the
world. We argued that these processes are having an increasingly
uneven impact on parts of cities and on different groups within
cities. Within the UK the resulting social polarisation is nowhere
more vividly displayed than in our case study boroughs. Consider
for a moment the way the City of London, including the Canary
Wharf bridgehead on the Isle of Dogs, sits cheek by jowl with the
inner city neighbourhoods of, for example, Finsbury in Islington
and Bethnal Green in Tower Hamlets. The gleaming, luxurious
office towers of the City contrast starkly with the adjacent
impoverished communities, each a kind of socio-spatial prison.
Inevitably, there is resentment. At one level this is mildly expressed –
for example, the residents of south Finsbury complain that the
Whitecross Street market has lost its character because it has
adapted to meet the needs of the lunch time 'yuppie' shoppers from
the City. At another level the protest is much more aggressive – as
when disillusioned teenagers use Stanley knives to scar the
paintwork of a Mercedes or BMW parked on 'their' turf.

The political origins of decentralisation in Islington

Having provided a brief profile of Islington and Tower Hamlets, we
now move on to consider the political origins and objectives of
decentralisation in the two boroughs. As the discussion unfolds it
will become clear that the decentralisation initiatives are fluid, not
static. They have evolved in response to changing pressures and
these pressures need to be examined and understood. By way of
introduction we would make two general points. First, the form and

significance of decentralisation is inextricably linked to the local political strategies for maintaining power adopted by the controlling parties in the two boroughs. Second, it is senseless to study decentralisation in any local authority in isolation from the broader context – a context which features constant interventions from central government in local authority policy-making, a continuation in many inner city areas of divison and tension within local communities, and a general atmosphere discribed to us by one local government officer as 'services under siege'.

The interest of the Islington Labour Party in both localisation and public participation goes back well into the 1970s – long before the new urban left began to gain momentum. Activists living in Islington were working over twenty years ago to make the local authority and other public service providers more responsive. For example, a group of tenants in north Islington, following tough negotiations, reached agreement with Islington Council and Circle 33 Housing Trust to create the Holloway Tenant Co-operative in February 1972 (Holmes, 1976). Various experiments with public participation took place in Islington during the 1970s and the Council's positive grant aid programme and its recruitment of community workers strengthened the voluntary sector and community groups (Smith, 1981). Miller takes the view that these developments were important in preparing the way for what was to come in the 1980s:

> for, without this ground clearing exercise, and the strengthening of the middle class groups in the local political culture, the urban left may have found it considerably more difficult to establish their dominance in a borough that historically was a traditional working class stronghold. (Miller, 1991, p. 125)

This suggestion is supported by other research on the emergence of the urban left – by the mid-1970s several councils, particularly in inner London, had younger, middle-class and more innovative councillors (Boddy and Fudge, 1984; Lansley *et al.*, 1989). In Islington it is clear that rapid gentrification in parts of the borough brought in several new professional middle-class councillors.

With the exception of 1968, Islington had for decades consistently returned Labour councils. However, the Conservative national electoral triumph in 1979 brought about an internal crisis within the

Labour Party out of which the Social Democratic Party (SDP) was founded in 1981. The SDP/Liberal Alliance had a fairly immediate impact on politics in both Islington and Tower Hamlets. In 1981 a large number of councillors and party members defected from Islington Labour Party to the SDP. They were drawn largely from the white working-class communities in the south of the borough although the figurehead was Michael O'Halloran, Member of Parliament for Islington North. Several of the politicians involved in the Islington Labour Party at this time have suggested to us that there was a rift, indeed an acrimonious battle, between the indigenous white working-class party members and the 'new, young professionals'. The defection of the right wing of the party to the SDP meant that control of Islington Council switched briefly to an Alliance group. In the 1982 local government elections the Labour response was emphatic – it won all but one of the fifty-two seats on the council.

The Labour Group which was returned to run Islington in 1982 was strongly identified with the 'Bennite' wing of the Labour Party. Its manifesto, a hefty 74-page document, gave much prominence to opposing Thatcherite policies – it promised no cuts in services. It was strongly committed to equal opportunities, local economic regeneration and solidarity with the struggles of oppressed communities at home and abroad. By the mid-1980s, along with some other London local authorities such as Hackney, Camden, Lambeth and Brent, Islington had become a target for media stories designed to discredit the work of, for example, women's committees.

Interestingly enough, the commitment to participation and decentralisation figured no more strongly than the commitment to a range of other radical policies in the 1982 manifesto. It insisted that:

> decision-making must be based on discussions across the Borough. . .There is a need to give fresh impetus to breaking down the bureaucratic isolation of much of the Council's activity. Involving more people will lead to services that more closely reflect needs, are better run, and have stronger support in the community. (Islington Labour Party, 1982, p. 1)

It went on to outline proposals for decentralisation although these were somewhat vague:

> Effective involvement of the community at large cannot be
> secured if the great majority of decisions are taken centrally. All
> service departments must be decentralised with local area teams
> or local facilities under a substantial degree of local management.
> The role of the Council will be to set the overall framework in
> terms of minimum standards, finance, responsibilities as an
> employer and co-ordination. (Islington Labour Party, 1982, p. 2)

There was no specific reference to the idea of neighbourhood offices.
While the overall thrust was clear, the specific way in which policy
objectives might be realised was not.

Most emphasis was placed upon developing participatory
structures for interest groups within a putative borough-wide
community. As the manifesto suggested:

> Community organisations are attempts by groups of people to
> organise to overcome their oppressions. In many cases the
> benefits of working together (making demands, managing
> services) may be as valuable as the services that the organisations
> provide, and community activity is valuable in order to combat
> the feelings of defeatism and despair that Tory policies bring in
> their wake. (Islington Labour Party, 1982, p. 4)

A sense of belonging to the borough was promoted by an appeal to
this imagined community of the oppressed, united in opposition to
the Conservatives and sharing, in a direct and concrete way,
ownership and control of the borough's valuable collective assets
and resources. In this light, therefore, we can see Islington's initial
commitment to decentralisation as part of a broader strategy of
constructing a 'community in struggle'.

The idea of the 'neighbourhood office' as a concrete and
practicable expression of this commitment to a new collectivism
appears to have taken shape immediately after the Labour victory.
By the end of 1982 the concept of a network of neighbourhood
offices delivering the mainline services of the borough and
connected to local neighbourhood committees had become a clear
model. What required elaboration was a more precise picture of the
services which should be based in such offices, their number and
location and the shape of the neighbourhood communities served by
each. In early 1983, therefore, a very extensive programme of public

consultation was undertaken with the residents of Islington as well as with council staff and trade unions. The resident consultation meetings were imaginatively run, they were clearly structured, use was made of small group discussions and so on. Out of this emerged the decision to go for twenty-four neighbourhoods, based wherever possible upon subjectively defined neighbourhood boundaries drawn from the resident consultation meetings.

The decentralisation strategy in Islington

The first years of the initiative focused upon getting the multiservice neighbourhood offices up and running. The first four opened in March 1985, the last in March 1987. Trade union resistance was considerable in places, particularly within the social services department whose staff were the last of those earmarked to take their place in the new offices (Heery, 1984). Towards the end of this period work started on the development of participatory structures which would operate alongside each office. Many of the borough's established tenants' organisations were wary of the notion of neighbourhood committees, seeing them as a means of bypassing their own consultation and negotiation machinery with the council. A great deal of energy was devoted to establishing a framework for neighbourhood participation which was as inclusive of all under-represented communities as possible but which actually gave local people very little decision-making power.

By this time, the initial political energy behind decentralisation was declining. The one councillor, Maurice Barnes, whose single-mindedness had been pivotal to the success of the initiative during its first phase, switched from being Chair of the Decentralisation Sub-Committee to Chair of the Housing Committee in 1986. Increasingly, the original radical objectives were being shed as leading Islington councillors began to see decentralisation as, essentially, a pragmatic strategy. Thus, Margaret Hodge, Leader of the Council, argued:

Our motives were highly pragmatic, concerned with the efficiency and co-ordination of the services that we provide . . . there are ideological reasons for undertaking decentralisation. In the context of Islington these are important but secondary. They concern the value of participation by the consumers of services in the planning and decision making process, they concern issues of local control over services and facilities. (Hodge, 1987, p. 32)

By 1987, the left in local government had experienced a number of defeats at the hands of the Conservative central government. The Labour-controlled metropolitan counties and Greater London Council had been abolished in 1986, central controls over local government expenditure had been greatly extended with the introduction of 'rate capping' in 1984, and the return of a third successive Conservative government in 1987 was followed by the introduction of effective restrictions on 'creative accounting' and moves to replace the rates with the poll tax. Indeed, 1987 was a watershed signalling a fundamental shift in the balance of power between central and local government. From this point onwards the decline of the left in local government, a decline which had been perceptible since 1985, began to accelerate as many of its leaders began to adopt the 'dented shield' strategy advocated by Neil Kinnock – that is, for Labour councillors to stay in power and do their best to avoid cuts in services and jobs (Lansley *et al.*, 1989, p. 45). 'Realism' and 'pragmatism' became the new order of the day both within the Labour Party nationally and within Labour-controlled local authorities.

Very little was actually achieved in the way of either managerial or political devolution throughout the 1980s. 'Above' the neighbourhood offices the rest of the council continued to operate very much within the same structures it had always used. The 'centre' remained top-heavy, support services such as finance and personnel continued to operate in a fairly unresponsive and bureaucratic fashion, and the political committee structures became increasingly complex and elaborate. Leaving aside the neighbourhood forums, the Council had twenty-two committees and sub-committees operating more or less throughout the 1986–90 period. Indeed, it almost seemed at times as if two entirely separate organisations were co-existing within the same local authority.

This co-existence of the old with the new was exemplified by the original internal management structure of the neighbourhood office – see Figure 3.2. Rather than there being a single manager responsible for all staff based within the neighbourhood office the four main groupings of staff present (housing, social services, environmental health and chief executives) were each primarily accountable via a principal officer to their own departmental hierarchy. The principal officer from the chief executive's department was formally accountable for the management of the office (but not most of the staff within it) and liaison with the surrounding communities via the neighbourhood forum. But s/he had no formal authority over the other neighbourhood services. It is a testimony to the commitment and inventiveness of Islington's neighbourhood office staff that this mix of departmental and integrated structures was made to work in a large number of offices.

The neighbourhood office structure, which existed largely intact throughout the 1980s, contained a number of inherent tensions – between local management and central control, between an integrated management structure and the traditional forms of professionally-based departmentalism – which led to a second wave of major changes in the early 1990s. In the 1990 local election – in London all councillors are up for election every four years – the Labour Party won all but three of the fifty-two seats on the council. The new Labour Group was committed to establishing a single Neighbourhood Services Department to replace the highly departmentalised structure illustrated in Figure 3.2.

From 1 January 1991, Martin Higgins, the existing Director of Housing, became Director of Neighbourhood Services. In the following months the new neighbourhood office structure was introduced and we discuss this further in Chapter 5. In essence, the housing, social services and chief executive functions were brought together within a single Neighbourhood Services Department and each neighbourhood office is now run by a single general neighbourhood manager. This arrangement is probably unique in UK local government. This second phase of organisational change occurred in the face of considerable opposition, particularly from senior staff in the then social services department. In 1992 the council decided to keep the twenty-four offices open but because of expenditure cuts has twinned sixteen of the neighbourhoods for management purposes (eight remain stand-alone). From 1993 there were, therefore, sixteen neighbourhood managers – eight managing a single office and eight managing a pair.

In summary, the implementation of neighbourhood decentralisation in Islington has involved both sharp and sudden transformations and incremental change over a ten-year period. The innovators

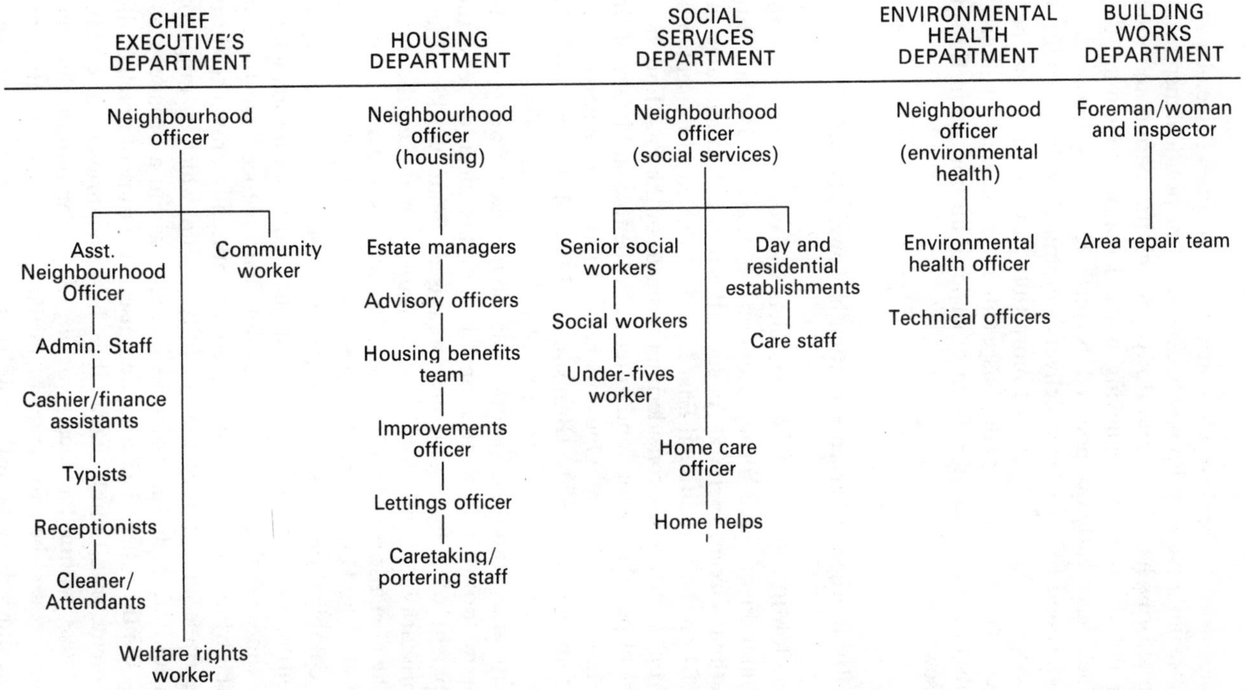

FIGURE 3.2 Typical structure of a neighbourhood office in Islington (1985–91)

have faced resistance from all quarters and at times it seemed as if the whole initiative was slipping backwards. The political inspiration for the reforms has ebbed and flowed during this period and much of the initial vision of achieving a participatory 'community of resistance' has clearly disappeared. Nevertheless, a distinct model of neighbourhood-based service delivery combined with an extension of local participation, discussed more fully in Chapter 7, has been achieved. The Islington model has excited a great deal of interest, not only in the UK but also from other local authorities in Europe and elsewhere.

The political origins of decentralisation in Tower Hamlets

The London Borough of Tower Hamlets was constructed from the amalgamation of three former London boroughs of Poplar, Bow and Bethnal Green, in 1965. As such, the borough constitutes the heart of London's traditional East End. It is difficult to disentangle myth from reality when considering the status of the East End, both in terms of popular history and in terms of the formal history of the British labour movement. One only has to think of the emergence of 'Poplarism' in the 1920s (Branson, 1979) and the rise of the Mosleyites culminating in the battle of Cable Street in 1936 (Piratin, 1980), to understand the pivotal role of the East End in labour movement politics. On the one hand this period sees the development of a homogeneous, organised, white working class built primarily around dock-related employment. On the other hand, the area also acted as the landing point for successive waves of migration – the Huguenots, the Jews and latterly the Bangladeshis.

This combination of a localised, occupationally-based working-class culture and waves of immigration has led to an unpredictable and, at times, explosive set of local political practices. On the one hand, the white working class has been continually drawn towards radical, transcendent forms of identity within which a range of diverse cultural traditions could be included within a broader class identity. On the other, the casual and insecure nature of much of the employment traditionally available has encouraged a certain defensiveness within the local working-class population that has provided the seed-bed for a set of insular and parochial attitudes which, at times, have been the soil from which racism has grown.

Since the Second World War, a number of developments have occurred which have undermined the solidaristic bases of the East End. First of all, there has been the decline of traditional sources of employment, particularly around the docks, a decline which was virtually complete by the early 1970s. Alongside the destruction of an important occupational base for community identity, the 1950s and 1960s in particular witnessed a massive wave of 'slum clearance', migration of young families to orbital new towns such as Harlow and Basildon, and housing redevelopment schemes, often 'high rise' in character (Willmott and Young, 1957). The combined effect of these developments was, to some extent, the creation of a working class population shorn of its own forms of labour and community organisation, living on the mythology of a vibrant, but past, community and led by a set of local Labour politicians, whose complacency was directly proportional to the total and continued absence of any kind of political opposition.

By the mid-1970s, Tower Hamlets was clearly becoming one of Labour's 'rotten boroughs'. It tended to be controlled by different cliques of old male councillors, very little by the way of innovation occurred in any service areas, and recruitment was almost entirely done internally. Relations between officers and members were very cordial, if not 'pally'. As one long-standing councillor noted, it was a Labour group which would not tolerate any criticism of its officers. As a succession of right-wing, Labourist, low-spending administrations came and went, an inertia set in which isolated the party from its electorate. Amazingly, the council consistently underspent on its housing investment by as much as 50 per cent. When squatters occupied some council properties in the mid-1970s, the council did not even know that it owned them. This was the context for the sudden and rapid emergence of a particular brand of Liberal politics in the borough.

The Liberal Party had no presence to speak of in Tower Hamlets before the mid-1970s. It was at that time that a few key Liberal activists, such as Eric Flounders and Bryn Williams, arrived in the borough. According to Flounders, the ward that he joined in Bow had been represented by the same Labour councillor since 1929. Flounders and Williams brought with them a quite new style of activism for Labour or Liberal politics in the borough. Interestingly enough, these activists organised themselves under the banner of 'Liberal Focus' rather than the Liberal party itself. This was the precursor to a brand of independent Liberal politics within the borough which has quite often set the local party against the national Liberal Party organisation.

The Liberal Focus initially concentrated its efforts upon the Bow ward within Tower Hamlets, and it was here that they achieved their first electoral successes, in 1978. In the 1982 election the Liberal Focus team won seventeen of the fifty seats on the borough council and by 1986 they became the majority group by one seat. Most of the elements of the decentralisation strategy which were implemented after 1986 were already assembled in the Liberal Manifesto of 1982. The seven neighbourhoods into which the borough has now been decentralised had already been identified by that time. In addition, by 1984, the Tower Hamlets Liberal Association was reorganising itself upon branches based round the seven neighbourhoods. By the late 1980s, the local Liberal Party had fewer than 160 members, but virtually all the members were very active.

More than one key Liberal activist referred to the organisation of the local association in terms of a democratic centralist model. Unlike many local Labour parties, the elected Liberal councillors also played a key role in the organisation of the constituency parties. In the 1970s, in particular, the local party operated a very strict regime. Candidates were not put forward for elections if the local party felt that it had an inadequate base in the area. Moreover, candidates had to live in the ward for which they were standing for election. It was these kinds of informal but strict rulings which brought the local Liberal Association quickly into conflict with the national Liberal Party.

It is useful to reflect on the specific nature of Liberalism within Tower Hamlets. On the one hand one might think of it as an extremely pure form of Liberal 'community politics'. Clearly there are strong elements of this, but there is also a strong sense of 'populism', which is perhaps the product of the confluence of Liberal politics within the strongly working-class local culture.

The Labour Party 'old guard' remained a strong residual force in the East End despite the emergence of a new urban left in many equivalent inner city Labour parties, including, as described earlier in this chapter, the Labour Party in Islington. Nevertheless, throughout the 1980s a deepening split developed within the Tower Hamlets Labour group, leading to the creation of a breakaway 'Tower Hamlets Labour Party' by some of this old guard. The

Labour Party's manifesto for the 1986 elections reflected entirely the political orientations of the new urban left. In a manner reminiscent of Labour groups in Liverpool, London and elsewhere, it called for a combined campaign by councillors, unions and community groups to defend local services against the Tory government.

In contrast, the Liberal 1986 manifesto, instead of mounting a campaign against the external Tory enemy, put forward an imaginatively populist strategy for tackling the rot within the borough itself. The Liberal manifesto opened with the following statement:

> What is pre-eminently wrong with the policies and structure of Tower Hamlets Council is that they are and have been the government of the bureaucrats, by the bureaucrats, for the bureaucrats. Council priorities have been theirs, not the people's. Services have been fashioned more for the convenience of the administrators, rather than to provide the services the people want, in the way they want. (Tower Hamlets Liberal Association, 1986, p. 5)

The Liberal manifesto attempted to make a clear distiction between Liberal and Labour approaches to decentralisation. Speaking of the Labour approach, the manifesto argues: 'To them it is providing local offices and local services; to us it is giving back power and control to the community' (p. 4).

Eric Flounders, who became Leader of the Council with the Liberal election victory of 1986, is particularly scathing about the kind of decentralisation carried out by some Labour authorities:

> They prat about, not knowing what they want or how to go about it – and they give in to every little demand by the unions, so that all they get in the end is a bigger, but decentralised bureaucracy. (Platt, 1987, p. 8)

The decentralisation strategy in Tower Hamlets

The key themes in the Liberal 1986 manifesto were concerned with issues of power, accountability and responsiveness. The manifesto sought to abandon the old specialist system of committees and replace it with a new set of committees related to neighbourhood rather than to professional functions. According to the manifesto, under the old system councillors frequently did not know (and possibly did not care) where the area being discussed was, so that they made either no contribution to the discussion or an ill-informed one. The manifesto promised an entirely new approach to political decision-making within the borough, based upon a system of neighbourhood committees controlled by the councillors elected for those wards. It is worth quoting the manifesto objectives in their entirety. There are just four:

1.   To restore political control to the elected councillors.

2.   To enable the decisions affecting each community to be taken by those who know best its needs and who are accountable to it.

3.   To make council services as accessible, as open and as responsive to the needs of each area as possible.

4.   To make council services provide value for money. (Tower Hamlets Liberal Association, 1986, p. 6)

Clearly, then, there is emphasis upon devolving control, enhancing accountability and increasing responsiveness. But this is conceived of within a very particular framework. Control is to be devolved to councillors who are, in this model, seen as the community. In Chapter 8 we explore in more detail this process of giving power back to locally-elected representatives. Additionally, responsiveness is seen almost exclusively in terms of the need to relate to and serve geographical communities rather than to those communities based upon, say, race, gender or other differences. This was clearly stated in the Liberal manifesto of 1986:

The principal and overwhelmingly most far-reaching proposal is that of total devolvement of power. In effect, it gives power back to the hamlets round the tower; it turns local government upside down, abandons centralised bureaucracy, and returns to the old 'parish' concept. It hands back to local areas and individuals the maximum possible control. That is what Liberalism is all about. (Tower Hamlets Liberal Association, 1986, p. 3)

In other words, the Liberals planned to rescue the old neighbour-hoods, neighbourhood loyalties and ethnic identities from obscurity, provide them with a new political autonomy and model local government around them. Interestly, this approach is very much in line with the ideology espoused by Seabrook in his discussion of the Labour Party-led decentralisation strategy in Walsall, although some of the ingredients are different. Seabrook talks of communities destroyed by unemployment and of the:

> untiring ideological assault on traditional working-class values, initiated and egged on by the media, with its shifting focus on threats and fears that undermine community – all the scares about mugging, or rapists or vandals; the scare about scroungers and idlers. . . Whatever the resilience, they do, in the end, have some effect. (Seabrook, 1984, p. 4)

He argued that a project which bases itself on the realities of neighbourhood life was engaging in one of the great ideological battles of our time. Notions of community and solidarity had been damaged by Thatcherism, but action at neighbourhood level could, he argued, enable people to fight back.

In Tower Hamlets, the eclipse of communities was couched in an intensely ethnicised language, and the sentiments of loss and disquiet of the once-dominant mix of white residents was intimately related to their position relative to new ethnic communities in the area. Old ties to place, fixed as parishes or older wards, and ties to neighbourhood, family and ethnicity held enormous political potential for any party bold enough to promote them as the basis for a vigorous political realignment. In Tower Hamlets, then, the Liberals recognised large, untapped feelings of imagined community and set about using them as the political foundation for their decentralisation policy.

Ultimately, this long-term policy initiative rested on reserves of deep-seated and unconditional support by self-identifying commu-nities. By transforming various imagined communities into institutional realities, they at once turned the fears and nostalgia, which were mobilised in times of defeat and threat, into a sense of political vigour. In turn, newly-won political strength had the potential to renew faith in the imagined community and guarantee support for its Liberal protagonists. In this regard, the Liberals were considerably assisted by the degree of ethnic spatial segregation in Tower Hamlets referred to earlier in the chapter. They were accused of manipulating white racism, and there is evidence to support these claims, as we show later in Chapter 8. Their response to this claim was that their strategy was more likely to empower the principal ethnic groups in whichever areas they dominated. In this sense the Liberals were committed to the notion of well-defined neighbourhoods developing their own priorities and strategy through committed local political leadership, even if that meant the enhancement of cultural difference and a significant degree of political divergence emerging within the borough.

Indeed, the Liberals were to shock the world of local government by handing over power in parts of the borough to their political opponents. Eric Flounders was able to claim that: 'We are the only local authority in Britain ever to have voluntarily given power to members of another political party' (Platt, 1987, p. 8).

The Liberals moved with astonishing speed to implement their strategy of devolving power to seven neighbourhoods. Immediately after the election on 9 May 1986, they told the officers that the traditional committee system had been scrapped, to be replaced largely by a system of seven multipurpose neighbourhood committees. Four of the new neighbourhood committees were controlled by the Liberals, the remaining three by Labour. The pace of change set by the council was startling:

> By the end of July it had held neighbourhood consultations, agreed in principle the specific locations of the new neighbourhood town halls and created seven new posts of neighbourhood Chief Executive, in effect disbanding the existing service directorate structure. (Morphet, 1987, p. 124)

The assumption on the part of the Liberal councillors was that everything that could be decentralised should be. All officers located in neighbourhood offices report to their neighbourhood Chief Executive and not to any departmental or service head outside the neighbourhood structure. This model was, then, rather different from the Islington neighbourhood structure introduced in 1982 – although, as we have mentioned, Islington did decide to introduce neighbourhood managers in 1990.

After losing a seat to Labour in a 1988 by-election, the Liberals lost control of the Poplar neighbourhood and maintained only overall control of the borough on the casting vote of the mayor. For a period, four of the seven neighbourhoods were Labour-controlled. In the May 1990 elections, however, the Liberals were victorious – they won control of five of the seven neighbourhoods, leaving Labour in control of just two. According to Peter Hughes, who became Leader of Tower Hamlets in 1990, decentralisation had contributed greatly to the success of the Liberal Party:

> The councils that have done well in the London elections are the ones that have paid attention to detailed, quality of service type issues. . . Our decentralised structure is much more knowledge-able and is able to see possibilities and push through changes.

In summary, the process of decentralisation in Tower Hamlets was on the 'big bang' model. There was a sudden and startling change in the spring and summer of 1986. Old structures, and some of the senior officers who were resistant to the new changes, disappeared almost overnight. The structure of the council has been transformed and the power of ward councillors has been substantially increased. A consequence is that, like the innovations in Islington, the Tower Hamlets model has attracted a great deal of interest within local government circles in the UK and in Europe.

Constructions of 'community'

As we explain in more detail in Chapter 9, the concept of community is an ambiguous and slippery one. Following Anderson (1983), we consider all communities not as naturally occuring things but as social constructions developed by groups which believe they have 'something in common' – typically a common interest, cultural identity or experience of place. By their nature, neighbourhood decentralisation strategies tend to give emphasis to the shared experience of place and, as we shall argue later, this is both a strength and a weakness.

Our analysis of the political emergence and evolution of decentralisation in Islington and Tower Hamlets enables us to extend the discussion of the geographical dimensions of decentralisation and to examine the different ways councils can work to bolster or foster the development of communities of place. First, we refer briefly to the size of the neighbourhoods, then we consider the construction of 'community'. Figure 3.1 on page 54 provides a map showing the neighbourhoods in Islington and Tower Hamlets. In Islington's twenty-four neighbourhoods population sizes vary from around 4000 to 11 000 and average around 6500. In Tower Hamlets, the neighbourhoods comprise groups of wards and are, on the whole fairly large – populations ranging from 14 000 to 32 000. This reflects the desire to strengthen the role of ward councillors. In Islington the neighbourhoods do not respect ward boundaries. Rather they reflect the aim of creating a very local service with the precise boundaries of the neighbourhoods emerging from discussion with local people. The Islington councillors felt that the ward boundaries did not relate well to people's experience of living in the neighbourhoods.

Comparing the way in which the idea of community was constructed through the decentralisation initiatives in each borough we can see how the Tower Hamlets Liberals based their strategy not on a desire to create communities, but on a wish to free existing communities from cultural anonymity and an alienating central bureaucracy. The Liberals' debt to historical precedent was evident in their choice of neighbourhoods. In Islington the size and shape of neighbourhoods were principally influenced by the commitment to provide convenient, short-distance access to multiservice delivery points. This resulted in the creation of many neighbourhoods with no prior historical reference or precedent. In marked contrast, the choice in Tower Hamlets was based upon six clearly recognised areas, each one rich in historical specificity and cultural identity – the one exception being Globe Town, an amalgamation of parts of Bethnal Green and Bow.

To retain such names as Poplar, Bethnal Green, Wapping, Stepney and Bow served to underline the council's commitment to the past and to the local imagined communities which inhabited it. In Islington, in contrast, in some of the new neighbourhoods, such as Beaumont Rise in the north of the borough, the new neighbourhood offices were not only placed in hitherto unrecognised 'neighbourhoods' but they also acquired names which meant nothing to local people.

There is another sense in which the Liberal initiative drew heavily upon cultural traditions within the locality. Their model expressed a notion of strong, representative local leadership whereas in Islington the emphasis was initially placed upon enhancing participation at all levels. In Tower Hamlets, in the past, this close association between neighbourhood and individual leadership was based on a voluntary commitment from local councillors and an intense loyalty from close-knit local communities. It gave rise to a specific form of political paternalism. The Tower Hamlets model of decentralisation continued with this successful recipe and provided the basis for the emergence of very strong forms of neighbourhood leadership formalised through the neighbourhood committee system – a pattern perhaps exemplified in Bow during the period 1986–90, when the neighbourhood was widely considered to be Councillor Eric Flounders' fiefdom.

While some of the neighbourhoods in Islington are new creations, the pattern varies across the borough. Thus, for example, Finsbury in the far south of the borough has an extremely strong sense of place and history – partly because there was a Finsbury Borough Council in the pre-1965 era. Elderly white residents living in high rise blocks in Finsbury felt they were living in 'the finest housing estate in England' and remember well the physical transformation of the area in the 1950s and 1960s. To some extent the council, by creating a neighbourhood forum in the area, has latched on to these feelings of solidarity. Some residents told us they felt the neighbourhood had 'a family atmosphere'. There is, however, an occasional sting in the tail for the councillors. Some residents make jokes about councillors getting paid child-minding money when they attend meetings and they were sometimes heard to say: 'We were better off when we were just Finsbury, weren't we?'

The nature of political innovation

The changes which occured in the organisation of local government in Islington and Tower Hamlets were led by local activists and the innovation that was achieved was enduring and radical. By radical we mean that they can be considered as discontinuous innovations, changes of pattern rather than changes within pattern. Other local authorities had similarly ambitious plans, some of which, such as the London Borough of Hackney's, collapsed before implementation (Hoggett, Lawrence and Fudge, 1984). In the area of neighbourhood decentralisation other local authorities, such as Birmingham, Camden and Lewisham, achieved some change in the 1980s, but these were partial, essentially adaptations to existing structures rather than root and branch reform. Moreover, as we have seen, changes in Islington have taken a full ten years to accomplish and, even now, many aspects of the traditional centralised and bureaucratic structure remain intact. Nevertheless we still feel that what has been achieved qualifies as a radical form of innovation. How was such innovation possible in Islington and Tower Hamlets but not in other Labour- or Liberal controlled local authorities of this period?

In Chapter 1 we examined some of the debate which has occurred about the importance of 'locality'. This debate is concerned with the possibility of autonomy at the local level; that is, the possibility that the sphere of local government and community action can be considered as a site for political struggle and innovation rather than simply as an extension of the central state apparatus. The latter position, one largely adopted by Cockburn (1977) in her analysis of developments in the London Borough of Lambeth, tends to draw upon forms of functionalist Marxism in which the state (including the local and welfare state) is viewed as a totalising and monolithic formation.

In the 1980s many criticisms of this perspective were developed (see, for example, Duncan and Goodwin, 1988) as a concern emerged to combine a class analysis with a recognition of the difference that locality can make. Ultimately this difference can be considered as the way in which various local cultures and traditions which permeate communities, cities and regions mediated by local economic conditions respond to, and impact upon, broader economic, social and political developments. Changes at one level of society cannot simply be read off from those occurring at higher levels – the national is not simply an echo of the international, nor is the local simply an echo of the national.

Local government is one element of the welfare state. In the UK the welfare state was a compromise forged between conflicting class interests after the Second World War. Local government consists of that part of the welfare state subject to direct local political accountability. So the welfare state, from the outset, served contradictory interests (Offe, 1975) and this affected its strategic role – to contain inequality while reproducing it, to give expression to the democratic impulse while restraining it, and so on. What emerged was a fundamentally technocratic set of institutions, protected by a political consensus which implied that social challenges and problems were amenable to professional and administrative solutions. Therefore, as it developed, the welfare state became the site for the articulation of a number of powerful, and often competing, structural interest groups – professional occupational communities, local political élites, public-sector trade unions, administrative and managerial personnel – who were able to combine strategies of self-interest with interpretations of the public interest.

This essentially contradictory foundation and complex, partly interlocking and partly conflicting structure presents a real set of limits to the kinds of change which can be achieved within the welfare state. But such contradictions and conflicts also provide change agents with their room for manoeuvre, they are the source of what Cockburn (1977) described as 'the play within the state'. The degree of change achievable will depend upon the balance of political forces – the extent to which the driving forces for change are confident, organised and organisationally intelligent, and the extent to which the opposing forces are complacent, divided or unable to match the wit or speed of manoeuvre of those driving change. The starting point however must lie in the perception of the need for change itself.

The problem for the two main political parties in the UK is that by virtue of their role in creating the architecture of the welfare state, they became accomplice to the particular technocratic form that this part of the state assumed. So even the most radical ideology of Labourism, in both its traditional and modern forms, exemplified a deeply technocratic and consensual model of socialism (Hoggett and McGill, 1988). Thus, it would be mistaken to believe that suddenly, in the late 1970s, a space opened up within the contradictions of the welfare state from which counter-hegemonic innovations began to pour. On the contrary, at the formal level the space for manoeuvre within the welfare state was already diminishing as expenditure cutbacks got underway.

What was new was the existence of a variety of grass-roots political, social and urban movements which pushed persistently at accepted boundaries. This point is made by Goss (1988) who argues that a 'blanket-like social consensus' around local service provision muffled the conflict between central and local government and inhibited the ability of local government to test its powers for much of the post-war period. She notes:

> So strong were the popular and professional assumptions about the role of local government that it never flexed its muscles. Hence, during this period, it could be argued that political constraints in the form of social assumptions and self-imposed political limits were stronger than formal constraints. (Goss, 1988, p. 162)

The radicalisation of local politics, in part a reaction to Thatcherism but in larger part a reflection of the impact of community-based, feminist and other forms of 'new' politics at the local level, corresponded to the partial and temporary abandonment of such subjective constraints by what Gyford called 'the new urban left' (Gyford, 1985). Given the defection of much of the old guard and working-class Labour to the SDP in 1981 the incoming Labour administration in Islington in 1982 was strongly influenced by this new political current.

The Liberals in Tower Hamlets, however, were quite different. In many ways they were as scornful of the new urban left ('trendy middle-class activists', as Tower Hamlets Liberals tended to call them) as they were of the old-guard Labourism which had dominated local politics in Tower Hamlets for decades. The Liberals, however, did bring with them another tradition, a newer tradition of Liberal community politics which had been forged as a grass-roots strategy by a party which had been, with a few exceptions, entirely without the experience of power at either national or local level for the best part of fifty years. We can speculate that, precisely because the Liberals had obtained no opportunity to establish any significant foothold within this part of the welfare state, their commitment to established conventions of political conduct was much looser.

The subjective constraints from which local Labour activists had to break free were therefore much weaker for Liberals, particularly in areas such as Tower Hamlets where Liberal politicians had only very recently obtained any form of representation. This may explain the paradox that while on the one hand the Liberal strategy was to extend traditional forms of representative rather than participatory democracy at the local level they did so in a way which was quite unprecedented. By handing over power to Labour councillors in the Labour-controlled neighbourhoods of Wapping, Stepney and the Isle of Dogs (three of the seven neighbourhoods) they defied one of the most basic conventions of representative politics – that is, having gained political control you do not then give any of it away.

For different reasons, therefore, party activists in Islington and Tower Hamlets were able to break free from the prevailing conventions and routinised assumptions which permeated the local welfare state. But this was not unique to these two boroughs. How was it that radical changes were implemented here but not elsewhere? In many ways Islington, in 1982, was already widely considered to be a modern and progressive local authority whose reputation attracted high quality professional and managerial staff, particularly in areas such as planning, architecture, social work and corporate planning.

Tower Hamlets was quite different. It was a pre-modern local authority, professionalism was weak, patronage strong and effective management virtually non-existent. But what existed in Tower Hamlets was a highly distinctive local working-class culture based upon a latent sense of defended community, a form of community largely lacking formal organisation or effective leadership. What the Liberals brought to this locality was strong leadership, a radically populist political strategy and the re-evocation of a lost history. In other words, the Liberals were able to harness a latent dynamic within the local culture to create a form of government which was uniquely congruent with local conditions.

In contrast, little in the way of cultural specificity differentiated Islington from many other inner-city areas. No single community, middle- or working-class, white or ethnic minority, dominated the local cultural landscape. The only convincing explanation for the political innovation that was achieved lies in the high quality of its political leadership. In particular it is worth noting the paradox that throughout the 1970s and 1980s the political leadership in Islington was tightly centralised – this both accounts for the success of Labour activists in implementing decentralisation in the teeth of trade union and professional opposition in the 1982–4 period, and for the resilience of the centrally-located bureaucracy which remained largely intact within the borough throughout the 1980s.

PART II
DECENTRALISED MANAGEMENT

4   Neighbourhood Decentralisation and the New Public Management

Introduction

The purpose of this chapter is to provide new ways of understanding the changing nature of management in local government. First we provide a context by examining the radically new approaches to the organisation of the production of goods and services which have emerged within both the public and private sectors during the last decade or so. Specifically we seek to examine some of the components of what has become known as 'the new public management' and to locate neighbourhood decentralisation as one strategy for giving particular shape to this. We provide a conceptual framework for neighbourhood decentralisation in which its four components – localisation, flexibility, devolution, and organisational culture change – are envisaged as interlocking and mutually reinforcing. We explore these four dimensions of decentralisation in some detail and offer numerous examples to illustrate how various models have worked in practice.

New forms of organisation and management

Profound changes in the organisation of the firm have taken place in Western-type democracies since the 1970s. Although the scale and nature of these changes are still contested, the giant industrial bureaucracies of the post-war years appear to be giving way to more internally and externally decentralised forms of organising production. These changes have found expression in the so-called 'post-Fordism' debate, a debate which was initiated by writers within the French 'Regulationist school' in the late 1970s (Aglietta, 1979).

The early phases of this debate were dominated by a tendency for over-generalisation from what may well have been rather specific developments within certain industrial sectors or regions (for example, Piore and Sabel, 1984). More recently, however, a number of analyses have emerged which, while recognizing the reality of the qualitative transformation in the organisation of production which seems to be occurring, nevertheless suggest that the particular form that restructuring assumes will vary from one economy and sector to another (Leborgne and Lipietz, 1987; Lane, 1988). Some writers, such as Clegg (1990), have also drawn attention to the way in which restructuring processes may also be 'culturally embedded' – that is, influenced by broader social and cultural traditions within particular nations and regions.

Some commentators have also drawn connections between the restructuring debate and the 'markets and hierarchies' perspective of Williamson (1985) by suggesting that the trend underlying many of the changes taking place is one in which a previously dominant paradigm of organisational control (control through hierarchy), is being displaced by a new one (control by contract). We should be careful however to understand that a variety of contractual forms of control appear to be emerging within and between firms, only one class of which corresponds to the classical free market model of open competition within an impersonal market. Indeed, some (Powell, 1990) have argued that in many regions and sectors relationships between and within firms are governed more by network-like forms of association than by arm's-length contractual arrangements.

Within organisations that have implemented radical internal decentralisation, the devolved operational units function on a contractual basis in relation to the firm's strategic core. A consequence is that the firm itself contains a kind of internal market for finance, information technology, training and other services. Where external decentralisation of production occurs this often involves a considerable element of inter-firm collaboration through which long-term partnerships between client and contractor organisations become the norm (Aoki, 1987; Dore, 1983). It is therefore useful to think of all markets for secondary goods and services as involving elements of competition and collaboration.

To summarise, a new organisational paradigm appears to be emerging which gives emphasis to radically decentralised methods in the organisation of production. Internal decentralisation corresponds to the process whereby management control, particularly at the operational level, is devolved within the firm, leading to the creation of internal business units typically engaged in trading with other units both within and outside the firm. External decentralisation corresponds to the process of 'contracting out' production and the control of horizontally integrated networks of subcontractors. It is vital to recognise, however, that the decentralisation of production is not equivalent to the decentralisation of strategic command. If anything, operational decentralisation has facilitated a much greater strategic centralisation – multinationals such as Benetton or Toyota have been able to exert much greater central control through the external decentralisation of production. It follows that decentralisation does not necessarily weaken the role of the centre. Indeed, it can be argued that effective decentralisation requires a strong and confident centre.

Irrespective of which form of decentralisation is pursued (and most large firms appear to have introduced a mix of each) the primary mode of control is through the medium of contractual relations. However, even in the case of inter-firm relations, such 'contracts' will assume a variety of forms – the legally-binding commercial contract being just one of these. Thus, we need to think of a contract as an agreement between two or more parties in which the rights and duties of each are more or less clearly specified.

The new public management

The organisation of public services in Western-type democracies has also witnessed dramatic changes since the late 1970s. This is partly through a process of imitation of developments within the commercial sector. Many of the contextual factors which triggered restructuring in the latter – for example, the impact of information technology, the rise of consumer expectations, the pace of change in political, social, and cultural environments – have also spurred change within the public sector. However, some triggering factors have also been specific to the public sector.

All Western-type economies faced similar problems in the 1970s, specifically a 'fiscal crisis of the state' which demanded the reining back of state expenditure (O'Connor, 1973; Pickvance and

Preteceille, 1991). From this perspective these governments were faced with the task of reforming state administration in a manner which gave emphasis to economy and efficiency: that is, to getting more from less. According to Hood (1991) this forced all governments to give emphasis to a certain set of administrative values, namely 'keep it lean and purposeful'. It is these values which have driven the search for new approaches to the organisation of public services and dominated the development of what has become termed 'the new public management' (Aucoin, 1990; Hood, 1990, 1991; Chapman, 1991). Hood (1991) summarises the components of new public management in terms of the shift towards the disaggregation of administrative units; the creation of explicit standards and measures of performance; an emphasis on results rather than procedures; the use of contract and franchise arrangements inside as well as outside the public sector; the promotion of competition; and a stress upon private-sector styles of management.

Once again, however, we should beware of thinking of the new public management as a single model of organisation – it assumes different forms in different nations according to their political, economic and cultural conditions. For example, a recent US contribution to these debates puts particular emphasis on entrepreneurial forms of management (Osborne and Gaebler, 1992). Moreover, even within a single country, such as Britain, the new management has been and will be shaped in different styles in different policy areas, at different levels of government, under different forms of political control.

Having said this, it is also true that successive Conservative governments have given a particular character to the new public management as it emerged in the UK. The emphasis has constantly been placed on the externalisation of production through compulsory competitive tendering, privatisation and 'opting out'. While in some cases – for example, the local management of schools – internally decentralised arrangements have been encouraged, it would seem that this was intended as a mere prelude to the promotion of competition and opting-out. Furthermore, government-inspired decentralisation strategies:

> have been developed with the explicit purpose of weakening and
> residualising local government and the rudimentary forms of

democratic structure residing at district level within the National Health Service. Power is being concentrated at the centre or dissipated into a disaggregated, sub-local arena of management agencies. (Hoggett, 1990a, p. 49)

The more the balance of power shifted towards central government in the 1980s, the more it was able to insert its own values, methods and language into the new management practices and the more difficult it became for local institutions to shape the new methods in their own image and for their own purposes. However, our argument is that despite this shift in the balance of power, a distinctive alternative approach to managing the public services did emerge at the local institutional level in the 1980s, one which harnessed the emerging post-bureaucratic paradigm to a set of values and purposes which had at their heart the reinvigoration of local democratic institutions rather than the supplanting or bypassing of them. This alternative gave emphasis to the radical internal decentralisation of public institutions, primarily on a spatial basis – that is, the creation of neighbourhood or area-based forms of service delivery structures, as a prelude to the promotion of community-based forms of institutional accountability.

Neighbourhood management

The impetus for change towards different forms of neighbourhood management has stemmed from a recognition of the kinds of concern set out in Figure 4.1.

Neighbourhood decentralisation was seen as a means of responding to many of these criticisms by introducing fundamental changes to the way in which services were organised and managed. This form of innovation was pursued most strongly by Labour- and Liberal-controlled authorities, two of which, the London boroughs of Islington and Tower Hamlets, are the subject of detailed examination in this book. These two were chosen because they represented, and still represent, the most radical forms of neighbourhood decentralisation to have been achieved in the UK. However, a large number of other authorities engaged in similar experiments throughout the 1980s and early 1990s. Thus Basildon, Harlow, Rochdale, Middlesbrough, Lewisham, Manchester, Rich-

1	Unresponsive	Front line staff do not have the authority to respond to the public.
2	Uninformative	Few people understand council procedures – they may know that they are number x on the housing waiting list and have y points, but they do not know what this means.
3	Inaccessible	Services are located in huge, hostile buildings miles away from where people live, and public meetings are unwelcoming.
4	Poorly co-ordinated	Despite the corporate management initiatives of the 1970s, departmentalism and professionalism have grown stronger.
5	Bureaucratic	Virtually every decision has to be made with reference to the 'rule book' or involves senior management. This requires large amounts of paperwork and causes long delays.
6	Unwilling to listen	Staff are trained to be more concerned with departmental and professional objectives than with listening to the problems of the public. Answering a public enquiry is often seen as a distraction from work.
7	Inefficient	There is massive waste as a result of duplication between departments and the application of uniform policies which have no flexibility to respond to local needs.
8	Unaccountable	Front-line staff and their managers cannot be properly held to account for poor performance if they lack control over the resources that are necessary to deliver services, nor can politicians be held to account for decisions made in remote central committees which have an impact in unforeseen ways on local communities.

FIGURE 4.1   Typical complaints about public service bureaucracies

mond, Stirling, Bradford, Birmingham and South Somerset have all pursued multiservice approaches to decentralisation in one form or another.

Walsall, Camden, Newham, Glasgow, Norwich, Sheffield and Southwark, among many others, have adopted strategies focusing primarily upon the decentralisation of the public housing service.

Many examples of neighbourhood- or locality-based decentralisation of the social services have also occurred (for example, in East Sussex, Devon, Berkshire, Hertfordshire, Cambridgeshire) but here the impetus has been primarily managerial and professional – in very few instances has the reorganisation been envisaged as the basis for new forms of accountability. Finally, within the National Health Service, Community Health Services within District Health Authorities have been reorganised on a 'patch' or locality basis in several areas – North Staffordshire, Devon and West Lambeth are probably the most interesting examples of attempts to do this in an integrated fashion for a number of services.

Given this diversity of interest and approaches, it is important to make two fundamental points about neighbourhood decentralisation at the outset. First, as we stressed in the previous chapter, decentralisation, in whatever form, is not an end in itself. Rather, decentralisation should be viewed as a possible route to the achievement of an organisation's strategic objectives. A public organisation that says its aim is 'to decentralise' does not know what it is doing – it needs to know *why* it is decentralising.

Second, and directly related to this, there are important choices to be made about objectives. Decentralisation can mean very different things to different people and, as with any purposeful approach to organisational change, it is essential for those leading the strategy to be as clear as possible about the objectives decentralisation is designed to achieve. The question for local authorities is not so much 'Should we decentralise?' as 'What form of decentralisation, if any, will further our values and policy priorities?'. In other words, decentralisation is a means, not an end in itself. Figure 4.2 identifies six overlapping yet distinct objectives.

Whatever the objectives involved, the principle of neighbourhood decentralisation underlies a discernable trend in the development of many of the public services over the last decade. Throughout this period we have worked closely as trainers, consultants and researchers with many of the organisations concerned. Over the years we have developed specific models or frameworks for understanding the nature of such developments (Hambleton, 1978 and 1988; Hambleton and Hoggett, 1984; Hoggett and Hambleton, 1987; Hambleton, Hoggett and Tolan, 1989; Burns, 1989). Building on this earlier work, we have been able to construct what we now see as an ideal-type model of neighbourhood decentralisation which

1	Improving services	More sensitive service delivery. Changing the relationship between public servants and the public: public at the top. Service planning and policy.
2	Strengthening local accountability	Enhancing public influence and control. Making performance more visible to the public. Strengthening the power of ward councillors. Promoting community development.
3	Achieving distributional aims	Targeting resources on different areas/ groups.
4	Encouraging political awareness	Winning political support for public services. Increasing public knowledge about local issues. Winning support for a political party.
5	Developing staff	Enhancing job satisfaction from working more closely with the public. Creating a friendly work environment. Encouraging neighbourhood loyalty.
6	Controlling costs	Developing management control to improve cost-effectiveness.

FIGURE 4.2   Possible objectives of decentralisation

1	Localisation	The physical relocation of services from a centralised to a neighbourhood or 'patch' level.
2	Flexibility	The promotion of more flexible forms of management and work organisation through multidisciplinary team working, multiskilling, local general and corporate management.
3	Devolved management	The devolution of decision-making powers to service delivery managers and staff.
4	Organisational culture change	The reorientation of management and staff values to promote quality of service and local democracy through greater user empowerment.

FIGURE 4.3   Neighbourhood decentralisation: an ideal-type model

consists of four interlocking and mutually-reinforcing elements. We outline this model in Figure 4.3.

Taken together, these four elements could constitute the organisational basis for a radical form of local accountability, what in Part 3 we call 'decentralised democracy'. Clearly, it also amounts to an ambitious programme of change for any public organisation to take on. Perhaps because of this many local authorities have pursued a partial strategy. Our experience tells us that this is to misunderstand the potential of decentralisation – the components of the model are highly interconnected. As a result it may only be possible to make a lasting impact if all four elements are addressed. There is little point, for example, in having accessible local offices if they cannot deliver anything because the local staff have little authority to act – or if the public has to wait even longer to get an answer to their queries because there are now more tiers of bureaucracy than there were before. In the remainder of this chapter we elaborate on the model and in Chapter 5 we use it to evaluate decentralised management in Islington and Tower Hamlets.

Localisation

Localisation refers to the physical relocation of services. It involves shifting services from centrally-located offices (often the town hall) to sites within local communities. There are now over a hundred local authorities that have localised one or more of their services. Localisation can be evaluated by the degree to which it is able to meet the objectives of: (1) physical accessibility; (2) openness; and (3) comprehensiveness.

1   Physical accessibility
There has been a considerable difference in the degree of localisation adopted by different authorities. While neighbourhoods in Birmingham cover populations of over 20 000 each, in Walsall each neighbourhood covers a population of nearer 7000. The concept behind the smaller areas is that they should be small enough to have a real 'neighbourhood' identity and be easily accessible to local people. Neighbourhood offices, as with any public service office should, of course, be designed to be easily accessible for people with disabilities. Unfortunately, this is not always the case.

2   Openness

The evidence suggests that it is not necessary to have a glossy finish on neighbourhood offices to ensure that the local service is used and supported. When the Labour Party lost control of Walsall council in 1982, the Conservatives tried to close certain neighbourhood offices. Even though these offices were housed in cheap prefabricated buildings, their closure was resisted with widespread protest. People felt they received a better service from the local offices than they had done from the centralised ones.

More important than the external design of the buildings is the way in which the offices are organised internally, in particular whether they are open-plan or not. The neighbourhood offices in Basildon are open-plan (Burns and Williams, 1990). This arrangement applies to everyone, including the office manager who sits with the rest of the staff. A degree of privacy is created through the strategic arrangement of indoor plants. In Basildon the offices are laid out so that specialists are located furthest from the public entrance and non-specialist receptionists are closest, but the public still has a right to walk in and talk to whoever they want. Similarly, in Walsall's local housing offices, the public has open access to all staff.

Other decentralised offices have resisted the open-plan arrangement, arguing that it prejudices staff safety. In 1986, Lewisham's housing staff went on strike over the refusal of the council to allow safety screens in decentralised offices (Thomas, 1987). In Norwich there are still high counters and although there are no glass divisions, there are emergency buttons which send metal screens crashing down on to the counters at the first sign of aggression. A compromise which seems to work effectively is one adopted in many of Liverpool's neighbourhood housing offices where reception areas have low, wide counters, so there is a reasonable distance between staff members and any potential attackers, but the atmosphere still remains informal enough to defuse potentially violent incidents. In addition, staff need to be trained in how to avert aggression.

Experience seems to suggest that the more open the environment the more likely it is that any potentially violent incidents will be defused. However, it is possible that incidents which do occur may be more extreme. So while we are convinced of the success of the open-plan policy, it is important to be aware of the potential dangers. It is also important to be able to respond flexibly because each local office faces different circumstances. On one estate we visited in Renfrew, housing office staff had their tyres slashed when they parked outside the office, they were abused and threatened as they left work, and the office was regularly vandalised. It would obviously be absurd to have a completely open work environment in these hostile circumstances. Nevertheless, such circumstances also point to the fact that solutions will not usually be found through technical means – for example, emergency screens – but rather in making sure that people are not working in isolation and can quickly enlist further human support.

3   Comprehensiveness

As we illustrate in the following chapter, there is often a trade-off to be established between making services really local on the one hand and providing a comprehensive service on the other. What should be decentralised? In practice the answer to this question has often been pragmatic. As we have already mentioned, there have been a large number of single service initiatives, primarily involving the decentralisation of either housing or social services.

When it comes to implementing a multiservice decentralisation initiative the debate has been more complicated. Harlow, Basildon and Islington have decentralised those services generally thought to be front-line services – such as housing, social services, environmental health and some form of community development function. Tower Hamlets has decentralised all services including planning and central support services such as personnel and finance, albeit to larger units.

There is widespread political support for the idea that all services which involve direct contact with the public should be decentralised, if possible, and that wherever this is impossible, services should at least be represented in the neighbourhood on a surgery basis or through some other arrangement. However, there has been considerable officer resistance to localisation. Greatest resistance has been encountered by those departments which have traditionally been most professionalised. While housing (the most recently professionalised) has formed the kernel of many decentralisation initiatives, other front-line departments (in particular social services) often argued that they were too specialised to be decentralised.

This problem was even greater for support services (such as finance, legal services and personnel), where staff tended to see themselves first as professionals and second as council employees. It was only the most radical councils, such as Basildon and Tower Hamlets, which in the 1980s had the courage to decentralise these services. Yet there is no logical reason why they should not be decentralised:

> One should not automatically assume that any central support service needs to remain centralised. Millions of small businesses and voluntary organisations are self suffiencient in terms of financial, personnel and IT services; no-one ever accuses such organisations of waste and inefficiency simply because they do not share such services in common. Thus there is no inherently logical reason for insisting that payroll, printing, catering or other services should be provided on a centralised basis. (Hoggett, 1990b, p. 19)

Some councils have attempted to overcome the problem of localising specialist services by offering 'one-stop' information and advice points which form a first line of service capable of dealing with many routine public enquiries before specialist help needs to be enlisted. Birmingham's thirty-five neighbourhood offices are an example of this model. North Tyneside also provides a comprehensive one-stop service which has been developed on the back of the network of neighbourhood housing offices it established in the late 1980s. Multiple service shops, drawing together both district and regional council services, have been developed both in Glasgow's East End and in parts of Fife such as Dunfermline. In more rural counties in England there have been a number of recent attempts to develop one-stop shops in small towns – thus, in Hertfordshire, for example, such initatives have brought together both county, district and town (that is, parish) councils. A final related model should also be mentioned – as local authorities are increasingly pushed towards being purchasing rather than providing organisations, some councils (for example, Thurrock) are beginning to think of one-stop shops in terms of 'local purchasing points' which not only provide information and advice, but are also involved in purchasing and commissioning a range of services at the local level.

Another illustration is the information service adopted initially by Manchester and more recently by Rochdale. Both were convinced that an effective central information source was a necessity for an effective decentralisation programme and as a result they both built large central information centres, Manchester in advance of the decentralisation programme and Rochdale in parallel with it. These information centres act as a central information and referral agency to the neighbourhoods and, where necessary, to specialist central support units. They were launched in recognition that residents have an information need, which in the vast majority of cases will not need further specialist support. In Rochdale evidence seems to vindicate this approach: During the first six months over 33,000 people were seen, most with multiple enquiries . . . only 610 of these required referral to a more specialist organisation or agency (Burns, 1990a). One of the offshoots of the decentralisation process has been a recognition of the critical importance of the reception service as the gateway to the council. Some, though perhaps not enough, decentralising councils have trained generic receptionists and financially upgraded the post.

The consequences of localisation

Localisation means that staff have more contact with the public and less contact with central professional support departments. This requires a change in the way that people work. As a result of more face-to-face contact with the public, staff need a variety of skills in, for example, interviewing, presentation, communication and negotiation. They may also potentially face greater aggression and will need to know how to deal with it. Decentralising authorities need to invest substantial resources into training to meet these needs.

This has meant that departments have quickly had to revise their systems of prioritisation. One of the ironies of decentralisation is that it can decrease waiting times for services through more effective local working, but, as news spreads that the service is working well, more and more people start to come through the doors. Waiting times can then rise as a result of increased demand so that efficiency may appear to go down (Hambleton, Hoggett and Tolan, 1989). Islington's neighbourhood repair teams are a classic example of this. Within a year they managed to get housing repair waiting times down from thirteen to two and half weeks, but as demand increased the waiting time rose to five or six weeks. Nevertheless, an increase in demand can be viewed as a measure of success. It is the people who are least in need of services who have traditionally made the best use of local government services (Bramley and Le Grand, 1992). Often the last people to approach the council are the people most in need, and many councils view localisation as a way of uncovering unmet need.

Another problem faced by decentralised staff is the emergence of a conflict of loyalties. Front-line staff we spoke to in Haringey and Rochdale felt that, as professionals based in a central housing department, their priorities were clear, but in the neighbourhoods they faced day-to-day accountability to the community. Many felt that they had become more accountable to the community than to the council. This was particularly strong in areas of community resistance, such as the Broadwater Farm Estate in Haringey. Yet few were prepared openly to admit their bias, with the result that a culture of subversion operated. Staff worked for the tenants' needs, but they could only do so by keeping quiet about it. A theme which we will develop throughout this book is that there needs to be consistency at all levels of the organisation. One of the biggest problems that decentralising authorities have faced is that while substantial resources have been devoted to changing the culture of the front line, little effort has gone into changing the views and ways of working of managers and support services at the centre.

Flexibility

Almost everyone who has had contact with local government has a tale to tell about the problems created by departmentalism. Ken Thompson, a Neighbourhood Officer in Walsall, has a nice one:

> But I underestimated the bureaucracy. I rang the environmental health department. 'There's rats in Goscote. Could you give us some advice?' 'Oh, you speak to public works.' So I ring public works. 'Where are the rats?' 'Goscote'. 'No, are they above ground or below ground? If they're below ground, they're our responsibility, if they're above, you'll have to ring the environmental health department'. 'You're kidding me'. 'No', they said, 'that's the way it works'. I said, 'Whose responsibility is it if they're in the bloody roof – the RAF?' It turned out that if

they were actually in your house the environmental health were in charge. (Seabrook, 1984, p. 41)

Integration brings services together in a way which enables corporate decisions to be made locally and enables workers to provide a service which does not artificially fragment the problems of local people. For example, it is well known that housing and social service problems are often highly related, but although the two services usually liaise, they rarely work together in joint teams. The development of more integrated and flexible approaches is an essential component of neighbourhood decentralisation as a way of compensating for the loss of some economies of scale which localisation inevitably entails.

In our experience, the development of such approaches is vital for the creation of a public-orientated service and can be seen as having a number of specific objectives:

- Preventing 'buck-passing' from department to department;
- Organising in a way that is most convenient to the public rather than to the organisation; and
- Preventing service duplication.

In the following sections we provide a description of some of the innovations in this area that have occurred during the past decade in the context of neighbourhood decentralisation. First, we discuss generic working, then we consider local corporate management.

Generic working

Generic working is non-specialist working. It springs from a philosophy that at the point of service delivery the public does not want to be passed from specialist to specialist, but wherever possible would rather see someone who has a competent knowledge of the whole of their problem. It is also founded on a belief that, even if front-line workers do not know the answer to a problem, they should take responsibility for finding out, thus preventing bewildered members of the public from wandering aimlessly around the council maze, buffeted from pillar to post, from department to department. During the past decade or so there has been a wide range of (largely undocumented) experiments with different forms of generic working.

The simplest form is where the whole range of services in a particular field is encapsulated in the job description of a single worker. Thus, in Walsall's neighbourhood housing offices in the 1980s, everyone in the office had the same job description and all carried out the same range of functions. These included housing benefits, estate management, housing advice and administration. The only distinction between local workers was their level of responsibility. A member of the public was able to walk into the neighbourhood office and talk to anyone as they wished. A similar approach has been developed in Tower Hamlets, where generic planning officers have job descriptions which include development control, transport, local planning and enforcement functions.

Norwich City housing department has varied the model slightly by creating a split between 'professional' housing officers and 'administrative' housing assistants. The professionals have a similar role to that of the Walsall officers but without the administrative function. The administrators have a generic job which includes reception, the processing of repair requests, monitoring and administration. Perhaps the most innovative generic system, which manages to combine the benefits of specialisation with those of genericism is that of Basildon. Every staff member of the neighbourhood offices has a primary specialisation, which takes up most of his or her time, and a number of secondary specialist interests. As well as creating a great deal of flexibility, it is also a good way to develop effective on-the-job training. In housing benefits, the primary specialist deals with the more complicated technical claims that require reference to new legislation and so on – s/he does not deal with day-to-day housing benefit calculation. Thus s/he is freed to carry out secondary specialisations. Other staff are able to learn how the housing benefits system works by taking on straightforward cases as part of their secondary specialisation. This system is particularly innovative because it has enabled workers to develop skills across traditional departmental boundaries.

Not all generic approaches involve changing the job descriptions of individuals. Patch-based multidisciplinary teams are a common form of decentralised working. Here a small group of specialists work to a small geographical area. A good example is provided by multitrade neighbourhood repair teams (Pilkington and Kendrick, 1987). These teams were formed in response to farcical problems which arose when staff from the Direct Labour Organisation visited a house to repair a tap, but were not allowed to fix the leaking toilet at the same time because they did not have a job ticket. They were also a response to problems with renovation programmes that were held up in their entirety because one trade had a backlog of other work – for example, plasterers waiting for plumbing to be completed. With a multiskilled team, the whole job can be completed more quickly. An average area repair team would consist of plumbers, carpenters, plasterers, labourers and brick-layers. There is evidence to suggest that this model has led to individuals taking on a more generic role, because plumbers working in close proximity to bricklayers and plasterers have learned each other's jobs (Burns and Williams, 1989). A variant on this model is the multidisciplinary project team. In Haringey, for example, teams of planners, architects, housing staff and surveyors were put together to work on housing schemes throughout the borough.

Most of these approaches have shown some measure of success. One area of controversy, however, has been in social services, where major doubts have been expressed about the ability of generic social workers to respond to complicated child abuse cases. This, in combination with the Community Care Act 1990, has created a trend towards, on the one hand, more generic local community care teams but, on the other hand, more specialist/centralised children's teams. Another problem confronting service integration relates to the increasing tendency to separate purchasing from provision, particularly when associated with compulsory competitive tender-ing.

Generic working has been strongly opposed by local authority white-collar unions such as the National Association of Local Government Officers (NALGO). The union has argued that making people into 'jacks of all trades' deskills them and is a way of getting one person to do the job of two or three: a route to job-cutting. In practice, however, the evidence shows that in the 1980s many neighbourhood decentralisation initiatives led to staff increases and higher wage levels. Trade union objections, however, should not be lightly dismissed. A detailed study of union activists in Islington (Miller, 1992) revealed that there is a balance to be achieved between responsiveness to the needs of service users and respect for the working conditions and experiences of staff.

The survey conducted by Lowndes and Stoker (1992b) of workers' experience of decentralisation in the Globe Town neighbourhood in Tower Hamlets revealed considerable satisfaction with many aspects of the new working environment. However, they noted that there was a fine line between the concept of job enlargement on the one hand and a kind of enforced 'genericism' on the other – one in which workers were forced to take on more and more responsibilities to prevent the cracks in the overstretched services showing.

The debate about deskilling is therefore a complicated one. On the positive side it can be argued that it is more useful for staff not to lose skills but to gain them. The argument of deskilling is often used to protect professional interests, job demarcations and thus hierarchies. However, people have an unexpected capacity to learn which is usually put down by the system. It should be noted that when Walsall decentralised in 1981, less than 50 per cent of the housing staff they employed to run the neighbourhood housing service had any professional qualifications.

The generic model of working in a decentralised environment is not new. It has been in operation for many years within the health service. GPs are, in some ways, the ultimate generalist workers. They usually serve small geographical areas. They provide a reception and screening service, they can offer a broad range of general solutions to issues which are not too complicated, and in many cases they have their own specialisations. If a patient needs more complex support s/he goes to the local hospital. But the GP takes responsibility for co-ordinating this, ensuring that the patient does not have to travel from department to department trying to find the right person to deal with his/her problem. This division of labour within the health service between generalists in the neighbourhoods and specialists at the centre is generally accepted as a model of good practice. It is one which other public-sector organisations could learn from.

Local corporate management

The sort of flexibility demonstrated in the Basildon neighbourhood offices could not come about if a traditional departmental structure had been maintained. Yet challenging departmentalism would probably have been beyond the agenda of most politicians before the mid-1980s:

> The departmental mode has a powerful hold on organisational thinking in local government. Until recently, the departmental was the only mode of working envisaged in local authorities. Alternatives lay beyond the boundaries of organisational assumptions. (Stewart, 1986, p. 142)

The advantages to be gained from the development of more flexible working practices will inevitably be undermined if the management structure of the organisation is built upon rigid departmental and professional boundaries. Three options have emerged for reforming the management structure: (1) the creation of local multi-professional management teams; (2) the placing of different service functions under the leadership of a single local general manager; and (3) the development of matrix management structures. Each of these options can be envisaged as a form of local corporate management. However, the problems of implementating such options cannot be examined in isolation from the broader problem of managing the tension between generalisation and specialisation in organisations.

The most radical option is the one adopted by local authorities such as Basildon and Tower Hamlets (and more recently Rochdale, Harlow and Islington) which have developed multiservice neighbourhood offices with general managers to whom all local staff (irrespective of their professional service) are directly accountable. These neighbourhood managers control a local budget and have the power to transfer money across departmental budget heads (a process known as virement).

This model, while fulfilling the demands of local flexibility, has been opposed by specialists who say that they cannot be managed by someone who does not understand their service. This view is strongly challenged by one Basildon neighbourhood manager: 'Management skills are more important than specialist skills. My knowledge of housing can be written on the back of a cigarette packet' (quoted in Burns and Williams, 1989, p. 35).

Nevertheless it is an argument which needs to be taken seriously. Many decentralising local authorities have responded by exploring the possibilities of matrix management (Hambleton, 1978; Peters and Waterman, 1982). Hambleton suggested that matrix management held out exciting possibilities for local government. The crucial feature of matrix management is that:

> there is a dual authority: each individual within the matrix reports to two managers. The non-functional manager may be concerned with an area, a project, a client group or some other issue cutting across functional perspectives. . . Matrix management can take many forms but to deserve the name, the non-functional manager must share authority in rewarding and penalising members of her/his team. (Hambleton, 1978, p. 300)

Examples of how matrix management works in practice can be seen within the health service. The Community Unit of North Staffordshire Health Authority has sector nurse managers who are responsible to locality general managers on a day-to-day basis, but accountable to a senior central medical manager for issues of medical practice. While clearly addressing many of the problems of departmentalism we outlined earlier, it must be acknowledged that such a system of matrix management is more complicated than the traditional functional hierarchy. Matrix management cannot be regarded as being helpful if it leads to role ambiguity and confusion. Peters and Waterman, drawing on industrial models, attempt to resolve the problem by suggesting that one dimension must have primacy (Peters and Waterman, 1982, pp. 307–8).

A number of local authorities have experimented with this approach which typically has involved the creation of area co-ordinator rather than area manager posts. In Bradford groups of officers from different departments meet in local teams which are run by an area co-ordinator. In Shipley, for example, the staff are all based in the same building, the old Shipley Town Hall. The area co-ordinator reports to an area committee comprising locally-elected councillors, but the committee also links into a network of neighbourhood forums based around local parish councils.

A similar system has recently been developed by the Liberal-controlled South Somerset District Council. Unlike Bradford, where traditional centralised political decision-making structures largely remain intact, in South Somerset the entire committee structure has been remodelled around four area committees, each of which links strongly to local parish councils and is served by an area co-ordinator. Another innovative model has been developed in Middlesbrough. Here the council has four area-based policy committees which are separate from the service committees. These are serviced mainly by officers working in the areas. The council's annual policy plan, which is a model of good practice, has a strong geographical dimension with clear maps showing the impact of proposals on different areas of the borough.

Arrangements of this kind not only enable services to be more responsive to local need, they also enable better strategic corporate policy to be developed across the whole authority. In the absence of corporate working at lower levels, disputes tend to escalate to the top of the organisational hierarchy because this is the only point of contact between the departments. This leads to a waste of senior management time and gives too great a weight to minor issues which could well have been resolved by staff at lower levels. Furthermore, decision outcomes often reflect departmental strength.

The main point we have sought to argue is that the traditional, professionalised way of running local authorities has led to excessive fragmentation both within and between departments. The departmental model has come to dominate virtually all thinking about how to organise local government. However, a growing number of councils are developing generic working and local corporate working which relate in a much better way to the needs of the public.

Devolved management

Earlier in this chapter, we referred to new forms of management which give managers a greater degree of autonomy but within a clearly specified and centrally-controlled set of boundaries – financial expenditure rules, service standards, policy guidelines, and so on. Figure 4.4 develops the 'freedom within boundaries' notion by identifying three levels of devolved resource control.

As we can see from Figure 4.4, the situation of nominal devolution differs little from conditions of bureaucratic control – there is simply some flexibility and looseness around the margin. In contrast, the devolved form introduces many of the modern approaches to resource management advocated by the Audit Commission (1989). Here considerable flexibility, particularly

Type of devolution	Freedoms provided to managers
Nominal devolution	Monitoring of 'shadow' budget; control over small budgets concerning special items, e.g. environmental improvements, good neighbour schemes.
Devolution	Control over revenue budgets and major capital budgets; non-restrictive rules of virement; opportunity for 'carry forward' of budgets at year end.
Radical devolution	Control over own establishment levels; some control over regrading; freedom to raise additional revenue through service charges and to raise additional capital (via control over capital receipts); freedom to contract out.

FIGURE 4.4   Levels of devolved resource control

concerning the management of local revenue budgets, has been introduced. Finally, radical devolution appears to provide the effective conditions for devolved units to become almost independent – all that would appear to prevent this is continuing central control of revenue raising and the allocation of this to operational units.

Devolved control can be evaluated according to how well it meets the objectives of (a) responsiveness, and (b) local flexibility. Initiatives to devolve control have crossed the political divide and to some extent have followed industrial trends towards franchise and cost centre management. In the period since 1987 Conservative government legislation has given budgetary control to GPs, case managers in health and social care, and head teachers in schools. Bradford City and Berkshire County councils, when under Conservative control, transferred much of the local authority on to a cost centre basis. Labour- and Liberal-controlled local authorities have also devolved budgets to neighbourhood managers through programmes of radical decentralisation. The Tower Hamlets, Harlow and Basildon models are the most radical – in these authorities, multiservice neighbourhood managers have control over all local staff and budgets. Devolved control has also been a feature of many forms of social service decentralisation, as in

East Sussex, Surrey and Devon, and some comprehensive models of decentralised housing services such as Sheffield's.

Devolved control is a response to the problem of 'buck-passing'. If authority is vested in the local area then decisions do not constantly have to be referred back up the line management hierarchy for authorisation. For many areas of decision-making, local managers are able to make better choices than are central ones. They are closer to the recipients of services and more able to judge the impact of risks that might have to be taken; they are better able to judge costs and benefits, and make priority decisions, particularly in times of scarce resources. Flexibility often means the ability to act quickly where the traditional centralised system can only react on a yearly cycle (Hoggett and Bramley, 1989). In this context we should note that:

1. The localisation of staff does not necessarily imply an accessible service because, if such staff and their managers lack control over resources, they have been given responsibility for service delivery without the power to deliver.
2. Control over essential resources allows staff to focus their energies on getting on with the job rather than lobbying and chivvying the centralised bureaucracy.
3. Control over inputs not only gives managers the flexibility to construct the most appropriate resource mix to produce reliable and responsive outputs, but also the incentive to operate efficiently and the space to innovate.
4. Where control over resources remains centralised, users and communities are placed in the position of being either complainant or lobbyist – only when control over relevant resources is placed in the hands of those delivering the service can genuine forms of democratic participation occur.

One of the ironies of devolved financial management is that it is supposed to create the conditions in which local managers are able to identify savings, yet unless those managers reap the reward for those savings there is no incentive to make them. This means that it is necessary to ensure that neighbourhoods can carry over a significant proportion of any savings into future financial years or transfer savings made in one area to provide additional expenditure in another.

In summary, devolved control should imply an acceptance that different neighbourhoods will do different things. It is based on the principle that good management involves some risk-taking. The only way it is possible for a risk culture to develop is if neighbourhoods are allowed to go their own way and try out different solutions to problems. This diversity is likely to lead to more creative solutions but is a concept which public service traditionalists find hard to accept. This brings us towards the vexed question of the relationship between 'the centre' and the neighbourhood, an issue we return to in our discussion of devolution in Tower Hamlets in the next chapter.

Cultural change

The contrast between bureaucratic and post-bureaucratic regimes can be underlined by using an analogy. Some parents attempt to 'solve' the 'problem' of controlling the behaviour of adolescent children by drawing boundaries very tightly – for example, 'you can only go out on certain nights, you must be in by a certain time, you will not mix with certain children, you will not smoke, drink, have sexual relations and so on'. Such regimes invite either submission and conformity or transgression. Broadly speaking, this is how bureaucratic organisational regimes operated. Other parents provide their children with much greater freedom within a set of loose but very clear boundaries – for example, 'if you're going to stay out at night you must let us know where you are'. The relationship is based upon trust and a belief that the child will be guided by a value system which he or she shares with the parents. Typically we refer to such families as 'liberal'. Here individuals exercise freedoms within agreed frameworks of conduct. Rules only tend to be invoked when such boundaries fail to contain behaviour and transgression occurs. Such regimes, which also apply to post-bureaucratic organisations, rely heavily upon the power of socialisation processes to regulate behaviour. Hence the paramount importance given to the concept of 'organisational culture' and 'culture change' within the management literature of the 1980s (Schein, 1985).

The types of decentralisation objective set out in Figure 4.2 (see page 88) cannot be achieved without major changes in the culture of the organisation. This means that both politicians and officers have to jettison old assumptions and take on new values. Effective managers in local government, as elsewhere, have always sought to promote certain values and norms as a way of motivating and controlling staff. In one sense, then, managers in both the public and the private sectors have, for many years, been concerned to shape the 'culture' of their organisations. What is new is that, in many organisations, managers are now giving explicit attention to ways of managing the corporate culture: 'Most are now aware of the symbolic consequences of organisational values, and many organisations have started to explore the pattern of culture and subculture that shapes day-to-day action' (Morgan, 1986, p. 138).

This development can be seen as a double-edged sword. On the one hand this interest in developing a shared understanding and belief system among employees can be viewed as a positive shift because it recognises the truly human nature of organisations and the need to focus organisational change on people and their values rather than on structures. On the other hand, critics feel that this trend is a potentially dangerous one as it may change the art of management into a process of ideological manipulation and domination. It is possible for the culture to be used to control rather than to express human character – to suppress dissent and harass staff who do not appear to have the 'appropriate attitudes' (Pollitt, 1990, p. 24). Clearly, the content of the values in 'value-driven' management is crucial to any intelligent evaluation of this kind of management strategy. These are often not that clear and we recognise that, in discussing cultural change, we are wrestling with an indistinct and elusive concept. Nevertheless we believe it is essential to consider cultural factors when attempting to assess the amount of organisational change achieved by reforms such as decentralisation.

We would stress that the 'culture' of an organisation is a complex phenomenon. In common usage 'culture' refers to a society's system of ideology, values, knowledge, art, laws and day-to-day ritual. The culture metaphor is used in organisation theory to suggest that organisations can be viewed as mini-societies with their own distinctive patterns of culture and subculture:

> Thus one organisation may see itself as a tight-knit team or family that believes in working together. . . Another may be highly fragmented, divided into groups that think about the world in very different ways, or that have different aspirations as to what

their organisation should be. Such patterns of belief . . . can exert a decisive influence on the overall ability of the organisation to deal with the challenges that it faces. (Morgan, 1986, p. 121)

Clearly, culture is not a distinct entity which can be separated from structural factors and procedural arrangements. Thus, the three sets of changes we have already discussed in this chapter can also have a significant impact on the culture of the organisation. Nevertheless, some critical cultural changes will not happen as a result of structural change. They need to be planned for, and made explicit. Our observation of decentralisation initiatives suggests that, at minimum, the following themes need to be addressed.

The back-line/front-line concept

One of the most important cultural changes which needs to take place in a decentralised organisation is a reversal of the perspective that the front-line is working for the centre. A new culture should start with the public. It should determine what the public needs, then assess what front-line staff need to fulfil the public need. It should assess what local management needs to fulfil front-line staff needs. In turn, the role of the centre or back-line is to meet the needs of local management. This approach inverts the typical organisation chart – the impetus comes from the point of service delivery and not from the centre.

This means that people who are working in the centre need to perceive themselves directly as being part of the process of service delivery. They need to be made aware of the direct impact their job has on the ability to deliver services. This cultural change is particularly important because of the physical isolation resulting from localisation. Because front-line workers and managers are physically further away from central staff, their ability to communicate with and challenge central staff is diminished. This means that central staff need to go through extensive training to redefine their roles. Walsall may be the only authority to have trained their central staff extensively for decentralisation.

The necessity for this cultural change is exemplified by many authorities' initial experience of devolved financial management. Because central accountants rarely perceive that accounting is part of the process of service delivery, the information they provide to local managers is often out of date and unhelpful. A consequence is that managers tended to adopt a conservative financial regime to ensure that they do not overspend.

Taking risks

It is common knowledge that people learn most effectively from their mistakes. In society at large we revere those who experiment and discover new solutions to problems. Yet in hierarchical public-sector organisations it is not acceptable to make mistakes. This means that such organisations become inefficient and extremely conservative. Similarly, few staff talk to their managers about the stress they are under because their managers are crucial to their promotion prospects. Yet it is often the people who acknowledge the problems they face and want to talk through ways of resolving them that have the most potential. It is vital for the decentralising local authority to deal with these management attitudes. There is no point in structurally providing front line staff with greater responsibility if they are too frightened to use it. The culture needs to encourage risk-taking.

A quality culture

Everybody is in favour of service quality these days yet many authorities have still to learn that you cannot expect front-line staff to deliver high-quality service if they experience poor-quality management and suffer from the consequences of inefficient and unresponsive support services. There are many approaches to quality currently being tried out in the public services – for example, the traditional approach, the 'scientific' approach, the managerial approach and the consumerist approach (Pfeffer and Coote, 1991). However, these approaches often neglect the cultural dimension. Interestingly, evidence from a study of neighbourhood offices in Birmingham suggests that there are close links between quality and decentralised management (Gaster, 1991).

Linking the components of decentralisation

Councils have progressed at different rates along the four dimensions of change that we have described. None has achieved major change in all the areas. We take the view that these components need to be integrally linked, and that the most effective decentralisation initiatives will involve change on all fronts. To accomplish this it is vital for politicians to guide decentralisation with a strong political will. Variations in political will have radically affected decentralisation programmes. Many politicians seem to have thought that all they had to do was to dream up a radical vision and tell their officers to implement it. In the 1980s many councillors did not realise the degree to which resistant senior officers could affect the process of change. The most closely-guided initiatives have been those of Walsall, Tower Hamlets and Rochdale. As noted in Chapter 3, Islington's change process has been marked by varying degrees of political commitment and it is possible to argue that the programme was on the point of going astray before strong political involvement was reintroduced in 1990. Basildon is probably the only really succesful programme where council members have not remained intimately involved with the process. This is largely because they employed a series of committed chief officers at the start and, when a hung council occurred, the officers maintained the momentum. Other decentralisation initia-tives have been less successful than they might have been because politicians have been too wary and 'hands off' in their approach.

Elected members have also proved to be powerful agents of cultural change. When councillors in Tower Hamlets and Basildon reorganised their own council committees, it was hard for officers to resist the change, not least because each department had to work to, say, seven committees instead of one. As a result many of the professionals agreed to change management structures because it was the only practical way of managing the changed work loads.

But as with any other change, structural solutions can only be part of the equation. For example, there are probably hundreds of local authorities with equal opportunities policies who, while stamping out the most obvious symptoms of racism, have failed to change many of the racist attitudes embedded in their institutions. Similarly, in a decentralised structure staff may acquiesce to the dominant political view but continue to resist real changes on the ground, often failing to fulfil the potential of the policies.

There is some evidence that changing the structure of the organisation can change its culture. Interviews we conducted with generic workers in Basildon (Burns and Williams, 1989) revealed that many had fiercely resisted this form of working, but once it was imposed, they could not imagine how they had previously worked any other way. In Tower Hamlets the sheer pace of change made it plain that things could not stay the same. People had to change attitudes just to keep up. Walsall Council created a new management culture simply by sweeping away those managers who clung on to the old values. The most succesful decentralisation initiatives have been those that have carried their staff with them. Hackney's decentralisation programme floundered on trade union resistance, and Manchester's programme was delayed for two years by protracted negotiations.

The decentralisation experience of a number of London local authorities, in particular Lambeth and Hackney, clearly demonstrates the dangers of physically decentralising services without devolving power. Lambeth's decentralisation of housing in the 1980s, for example, involved the creation of many local estate offices, area offices and district offices grafted on to the old central housing department. But the housing officers who managed these offices were given no local control. This meant that every time there was an issue of contention it had to travel back up the management hierarchy. Following 'decentralisation', instead of going directly to a central senior manager the issue went first to the district, next to the area office, and finally to the centre – often getting lost on the way. This made the decision making process more inefficient than it was in the first place.

Similarly, it is far more difficult to decentralise physically without planning greater flexibility. As we have indicated, generic working can be an appropriate response to problems of lack of specialist staff and cover. Furthermore, localisation exposes staff to the public more and separates them from central colleagues. This can create problems of isolation. This needs to be countered by effective team support and local peer group problem solving mechanisms which result from integrated approaches to work.

Devolved power and integrated working are also mutually supportive. As we explained in Chapter 3, the decentralisation programme of Islingon Council demonstrates very clearly the way in which the system was reformed over time to compensate for the fact that localisation was introduced without sufficient attention being given to the importance of devolved power and service integration. In particular, the council realised that, in order for local service delivery to be really effective, there had to be a corporate neighbourhood manager.

To conclude, we must stress that the key dimensions of decentralisation are connected and interlocking. The pursuit of one dimension in isolation from the others will often create as many problems as it solves. Decentralisation is not something that can be bolted on to another structure. It has an internal logic of its own, and to make it work, radical change must be considered at all levels. In the next chapter we use the framework developed in this chapter to evaluate decentralised management in Islington and Tower Hamlets.

5 Shaking up the Bureaucracies

Introduction

In this chapter, we assess the degree of organisational change achieved in Islington and Tower Hamlets and, where possible, the impact of this upon service delivery. Do the new arrangements constitute a radical departure from the traditional bureaucratic forms that Weber (1948) outlined? In classical terms, bureaucracies have been perceived as ordered hierarchies of centralised command, relying heavily upon specialisation and formal procedures. In the context of governmental institutions the bureaucratic form has influenced the development of a particular kind of social relation between these institutions on the one hand and individuals and communities on the other – one characterised by the remoteness and impermeability of the organisation.

In the previous chapter we provided a model of neighbourhood decentralisation which consisted of four dimensions: localisation; flexibility; devolved management; and organisational and cultural change (see Figure 4.3 on page 88). We recap briefly on each of these four dimensions. The localisation of service delivery corresponds to the spatial dispersal of productive operations within the organisation – again a phenomenon one can see at work within the private sector. Such dispersal was impossible as long as organisations relied primarily upon principles of control 'derived from the hierarchy of offices . . . in direct surveillance and supervision, as well as the standardised rules and sanctions' (Clegg, 1990, p. 178).

Flexibility involves reversing the phenomenon which Clegg argues was the hallmark of the bureaucratic system, namely the 'maximal specialisation of jobs and functions and an extensive differentiation of segmented roles' (Clegg, 1990, p. 179).

Devolved management is not an automatic consequence of the physical dispersal of operations to local offices – a council can open a network of local offices without devolving decision making authority to the local level. It is essential to understand that the devolution process in both the public and the private sectors has been shaped to have an impact primarily upon operational rather than strategic levels of management. Indeed, we have argued elsewhere that post-bureaucratic models of organisation involving decentralised forms of working have provided the framework for a strengthening of centralised strategic control (Hoggett and Hambleton, 1987; Hoggett, 1990a, 1991). What we often see is 'the decentralisation of operations and the centralisation of command' (Murray, 1983).

Finally, the fourth dimension of cultural change highlights the way post-bureaucratic organisations attempt to shift from regimented and overregulated regimes to ones that function on the principle of 'freedom within boundaries' (Hoggett, 1991). Such regimes rely heavily upon socialisation processes within the organisation to ensure that personnel become, to a degree, self-regulating. Hence the growing importance of 'managing the organisation's culture' (Schein, 1985).

In order to assess the degree to which Islington and Tower Hamlets have been able to depart from the bureaucratic model, we now apply this four-part framework to their experience. But before going into detail we should note that there are important variations within each borough – more so within Tower Hamlets, where the neighbourhoods have more autonomy. In Islington the organisational and political arrangements are relatively standardised across the twenty-four neighbourhoods. In Tower Hamlets the seven neighbourhoods have developed quite different organisational and political arrangements, with the result that it is not possible to compare a 'standard neighbourhood' in Tower Hamlets with its Islington counterpart.

The organisational and political structures in Islington and Tower Hamlets

The way the different approaches to decentralisation in Islington and Tower Hamlets emerged and developed was discussed in Chapter 3. The basic features of decentralisation in the two boroughs are outlined in Figure 5.1. In Islington, neighbourhood offices were designed to be within ten minutes' walk for the average able-bodied resident. As we note later, the emphasis on accessibility also found expression in the physical design and layout of the offices

	ISLINGTON	TOWER HAMLETS
Number of neighbourhood offices	24	7
Average population of neighbourhoods	6500	24 000
Other neighbourhood structures	None	Housing services further decentralised into system of estate bases within each neighbourhood.
Type of neighbourhood office	Mostly new-build, standardised, open-plan format	3 new-build, 4 conversions, no standard design
Numbers of staff per office	40–50	Typically 200 +
Services based in neighbourhoods	Housing, social services, environmental health, chief executive's (administration, reception, welfare rights, community work)	Virtually all direct services except highly specialised ones such as Occupational Therapy. Virtually all policy and support (e.g. legal, personnel) services
Neighbourhood management	1984–92 Neighbourhood Co-ordinator, plus three heads of professional service. 1992– Generalist Neighbourhood Manager. Twinning of 16 neighbourhoods for purposes of management	Generalist neighbourhood Chief Executive
Organisational structures	1984–92 Neighbourhood offices subordinate to professional departments 1992– Housing, social services and chief executives's functions combined into single Neighbourhood Services Department	Professional departments broken up and subordinated to neighbourhood structures. 'Compromise' established between Neighbourhood Chief Executives and Director of Housing and Social Services regarding responsibility for professional aspects of childrens' social work.
Democratic structures	Neighbourhood forums established alongside all neighbourhood offices. Basically, advisory and consultative bodies with limited delegated powers. Energetic efforts to widen public involvement in neighbourhood decision-making	Neighbourhood committees with fully delegated powers consisting of locally-elected councillors. A variety of neighbourhood consultative bodies alongside neighbourhood committees. Estate based forums in some neighbourhoods (e.g. Bethnal Green)

FIGURE 5.1   Basic features of decentralisation in Islington and Tower Hamlets

– modern open-plan buildings often referred to locally as 'Pizza Huts'. The offices were designed to cater for a catchment area with an average population of 6500, compared with 24 000 in Tower Hamlets and are consequently much smaller.

The capital costs associated with opening neighbourhood offices are difficult to estimate. The average cost of the sixteen new buildings in Islington (eight were conversions) was £450 000, but no comparable data is available in Tower Hamlets. Indeed, some of the neighbourhoods under 'Labour control, such as Wapping, steadfastly refused to engage in any major new capital projects involved with the mini-town-hall concept. What is not known in either borough is the amount of capital receipts derived from the sale of council buildings which were vacated when staff were transferred to the new offices.

Figure 5.2 provides a description of the management structure of the neighbourhood office in Islington after the changes introduced in 1991/2. No standard model exists in Tower Hamlets because neighbourhoods were free to devise their own management arrangements. Some neighbourhood Chief Executives had assistants or deputies; some did not. Some neighbourhoods, such as Wapping, were run by a small management board of six heads of service together with a larger group of senior officers which met on a less regular basis. Other neighbourhoods, such as Bow, were run by a single board of ten senior managers. By way of example Figure 5.3 shows the organisation structure of the Globe Town neighbourhood. Here the neighbourhood Chief Executive introduced a fairly flat management structure with a high level of informality and openness (Lowndes and Stoker, 1992b).

Labour neighbourhoods tended to favour having their own policy units comprising specialist equalities and research/policy officers, a system largely eschewed by Liberal controlled neighbourhoods. All neighbourhoods, however, would have their own committee services section which supported the running of the neighbourhood committee and advisory forum.

Localisation – getting closer to the public

At first sight the different approaches of Islington and Tower Hamlets to service localisation are striking. Islington has twenty-

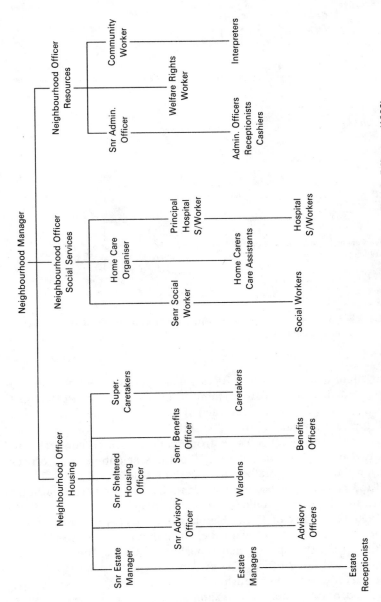

FIGURE 5.2 Typical structure of a neighbourhood office in Islington (1992)

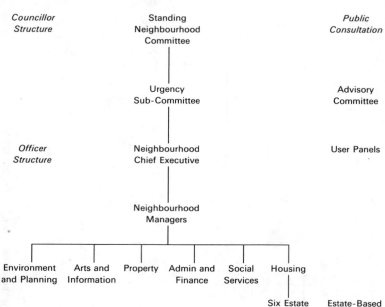

FIGURE 5.3   The neighbourhood office structure in Globe Town, Tower Hamlets

four small neighbourhood offices which typically contain between forty and fifty staff. Tower Hamlets, on the other hand, has just seven neighbourhood centres, each of which constitutes a mini town hall typically containing over 200 staff.

The evidence of office usage from market research conducted in the two boroughs indicates that Islington's neighbourhood offices are, on the whole, more heavily used by local people. In 1987 over half (53 per cent) of Islington residents had used a neighbourhood office and 71 per cent could locate it correctly (MORI, 1987, p. 132). In 1990, two in five of Tower Hamlets residents (41 per cent) had at some time been in touch with their neighbourhood office (MORI, 1990, p. 103), the smallest neighbourhood – Globe Town – having the most well-used office. The evidence suggests, not surprisingly, that larger-sized neighbourhoods inhibit public access to the neighbourhood office. For example, our own interviews with residents on the Limehouse Fields Estate in Stepney revealed that only a tiny fraction had ever been to the local neighbourhood centre, some 20 minutes' walk away.

Although the Tower Hamlets MORI survey did not ask respondents to locate their office correctly, it did ask them if they were aware of the neighbourhood in which they resided. Interestingly enough, not only did over 80 per cent of residents in Stepney and the Isle of Dogs identify their area, but over 80 per cent in Globe Town as well. Globe Town was the only one of the seven neighbourhoods to be 'artificially' created (that is, it was not based upon any historically pre-existing community). The final point concerns who uses neighbourhood offices. Although no survey data are available from Tower Hamlets, data generated by a consumer survey (MORI, 1987) and 1991 neighbourhood office exit polls suggest that women, ethnic minorities, pensioners and council tenants all use Islington's neighbourhood offices more frequently than their numbers in the general population would lead one to expect.

It is important to note that the mini town halls represent just one element of service localisation in Tower Hamlets – within each neighbourhood the estate bases provide a physically accessible network of service points. Although these bases only deal with housing and related issues we can note that housing-related enquiries, particularly concerning repairs and maintenance, are the most common reason for people getting in touch with their local authority in most urban areas. For example, the survey evidence for Tower Hamlets indicates that 53 per cent of those who have contacted the council did so with a concern about housing repairs (MORI, 1990, p. 89). In Islington, enquiries relating to housing and building works account for 54 per cent of the total (MORI, 1987, p. 141). Failure to deal satisfactorily with such enquiries was the most common reason for the gap, identifiable in both boroughs, between satisfaction with the way in which service users felt they were treated (80 per cent satisfaction levels in both boroughs) and their satisfaction with the result (60 per cent in Islington and 47 per cent in Tower Hamlets).

While both councils have successfully attracted more people into local authority offices as a result of being physically present in local neighbourhoods, this change has not come without problems. Here is the view of an environmental health officer based in a neighbourhood office in Islington:

The neighbourhood office is on the whole a good idea from the point of view of effective service delivery and job satisfaction. You are amongst the people and you understand the area. However, there is a certain amount of isolation from professional colleagues and there can be communication problems with the centre. We need specialist support and we can't always get it as quickly as we would like.

There are other potential problems relating to localisation which go beyond the concerns of those involved with specialised services – these revolve around the importance of maintaining a reliable service. The smaller the size of a neighbourhood team the greater the problems of covering for vacant posts, sickness and other absences. Research in Islington by Miller (1992) has revealed a fairly widespread view among neighbourhood office staff that even the less specialist services have been spread too thinly. This view is usefully represented by the following remarks of a home care organiser in one of the neighbourhood offices:

We don't have a lot of flexibility. The numbers of home carers fluctuates – new jobs, sickness, leave – and we don't get a replacement. It's different from the old system where people would be shuffled around. For instance, when you go on leave for two weeks you have to forward plan for those weeks. Well, a lot can go wrong in those two weeks and so you can never get the job out of your mind. People contact me at home while I'm on holiday to sort things out. That would never have happened in the centralised office because there was always someone there to cover. (Miller, 1992, p. 209)

As this experience indicates, problems of cover can be particularly acute for line-management staff within neighbourhood structures. However, there are avenues available for compensating for such difficulties. Research on developments within the private sector indicates that small production teams can overcome such potential inflexibilities by creating more multi-skilled and generic forms of team-based working. As we note later in this chapter, Islington has made little progress in developing generic work structures and this exacerbates cover problems. Another strategy is to create a small pool of workers who can be used on a peripatetic basis to cover for absences in particular offices. This is now used as a way of covering for absent home care organisers in Islington. The point remains, however, that as a general rule, the more physically dispersed a service is the greater the potential for problems with cover. This is one of the factors Islington took into account in its review of the neighbourhood office system in 1990 and partly explains why, as described in Chapter 3, the council decided to twin eight pairs of offices for management purposes.

The importance attached to the quality of the service encounter will influence the degree of localisation chosen. In opting for relatively small neighbourhood offices Islington has, it can be argued, created structures which are small enough to avoid being experienced as impersonal and alienating by service users and providers. Like Tower Hamlets, Islington has been criticised for the cost of its neighbourhood offices. However, this cost must be measured against the unique style and ambience that these striking, largely open-plan offices create.

The split-level offices have a modern, colourful design – they are lively and bustling. The open reception areas feel informal and welcoming – notices of events or classes, leaflets on benefits, advice and so on clamour for attention. Coffee machines, play areas and community rooms add to the sense that this is not a typical local government office but a place which sees itself as a resource for the community – as an enterprise concerned to engage with local people.

We noted earlier how one of the major dysfunctions of traditional bureaucracies is their impermeability to the environment. Islington's neighbourhood office concept is a bold attempt to project in physical terms the new organisation's greater openness to its environment. Each office is like a large window through which providers and users of services can look upon one another. These design features coupled with considerable investment in staff training have, on the whole, had a beneficial impact on the quality of the service encounter – not least because they have helped to promote positive attitudes among staff working in the neighbourhood offices. Thus the great majority of respondents to Miller's survey of the attitudes of staff working in Islington's neighbourhood offices, many of whom were trade union activists, felt not only that the offices had facilitated greater access to services, but also that the arrangements had enabled service users to develop a better understanding of why decisions concerning themselves had been taken.

The council where I used to work was a faceless, unapproachable body. That isn't the case in Islington. People can walk into any office, sit down and talk to someone (female housing advice worker). (Miller, 1992, p. 204)

Another factor which enhances the service encounter in localised offices is the way users and providers get to know one another. One housing benefit worker in an Islington office put it to us this way:

There has been quite a bit of stability in our section. The claimants have got to know us. This makes them feel more secure. Before decentralisation I used to work in one big office dealing with all council tenants in the borough. You just didn't know the people. Here the claimants tell us more – sometimes we can get substantial sums for them because of this.

Although the changes have been less marked in Tower Hamlets, a recent case study of the operation of the Globe Town neighbourhood found that 61 per cent of the staff who responded felt that, as a result of their increased exposure to the public, their relationship with the public was more productive than before decentralisation (Lowndes and Stoker, 1992b). A majority also felt that the new working environment was more stressful but this stress was attributed primarily to the gap between the demands placed upon them and the resources available rather than close physical proximity to the public.

This raises a further interesting issue concerning the theme of post-bureaucratic organisational control. Research on contemporary 'interactive service organisations' in the USA by Fuller and Smith (1991) has suggested the emergence of a new, non-bureaucratic control strategy within service organisations which they refer to as 'management by customers'. They argue that this strategy has become linked to the contemporary corporate ideology of 'service quality' reflected in managerial assertions that 'customers' loyalty depends on the treatment they receive from service workers' (p. 2). They point to the fact that quality service requires the use of judgement, affective and interpersonal skills 'which cannot be successfully codified, standardised, or dissected into discrete components and set forth in a company handbook' (p. 3). Methods employed to achieve management by customers include market research, complaints procedures and the use of bogus service users. Measures of this kind represent an attempt to augment managerial with customer power.

Such developments should give us pause for thought when reflecting upon the localisation of public services. Many workers we spoke to, both in Islington's neighbourhood offices and in Tower Hamlets' estate bases, made the comment that they now felt constantly accountable to service users because their performance was now far more visible. On the one hand, from the perspective of the service user, this would seem to be a welcome development. On the other, such shifts may, from the perspective of the local worker, appear somewhat ambiguous. Many of the neighbourhood office staff we spoke to had developed strong feelings of neighbourhood loyalty and commitment. However, many also said that localisation put them under considerable pressure.

The impact of localisation on service priorities

While decentralisation has undoubtedly led to more people coming though the doors, and many of these people could be considered those most in need, there is a real risk that just coping with numbers will make the service almost entirely demand-led. The social work task in Islington has been particularly vulnerable to these pressures, and it is worth examining some of the key issues which have emerged in this field.

Starting with the broader picture for a moment, we can note that much of the task of social work involves intervention in the emotional lives of individuals and families. The relationship between material deprivation and emotional distress has long been considered an important one. But in the 1970s a split began to emerge within social work practice between those who saw the primary task as working to improve the material circumstance and personal confidence of clients and those who persisted in emphasising the therapeutic nature of the social work task. By the late 1980s the primary task of mainstream social work had been to some extent redefined as the prevention of (physical and sexual) child abuse. This development helped to unite many of those involved in social work practice. Nevertheless a tension still remained and the connection between personal distress and material circumstance, which had been such a hallmark of radical social work, continued to be sustained in some of the more progressive inner city areas such as Islington.

The neighbourhood concept in Islington had a strong appeal to social workers with radical values, many of whom were drawn to the borough to work in the new neighbourhood offices. The strong emphasis on equal opportunities and welfare rights, the connection made between social work problems and material difficulties concerning housing and health, the importance attached to the anti-poverty campaign and so on, all symbolised an approach to the social work task which focused upon rights, entitlements, community action and empowerment.

But the strength of Islington's approach was perhaps also a weakness as there is a danger that the emphasis upon the material and public becomes a means of denying that individual stress also concerns the emotional and private. It can be argued that the emphasis upon providing a responsive service to the public masks the fact that many social work clients are involuntary recipients of state intervention, scrutiny and complex legalistic practices. Some of the problems attendant upon Islington's approach were revealed by the Liam Johnson Review, an inquiry commissioned internally by the Social Services Department in 1989, after the death of the 3-year-old child, Liam Johnson, at the hands of his father in 1987.

Mr Johnson was convicted of manslaughter in June 1989. The inquiry cleared social workers, neighbourhood officers and other care agencies of any blame for the toddler's death but went on to say that 'the present neighbourhood office structure is a time bomb waiting to go off' (Lawson *et al.*, 1989, p. 163). The panel felt that the pressures of maintaining the service were so great that there was no proper time for reflection and planning. The social work task had become almost entirely a matter of reacting to crises rather than undertaking effective preventative work. These are important points. On the other hand, it would be difficult to find any inner city local authority that did not face these problems. And if all these new people turned up at the central offices of the old department, there would probably have been even worse problems. The panel also noted that 'No one who has spoken to us is opposed to the idea of the neighbourhood office system and all seem genuinely committed to the idea of trying to make it work' (p. 153). Nevertheless, when in a telling analogy the report states 'a present emphasis on provision of demand-led services to the public is analogous to seeing the role of the general practitioner as being to sit in his surgery and write prescriptions' (p. 158), it is raising an important issue for many social work staff who note the paradox that, in those neighbourhoods most under pressure, the social work service has tended to become highly reactive and crisis-orientated. Community-based work comes to be seen as a luxury. It is important to realise that localising not only raises practical dilemmas but implicitly asks questions about the very nature of the service that is delivered.

The pressure to respond to increased demand as a consequence of localisation is also illustrated by the development of the home care service in each borough. Using the Social Services Inspectorate's 'Key Indicator' profiles for the two boroughs and for inner and outer London as a whole, it was possible to develop an approximate picture of the extent to which this service was targeted at those most in need. The concept of 'targeting' is an ambiguous one for, on the one hand, it suggests a service focused where need is greatest, while on the other it signifies an important shift away from the idea that certain kinds of service are a right to be expected according to age, degree of disability and so on. Thus, until very recently, the majority of Labour-controlled local authorities regarded the generous provision of home care services as an index of their socialist commitment to the welfare of elderly people.

A universally orientated service provides a high total level of service covering a high proportion of those deemed to be eligible for it but offers a comparatively low intensity of provision. A targeted service, on the other hand, restricts coverage in order to increase the intensity of service to those deemed to be most in need. Social service activity returns suggest that in the late 1980s, the overall level of service in both boroughs increased, although compared with other inner London boroughs, Islington provided a higher level than average, and Tower Hamlets a lower level. More importantly, if we take the '75+' age group as a proxy for the most vulnerable, then it is clear that during this period the home care service became less targeted at those most in need in both boroughs. The evidence available appears to suggest that the initial effect of decentralisation was to shift the service in a direction which was more responsive (or 'reactive', depending on your viewpoint) and universalistic; in fact, in a direction counter to the emerging wisdom of the government and of many within the policy community itself. In other words, the home care service in Islington and Tower Hamlets came to be construed primarily as a popular service which was spread thinly over a generously defined stratum of those entitled to receive it. We are not suggesting that localisation inevitably has an impact on services in this way, rather that it is an issue which decentralising authorities need to consider.

Restructuring for flexibility

Within any decentralised system, the disadvantages arising from the loss of economies of scale will be considerable unless the shift towards decentralisation is accompanied by the introduction of more flexible management and work patterns. Within the private sector what are sometimes referred to as post-Fordist organisational forms are characterised by more '*ad hocratic*' management practices (Mintzberg, 1979). This means that they develop looser, less permanent, more lateral and matrix-like structures and that they encourage, even insist on, moves to more flexible forms of skill use, such as multi-skilling (NEDO, 1986). We have found it helpful to consider restructuring for flexibility at three levels: (1) service delivery; (2) operational management; and (3) strategic management.

Flexibility in service delivery

As we noted in the previous chapter, the pursuit of flexibility at the service delivery level can be achieved through two basic methods – the creation of more generic working patterns, and the creation of multi-disciplinary teams. Both of these methods have been adopted within the two boroughs though there has been more emphasis upon the latter rather than the former. The neighbourhood housing service in Islington, for example, retains specialist housing advice and benefits workers, lettings officers and improvements officers alongside an estate management team.

The degree of retention of specialist posts is further illustrated by the fact that each neighbourhood office in Islington also has a specialist welfare rights worker and part-time (originally full-time) community worker. As a result, Islington probably boasts more of these specialist posts than any other equivalent local authority in the country. This clearly contributed considerably to the costs of decentralisation. As the borough's official guide to its neighbourhood approach indicates, decentralisation was accompanied by the creation of twelve new welfare rights advice posts, sixteen additional area improvement officers, twenty extra housing advice workers, twenty-five estate managers, thirty new social workers and sixty administrative staff (London Borough of Islington, 1986, p. 10).

The advantage of this system is that it provides a comparatively high level of specialist competence at the local level. In Tower Hamlets the degree of specialisation at local level is generally not so high and, in virtually all neighbourhoods, job responsibilities tend to be fairly broadly defined. Estate management staff in the outposted estate bases find themselves having to respond to the same range of demands that Islington's system caters for, but simple pressure of work inevitably means that the most pressing demands, for example responding to housing repairs requests, tend to take precedence over other needs.

In Tower Hamlets many enquiries concerning rights and benefits tend to be dealt with by the One Stop Shops in or near the mini town halls. Enquiries registered at the seven One Stop Shops in 1990 totalled over 240 000, more than double those in 1989, despite incomplete statistics from the Isle of Dogs. Although housing enquiries continued to predominate in all neighbourhoods (ranging from 30 per cent in Globe Town to over 55 per cent in Bethnal Green Neighbourhood), enquiries about the poll tax and rates numbered more than 29 000 and comprised over 12 per cent of the total in 1990. The popularity of Bow's One Stop Shop, which has acquired a national reputation for being a particularly effective service model, is illustrated by the fact that in 1991 it dealt with 107 051 enquiries!

In comparison there are very few examples of generic work organisation in Islington. Since September 1988 neighbourhood administrative staff have all worked to a common job description. These administrative staff provide support to all sections of the neighbourhood office – housing, social services, environmental health and chief executive's – and have a job description which increases in content and complexity as post holders progress towards a senior career grade. Interestingly enough the introduction of this generic career grade was opposed by the white collar trade union organisation in Islington, NALGO, largely because of the way in which it departed from traditional forms of job description. To the dismay of the local union branch, the neighbourhood administrative staff themselves took a different view. They saw in this new career grade an opportunity for the kind of internal progression that more professionalised staff take for granted.

In addition to providing administrative support these workers help to manage and staff reception, deal with much of the repair-taking and progress-chasing work, and supply information to the public on a range of council and other services. Competition for the pooled generic administrative support has at times symbolised and, to some extent exacerbated, interprofessional rivalries within the local offices. Each professional group has tended to cling to the belief that their effectiveness would be increased if they had their own dedicated administrative support system. This has led many proponents of decentralisation in Islington to dismiss criticisms of neighbourhood administrative support as professional 'sour grapes'.

A great strength of the neighbourhood approach in both boroughs, and one that is particularly pronounced in Islington, is the delivery of services through small, interdisciplinary teams which work together within a tightly defined physical area under a common, locally-based manager. A further method, common to both boroughs, should be mentioned. This consists of the creation of local, non-functionally based, interdisciplinary groups organised on a temporary basis. Virtually all of the neighbourhoods within Tower Hamlets have assembled Capital Programme Teams in this way. The startling productivity of these teams is discussed later in this chapter. There are many other examples which could be added of effective collaborative projects undertaken at neighbourhood level. Among those developed in Islington we can mention: the neighbourhood environmental improvement projects – bringing together local planners, community workers and officers responsible for private-sector housing improvements (Barnard, 1991); neighbourhood anti-racial harassment and anti-crime initiatives; and the development of co-ordinated cold-weather strategies between housing and social services workers to support elderly people during 'cold snaps' in winter.

Flexibility at the level of operational management

So far we have examined methods of introducing flexibility at the point of service delivery within the two boroughs. In this section we move on to consider how flexibility has been introduced at the level of operational management. Here we find quite different strategies adopted within the two boroughs and (as we outlined in Chapter 3) in the case of Islington, a process of learning from the problems associated with their initial strategy and a decision taken in principle in 1990 to move, in some respects, to a model more closely resembling the one adopted at the outset within Tower Hamlets.

Islington's initial neighbourhood office management model was essentially a compromise – a recognition by the members and officers charged with implementing decentralisation in the early 1980s of the power of the professional departments and the trade unions within Islington. But the controlling Labour politicians in Islington were also implicated in this compromise because as long as the main professional departments remained, so too would the traditional committee structure. Councillors drawing their power from the existing service committee structure had a vested interest in preserving existing departmental structures.

As a consequence the neighbourhood officers from the Chief Executives department were placed in the invidious position of being seen by the community to be responsible for the overall performance of the local office yet had no executive power over most of the staff based within it. There was a clear expectation, which later became formalised, that neighbourhood offices should be run by a management team comprising the four principal neighbourhood officers – see Figure 3.2 on page 63. In many neighbourhoods these teams worked very effectively but this was largely due to the existence of goodwill, effective interpersonal skills and a commitment by local officers to work through problems and tensions between the four service teams. In some offices, however, some or all of these conditions were absent and as a result relations between services within the neighbourhood were not always smooth.

The recent reorganisation within Islington brings the operational management arrangements very much into line with those introduced at the outset in Tower Hamlets – see Figures 5.2 and 5.3 on pages 115 and 116. Here the seven neighbourhoods are each led by a Neighbourhood Chief Executive who has full line management control over all professional services within that area. Each neighbourhood is run by a corporate management team, though the composition of these teams varies between neighbourhoods. Management teams meet on a weekly or fortnightly basis and are responsible for the development and implementation of local policies and for day-to-day management issues within the neighbourhood.

The contrast between Islington and Tower Hamlets before 1990 was striking. In Islington there was little doubt that even after several years of decentralisation the primary loyalty of the vast majority of neighbourhood based professionals and their managers was to their own departments rather than to the neighbourhood. In Tower Hamlets, on the other hand, all the main professional service departments and their attendant committee structures had been abolished. There can be no doubt that this startling move had an impressive impact on staff attitudes – officer loyalties altered dramatically and commitment to the new neighbourhood structures emerged with astonishing speed, even within those neighbourhoods under the political control of the opposition Labour Party.

Indeed, the development of neighbourhood loyalties grew so quickly that new kinds of rivalries, replacing the old departmental ones, soon emerged. Clearly the Liberals' political strategy, enshrined in their 'principle of neighbourhood autonomy', encouraged such developments and, as we shall see later, this has led to a number of retrograde developments within Tower Hamlets. Nevertheless it soon became apparent that neighbourhood loyalties were so intense that even the Labour-controlled neighbourhoods found it hard to bring themselves to develop collaborative strategies with other neighbourhoods – for example, around joint tendering for refuse collection contracts. This has raised important questions – not least that corporate managers with powers of virement across all budget heads will, in the face of competing priorities, make different decisions in different neighbourhoods. In other words, increased local flexibility can only be achieved at the cost of uniformity. And the lack of uniformity almost inevitably puts neighbourhood managers into conflict with senior professional managers at the centre.

Such conflicts occurred repeatedly within Tower Hamlets social services in the 1989/90 period. On two occasions, a series of decisions were made by local neighbourhoods which put child protection work in those areas at risk because of dangerously low staffing levels. On each occasion, local service managers were forced to appeal above the heads of their Neighbourhood Chief Executive and local councillors to the Director of Social Services for support. In a third instance, a case of multiple child abuse perpetrated by a local man who was HIV positive led to further internal tensions as the need to assemble a team of expert staff rapidly from across the whole borough to deal with the crisis was at first frustrated by the tardiness of non-affected neighbourhoods in releasing 'their' social work staff. Problems such as these dogged the brief period during which Neil Walker was Director of Social Services in Tower Hamlets. Tensions between Walker and the then Leader of the Liberal Group in the borough, Brenda Collins, and other influential councillors led to his resignation in early 1990 amid accusations within professional journals that social services were becoming 'Balkanised' in the borough (Insight, 1989).

Flexibility at the strategic level

In the context of decentralisation, strategic management involves taking a broader view of the issues and opportunities in the neighbourhood. It requires officers to escape from the traps and limited horizons of operational management and needs local councillors and others involved to stand back from everyday concerns and adopt a longer-term perspective. Most local authorities are incapable of developing a strategic approach to the needs of particular areas within their jurisdiction. This is because their centralised departmental structures present formidable obstacles to those concerned to develop local corporate planning and interagency working. This is a significant disadvantage for the conventionally organised authority because many of the problems councils confront – particularly in urban areas – are highly interrelated on the ground. They require a concerted response, not just by the various council departments, but also by other agencies – public, private, and non-profit – working in close collaboration with the council. A major advantage of a decentralised structure is that it can provide a framework within which local strategic management can take place.

Both Islington and Tower Hamlets have taken steps to develop a capacity for strategic management at the local level by introducing neighbourhood-based planning. The models of planning being developed at local level have interesting differences. These contrasts reflect not only the fact that the sizes of the neighbourhoods in the two boroughs are rather different, but also different philosophies about the nature and purpose of planning. As we explain in Chapters 7 and 8, the Tower Hamlets strategy for empowerment has put the emphasis on strengthening the position of ward councillors, whereas the Islington model involves experimenting with new forms of participatory democracy.

The action plans developed by the neighbourhoods in Tower Hamlets resemble the corporate plans produced by small local authorities. Despite there being variation across the borough our general impression is that considerable effort goes into the preparation of these plans and that they have considerable officer commitment. Unlike Islington, the planning department has been decentralised and we spoke to several planners who, while they found the changes unsettling at first, have come to realise that their skills are valued and that working at neighbourhood level has significant advantages. One neighbourhood planner said:

> It's good that the planners went into the neighbourhoods early – planners have gone up in influence. We were out of touch in the Town Hall. Down here you know what's going on and you can have a much closer link with members. And inter-departmental working is much better – we have a fortnightly management board meeting which is excellent at keeping departments in touch with each other.

The Bow Action Plan provides an example of the kind of strategic document being produced at neighbourhood level. It presents a picture of services in Bow as seen by local officers to provide 'a basis for defining aims, objectives and priorities as part of a comprehensive strategy' (Bow Neighbourhood, 1989). The position statement covers all council services and sets out performance targets and standards for the following year.

In Islington, strategic flexibility at neighbourhood level is being promoted through the preparation and rolling forward of Neighbourhood Action Plans. These represent a bold attempt to develop a new kind of very local, highly engaged planning. A key underlying thrust is the desire to use planning to give local people more power over events that influence on their lives. It was pointed out to us by the officer leading the development of the new approach that, too often, what neighbourhoods struggle for is a negative power – the power to stop other institutions and agencies taking decisions. She put her vision of a more creative approach to one of our seminars this way:

> Bringing about the decentralisation of power requires an organisation and practice of planning for action. Planning for services and development provides a positive power which we are attempting to shift in the direction of communities. It involves people in identifying what they can do now, what could be done if other institutions or parts of their own institution could be made to work in the same direction, and things which after analysis and discussion people realise can only be achieved if there are some other big changes. (Thomson, 1990)

The basic planning conditions which the Islington approach is attempting to fulfil are: involving people inside and outside the authority; clarifying the scope of local planning power; providing information about the locality and existing services; organising to plan, to act and continually to assess impact. Pilot plans for two neighbourhoods – Gillespie and Highbury – were produced in 1990 and all neighbourhoods prepared plans in 1991. The plans, which are to be updated annually, assess local problems and opportunities, examine local needs, review services, and specify performance targets for the coming year. The plans are not hefty documents – the pilot examples are less than twenty pages in length. The Bow Action Plan, admittedly for a much larger area, is over fifty pages and is less readable and accessible than the ones emerging in Islington.

Much more important than the documents is the impact of the plans. The Islington approach is much stronger on public involvement – thus the neighbourhood forums are heavily involved in plan preparation and review. The 1990 Gillespie Neighbourhood Action Plan put it this way:

> The plans are compiled in such a way as to enable monitoring and local accountability to local residents. . . They will allow members of the neighbourhood forum to check that targets are being achieved and policies are being correctly applied. This experience

will feed into future years' plans, suggesting areas where policies may require change at borough or local level to improve effectiveness (London Borough of Islington, 1990).

It is too early to say how effective these arrangements for local accountability will be, although we can note that, in relation to operational management, most of the forums have already shown themselves to be well able to spot failings and bring issues to the attention of their local office. In relation to performance monitoring, the action plans in Tower Hamlets rely heavily on local members. It is at least arguable that this places too great a burden on them – the plans, which cover large areas, include a daunting mass of detail. Have councillors got the time and the inclination to monitor so many variables? The Islington approach has the virtue of strengthening local 'voice'. As a result, there are more people monitoring fewer targets. This could well turn out to be a more effective way of ensuring that plans are implemented than by placing all the burden on local councillors.

Devolved management

Of the four dimensions to organisational change that we have argued comprise decentralistion it is the shift towards devolved forms of decision-making which is the most crucial. A comparison of the degree of devolution achieved in Islington and Tower Hamlets suggests that Tower Hamlets has gone much further. Indeed, whereas Islington has slowly moved from forms of nominal to actual devolution (see Figure 4.4 on page 102), at one level Tower Hamlets probably represents the most radically devolved local authority in Britain. However, as we shall see, although radical forms of devolution to the neighbourhoods have occurred within Tower Hamlets the extent of devolution below the level of the neighbourhoods is patchy. A final issue that must also be considered where radical devolution occurs is the question of how resources are to be allocated to areas.

Within Islington, financial devolution developed in an extremely piecemeal fashion as more and more budgets for particular, one-off items were handed to the neighbourhoods. Thus in the late 1980s each neighbourhood had its own environmental improvement budget, a small grants budget for local community organisations, an office running costs budget, and so on. What had not been achieved was the transfer of staffing budgets to neighbourhoods. These were still held centrally. Thus, for example, each of Islington's twenty-four home care teams had a nominal home care hours budget (allocated on the basis of 1981 census data), but the actual budget was still held by a senior social services manager who had the power to determine which vacancies at local level were to be filled and when. This presented neighbourhood home care organisers with tremendous difficulties – many had experienced delays of more than six months in filling vacancies within their small and often overstretched teams. As we noted in our discussion of localisation, there are inherent dangers in spreading services too thinly. Where local managers lack control over recruitment then problems of cover can undermine the reliability of the service being provided. The council was aware of these problems and the creation, in 1991, of the new Neighbourhood Services Department and the introduction of Neighbourhood Managers in each local office provided the borough with an integrated organisational framework within which devolution of staffing budgets to neighbourhoods could proceed.

In one respect, within Tower Hamlets things could hardly have been more different. From the outset the seven neighbourhoods were allocated actual budgets for all operations conducted within their boundaries, including the running costs of major facilities such as libraries and residential facilities which were used by residents outside their own area. Having said this, the units to which devolution occurred were actually fairly large and the degree of devolution within the neighbourhoods varied considerably. Initially budgets were allocated to neighbourhoods on the basis of historical expenditure patterns. This involved an extremely time-consuming process of reconstituting budgets from a functional to a spatial basis. A decision was made that recharging for use of facilities by non-neighbourhood residents would only apply to certain social services facilities as realistically it was unimplementable for services such as libraries and leisure facilities.

However, in 1988, work began on developing a more needs-based approach to the allocation of neighbourhood budgets. A report to the borough's Performance Review Committee in 1989 highlighted the essential characteristics of the method to be adopted:

The Government's Grant Related Expenditure system, which assesses the need of local authorities for grant purposes, was used to determine appropriate shares for neighbourhoods of resources available for neighbourhood services. . . Expenditure on borough-wide services, such as Victoria Park, by neighbourhoods was separately assessed and added to neighbourhood's allocations. . . Expenditure on rechargeable neighbourhood services, eg social services' residential homes, was separately identified and adjustments were made to target allocations so that they could be compared with needs based allocations on a like for like basis.

The report indicated that the gainers of a needs-based approach would be Bethnal Green, Poplar and Stepney, whereas the losers would be Bow, Globe Town, Isle of Dogs and Wapping. Some of the neighbourhoods, such as Stepney, stood to gain an increase of over 20 per cent on their 1989/90 allocation whereas others, such as the Isle of Dogs, stood to lose over 15 per cent of their allocation. The report also usefully listed the disadvantages of such an approach – the complexity of the formulae used makes it difficult for neighbourhoods to challenge; the use of outdated 1981 Census data was questioned; the absence of separate provision for administration leads to failure to allow for loss of economies of scale for smaller neighbourhoods and the administrative costs of maintaining recharge mechanisms are significant. Despite these provisos approval was given for the exercise to proceed and, eventually, a formula based upon the government's newly introduced Standard Spending Assessments (SSAs) together with a 'small neighbourhood' element was used to construct final allocations. The new system, introduced on 1 April 1991, was to be phased in over a four-year period.

While a variety of objections can be raised against any formula-based approach there can be no doubt that it constitutes a more equitable and less serendipitous method of budget allocation than past spending. The area resource allocation system developed by Tower Hamlets may not be unique in British local government but it goes a lot further than most councils in attempting to bring about a fair geographical distribution of resources.

Having discussed the way Tower Hamlets distributes resources to the neighbourhoods we now examine the amount of discretion exercised at local level. To the surprise of many outsiders, the neighbourhoods have virtually unlimited powers of virement within their overall budget – the only exclusion is the housing revenue account, which is ring-fenced (that is, this budget is earmarked for housing and cannot be spent on other services). Neighbourhood budgets are monitored on a regular bi-monthly basis by the Performance Review Committee, which also scrutinises neighbourhood assumptions regarding capital receipts. Neighbourhoods are allocated a share of the borough's housing capital programme on a pro rata basis according to the size of the housing stock contained within their area, and the social services capital programme remains centrally administered.

The neighbourhoods have complete autonomy to bid for central government grants, such as Estate Action money, and they retain their own capital receipts. This clearly provides neighbourhoods with the incentive to maximise additional income-raising strategies. This had a significant impact upon the performance of the neighbourhoods' capital programme teams whose interdisciplinary character was mentioned earlier. As Table 5.1 indicates, until decentralisation, the borough's housing department was unable to spend even its central-government allocation. Since 1987, spending has consistently outstripped allocation. In 1989/90, the last year before the Conservative government increased restrictions upon local councils use of their capital receipts, the capital programme in the borough was considerably higher than any equivalent sized housing authority in the UK. This was partly because the Liberals escaped the government's capital controls by introducing a leasing scheme in relation to central heating, lifts and other items. This was an important central initiative. Even so, the achievements of the neighbourhood teams were remarkable.

Clearly, however, the model developed in Tower Hamlets is one which tied a neighbourhood's capital spending to its willingness and capacity to act entrepreneurially rather than to its degree of housing need. Comparing the capital programmes of the seven neighbourhoods over the four-year period 1987–91, it is noticeable, for example, that Globe Town, with a smaller housing stock in a better condition than Stepney's, had a programme amounting to £38 million compared to the latter's £31 million. It could be argued that this approach is one guaranteed to produce unnecessary spatial inequalities. The Liberals' answer would presumably be that even Stepney's capital programme was considerably higher than it would

TABLE 5.1   Borough-wide housing capital expenditure and allocation in Tower Hamlets, 1982/3–1990/1

Year	Allocation £000s	Spending £000s
1982/3	10 542	5 777
1983/4	12 000	8 724
1984/5	12 311	8 571
1985/6	11 644	9 226
1986/7	17 504	17 187
1987/8	19 507	20 345
1988/9	22 985	29 803
1989/90	20 517	124 597
1990/1	31 973	46 438

have been under a centralised system and, if the local electorate are unhappy with the policy, they can always vote the neighbourhood's political leaders out. Interestingly enough, Stepney's Labour leadership was voted out in the 1990 council elections and many felt that the poor Labour record on basic housing issues such as repairs and improvements was an important contributory factor.

Central control and local autonomy

This discussion of devolved management has referred to some of the tensions which exist between a desire for authority-wide consistency and fairness and the need to recognise diversity and encourage entrepreneurial behaviour at local level. As Tower Hamlets has such a radically devolved organisation, the experience of the borough deserves further exploration. Note that the neighbourhoods have freedom to spend their revenue budget more or less as they like, provided they stay within statutory guidelines. They have the power to set their own establishment levels within budget. They have control over gradings of posts, which has led to some inter-neighbourhood poaching as staff find that the rate-for-the-job is better across the neighbourhood border. They can generate and retain their own capital receipts. They can contract out services where appropriate and they can enter into partnership deals with the private sector. In many ways, the neighbourhoods resemble seven mini local authorities, which is precisely what the Liberals intended – this is the realisation of their 'principle of neighbourhood autonomy'.

Tower Hamlets constitutes a unique phenomenon in British local government because it has been bolder than any other local authority in checking and undermining the power of what local Liberals see as the centralised bureaucracy. Indeed, in some ways the Liberals appear to have made a fetish of 'the centre' which at times had led them towards illogical forms of reorganisation. The former Director of Social Services, Neil Walker, described this anti-centralised ideology simply as 'if it's central it's bad'. With regard to the planning function, the former Chief Executive, John McBride, made the point that despite having more urban development taking place than virtually anywhere else in the country, Tower Hamlets had no central planning and development committee. Many neighbourhoods, particularly those under Liberal control such as Bethnal Green, were entrusted with handling major development sites such as Whitechapel Market where hundreds of millions of pounds were at stake. Clearly this gave less senior planning officers an experience of handling major developments, which they would never have obtained in more hierarchical organisations. On the other hand, was it reasonable to expect comparatively inexperienced officers to take on the well-resourced planning consultants hired by big development companies?

Often, when decentralisation is considered in the academic literature, the question is asked as to what extent the new arrangements permit the adaptation of central policies to local needs and conditions. In Tower Hamlets the question seems to miss the point. The powerful policies that exist are, by and large, those that are locally created.

The struggle betwen central control and neighbourhood autonomy in Tower Hamlets has been particularly interesting in the case of housing allocations. Prior to the Liberals gaining control of the borough in 1986, Tower Hamlets had been subject to investigation by the Commission for Racial Equality (CRE) over allegations of racism in the management of its housing service. As a result, the CRE issued a Notice of Discrimination against the housing department in 1987 which forced it to introduce a number of practices, such as the creation of effective ethnic monitoring within the housing allocation system, to overcome discrimination against the Bangladeshi community in particular.

The notice of discrimination posed a challenge to the Liberals which they responded to in a novel fashion. The major source of discrimination occurred in the rehousing of homeless families within the borough, a group who were disproportionately Bangladeshi. In early 1988 control over housing allocations had been devolved to the seven neighbourhoods. A procedure was introduced whereby each neighbourhood was given an annual quota of homeless families to rehouse, a quota originally based on the size of the neighbourhood's housing stock and later upon the number of vacant properties available to let in each neighbourhood. Failure to rehouse this quota meant that the neighbourhood would be penalised the equivalent of the average cost per month of keeping each family in temporary accommodation.

Such attempts to assert a greater degree of central control have not been introduced without resistance. For a considerable time Bow refused to introduce a neighbourhood ethnic monitoring system for its housing allocations even though, under the CRE notice, this was effectively a legal requirement. This eventually led the CRE to begin action to prosecute Tower Hamlets for failure to comply with its notice. Eventually Bow reluctantly complied with the procedures. This, however, was not before the borough's Chief Executive had stepped in to instruct officers within Bow to ignore the wishes of their local councillors and comply with the terms of the non-discrimination notice.

Similarly, the system of quotas and penalties for rehousing homeless families has met with innumerable problems. Many neighbourhoods failed to provide accurate information regarding the number of vacant properties available to let in their areas. As a result the more honest neighbourhoods ended up receiving a disproportionate number of homeless families to rehouse. This was partially overcome when an independent means of monitoring the number of vacant properties became available using a computerised rent account system.

The basic problem with the new homeless families allocations system, however, is that some neighbourhoods have simply chosen to incur the financial penalty of not meeting their quota. They see this as the necessary price to pay for pursuing their own local lettings priorities. By 1990 most of the Liberal-controlled neighbourhoods had decided to give greater emphasis to 'sons and daughters schemes' by setting aside a small number of allocations for the sons and daughters of existing tenants within the neighbourhoods. Because such schemes tend to discriminate in favour of the families of tenants already occupying council property they tend to favour the indigenous community and to penalise groups, typically the black and ethnic minorities, who have arrived more recently in the area. Because the supply of council housing in Tower Hamlets is limited when compared to demand, the policy of giving priority to 'sons and daughters' can only be achieved by lowering the priority given to rehousing homeless families and risking the financial penalty.

The targets and penalties system introduced in Tower Hamlets is probably unique. Paradoxically, although it was formulated by some leading Liberal activists in the borough it has also been strongly resisted by Liberal councillors in some neighbourhoods. The nature of the resistance is twofold – the system is resented as an intrusion by 'the centre' upon local decision-making and it is seen as a means by which 'outsiders' who are in some respects seen as 'undeserving' can gain access to scarce council accommodation. Given that the overwhelming majority of homeless families in Tower Hamlets are Bangladeshis, we can see how housing allocations, the relationship between the centre and the neighbourhoods, and the politics of race have become inextricably bound together. This was vividly illustrated at the council by-election for the Millwall ward in the Isle of Dogs in September 1993. Derek Beackon, the successful British National Party candidate, made headline news by pursuing a racist campaign against the housing of homeless families in the area.

Clearly, the existing system disadvantages homeless families in their struggle for rehousing in the borough and results in a skewed spatial distribution of lettings to such families. Some Liberals would clearly say that they and their electors are willing to accept this. The problem is that penalty systems are not designed to cope with deliberate and systematic transgression by what are effectively seven mini housing authorities within the same borough. In a situation where the strategic core of a housing department has been dismantled and the centre has no formal power – for example, to discipline or sack officers – over those making operational decisions, then systems which are even more inventive than that designed in

Tower Hamlets are going to be necessary if some degree of equity is to be preserved.

Devolved management and service efficiency

What has been the impact of devolved management on the efficiency of service delivery in Islington and Tower Hamlets? Our evaluation study focused on three areas – the target efficiency of the home care service which we referred to earlier in this chapter; the question of administrative overheads; and the impact on rent arrears recovery. We focus first on the latter because it is one of the few areas where comparable performance data is easily available for the two boroughs. Throughout much of the 1980s Islington was fairly notorious for not keeping comprehensive data on service performance levels, a weakness which it only began to rectify in the late 1980s when it introduced a borough-wide service quality initiative. Using data compiled by the London Research Centre in 1991 (see Table 5.2), it is clear that Tower Hamlets has consistently performed well compared with other London boroughs on this indicator.

TABLE 5.2   Rent arrears: Islington, Tower Hamlets, all London boroughs

	1980/1	81/2	82/3	83/4	84/5	85/6	86/7	87/8	88/9	89/90
Islington	13.9	13.7	18.7	15.6	16.1	20.2	N/A	27.4	28.9	12.1
Tower Hamlets	7.7	7.1	8.1	6.6	6.6	13.1	N/A	4.9	4.7	6.1
All London boroughs	9.4	7.8	9.9	9.8	12.4	13.0	N/A	13.1	16.3	16.1

Note: Figures show total arrears as a proportion of gross rent collectable.
Source: London Research Centre, Comparative Housing Statistics, 1990.

With the introduction of decentralisation, performance in Tower Hamlets, which had been deteriorating under the former Labour administration (see the 1985/6 figure), was turned around dramatically. Moreover, the reduced arrears levels have been achieved against the general trend within London, in which arrears have been rising since 1981/2. Islington, on the other hand, has returned consistently higher than average arrears figures since 1980/1, with large increases in the period 1985 to 1989. However, in 1989/90, Islington managed a dramatic improvement in its performance, reducing the arrears level to below the London average for the first time.

In accounting for these figures, a number of factors need to be considered. The achievement of Tower Hamlets is largely due to the existence of specialised arrears recovery teams, which since decentralisation have been located within each of the seven neighbourhoods. An innovative incentive/sanction scheme also operates, whereby central arrears targets are given to each neighbourhood; success in reaching above the target enables the neighbourhood to transfer or vire the surplus into the local repairs and maintenance budget, whereas failure penalises the neighbour-hood's repairs budget in a similar fashion. In Islington, arrears recovery has been an aspect of the generic responsibility of estate management and has therefore competed for priority with other tasks that the neighbourhood-based estate managers have had to perform. However, in the late 1980s, in response to the escalating levels of arrears in the borough, the Housing Department began to develop neighbourhood arrears monitoring systems and neighbour-hood targets. This innovation appears largely to be responsible for the considerable improvement in performance in this indicator, in 1989/90. However, there has been a price to pay for this, as for many neighbourhood estate managers now complain that much of their function has been reduced to that of 'arrears chasing'.

Tower Hamlets has also developed a sophisticated model of comparative neighbourhood indicators which provides easily-understood figures for citizens. The figures reveal a correspondence between performance levels and political control – Bethnal Green, Bow and Globe Town, all under Liberal control since 1986 – have performed better than the other neighbourhoods. Within many of the neighbourhoods in Tower Hamlets, scrutiny can be taken further by revealing variations between estate bases within the neighbourhoods. Such kinds of information system which have great sensitivity to spatial variations in performance are in many ways vastly superior to the traditional performance management information systems found in many councils. In particular, they provide information to service users which is meaningful and relevant to their needs, enabling them to compare the performance of officers in their neighbourhood or on their estate with others doing similar jobs. On more than one occasion we witnessed tenants at neighbourhood meetings calling upon embarrassed local housing officers to account for what the tenants felt was poor performance.

The impact of decentralisation on arrears recovery reveals a number of interesting issues. The objective of controlling and reducing arrears levels has itself by no means been unproblematic. The contrast between the performance of Labour- and Liberal-controlled neighbourhoods in Tower Hamlets should not be understood simply in terms of variations in managerial effectiveness but also in terms of contrasting political priorities. However, where arrears recovery is an agreed priority, it seems clear that the organisational arrangements developed in Tower Hamlets, combining decentralised specialised teams with neighbourhood monitoring and incentive systems, can be particularly effective. This suggests a need to give further consideration to the balance between specialisation and genericism within localised teams. While genericism can clearly provide a more flexible and responsive service, the danger is that it introduces a system which transfers on to front-line staff, such as estate managers and field social workers, the responsibility for managing competing priorities. As a result of this, specific aspects of performance may, sometimes inadvertently, suffer if effective monitoring systems are not in place to act as an early warning system.

Paying for local democracy?

The creation of seven highly devolved neighbourhood structures has not been without its costs, however. Audit Commission profiles of Islington and Tower Hamlets for the period 1989-90 revealed that while administrative staffing levels in Islington were slightly lower than the average for inner London boroughs, in Tower Hamlets they were much higher. Table 5.3 provides a breakdown of staffing levels for the different categories which fall under the 'central administration' heading within the Audit Commission profiles.

Clearly, the decentralisation of Chief Executive's staff, legal and personnel has corresponded to dramatic losses in economies of scale. This is most striking for 'Chief Executive staff' such as committee services, research and policy, publicity and communications, etc., all

TABLE 5.3 'Central' staffing levels in Tower Hamlets

| | Central staff/1000 FTE all staff | |
	Tower Hamlets	Inner London average
Financial	57.9	52.4
Chief executive, legal and secretarial	109.9	58.5
Computer	10.1	14.0
Personnel and management	27.1	13.2

Source: Audit Commission Profile, Tower Hamlets, 1989–90.

of whom have been decentralised to the neighbourhood level. Although none of these staff are direct service providers they are all tied in closely with the development of neighbourhood democracy in Tower Hamlets – providing committee services for local Neighbourhood Committees, developing neighbourhood-based information and publicity materials, conducting local market and policy research and so on. In other words, while they may not directly contribute much to the quality of services in the borough they do contribute to the quality of local government and democracy.

Cultural change

We have already seen how localisation can encourage the development of user-orientated attitudes among many staff and how, in some cases, staff transferred out from the town hall have developed a commitment, even a loyalty, to the neighbourhood. We have also referred to the way restructuring has brought about more flexible patterns of working at local level including new kinds of collaboration between different departments. Indeed, one of the most striking findings to emerge from our investigation of neighbourhood offices in both boroughs was the way in which closer physical proximity of staff enhanced communication and co-ordination. The following comments from staff in the Stepney neighbourhood, typical also of those that we heard from other neighbourhood offices, imply significant shifts in the culture of the organisation:

> There is better communication altogether – if I want to see the surveyor, I've just got to go upstairs. (Housing Allocations Officer)

> Decentralisation has definitely brought me closer to both housing and meals on wheels. (Home Care Organiser)

> Environmental health officers will often come down and report their concerns about old ladies. (Team Leader, Social Services)

The organisation of the home care service in Islington revealed a similar phenomenon. Informal co-ordination was a result of people working together, on the ground, on an everyday basis:

> It's very handy being in an office like this with housing upstairs. If a client has bronchitis and a problem with damp you can get a quick response. (Home Care Organiser, Beaumont Rise, Islington)

> We have a very good welfare rights person who'll go out to elderly clients – he's very approachable when the carers pop in as well. (Home Care Organiser, Finsbury, Islington)

These various shifts in the way people work together arise mainly from the proximity of staff and the fact that both boroughs, but more so Islington than Tower Hamlets, have given some, although arguably not enough, attention to staff training designed to encourage collaborative working. But because collaboration is stimulated by the proximity of staff working within neighbourhoods, one tends to find that the further one goes up the hierarchy, the more traditional boundaries and assumptions are maintained.

Changes to the culture of the organisation can also be pursued in a more deliberate and direct way by giving explicit attention to organisational values. The Islington approach to equal opportunities provides a good example of this strategy. From the outset the Islington councillors were keen to ensure that the decentralisation proposals would further their equal opportunity objectives. One councillor put it this way: 'If local services aren't run in line with strict equal opportunities guidelines all that disadvantaged groups gain is easier access to discrimination and inequality.' A great deal of effort has gone into cultivating an atmosphere within the organisation which makes discriminatory behaviour unacceptable. Our experience of being in the neighbourhood offices in 1989 and 1990 suggests that a commitment to equal opportunities is an organisational value that enjoys widespread support at local level. This comes across in the style and manner of many neighbourhood officers, and is reflected in innovation within the offices – for example, the creation and implementation of clear guidelines for dealing with racial harassment – and is demonstrated by imaginative efforts to reach out and engage the interests of minorities living in the neighbourhoods – for example, by providing interpreting services in the neighbourhood offices and by the creation in some neighbourhoods of a black members' forum.

While Islington has successfully introduced a culture of equal opportunities which has permeated much of the authority, it has barely begun to create a risk culture. Rules remain rigid, and responsibility remains with senior professionals. In Tower Hamlets, as we have seen, risk is implicit in the whole strategy. One can debate the relative merits of this sort of risk-taking, but there is no doubt that it represents a radical departure from the bureaucratic culture which has until now dominated the public sector.

The experience of Tower Hamlets and Islington also offers lessons about the management of change. For example, the simple fact that Tower Hamlets councillors changed their own decision-making structures before they changed the officer structure unambiguously signalled their intentions and made it very difficult for officers to resist. Furthermore, the fact that Tower Hamlets councillors personally managed the process of change prevented it losing its direction. In Tower Hamlets during the process of change the decentralisation committee became effectively the only important committee. It had almost unlimited power, and all the key councillors sat on it. In contrast, Islington's decentralisation committee was a sub-committee of the policy and resources committee. Notwithstanding the energetic efforts of the chair, it had relatively little power and was rarely attended by most councillors. If anything, this implicitly signalled that councillors were not taking the process seriously, and it allowed officers to think in the same way. It is precisely because of this that the Islington programme appeared to lose its way during key periods of transition.

Conclusion

In this chapter we have considered in some depth four dimensions of decentralisation: (1) localisation; (2) restructuring for flexibility; (3) devolved management; and (4) cultural change. We have used this framework to structure our comments on the amount of organisational change that has taken place in our two case study authorities and we have attempted to weigh the strengths and weaknesses of alternative organisational change strategies.

What is startling about both Islington and Tower Hamlets is that, in spite of an unhelpful and intrusive central government, they have shown that it is perfectly possible to embark on bold and far-reaching change strategies for public service organisations, even in inner city areas faced with huge social and economic problems. The achievements of Islington and Tower Hamlets disprove assertions that local government is incapable of taking forward self-driven transformation.

None of this is to imply that all the organisational changes introduced in Islington and Tower Hamlets have been without difficulties, nor is it to suggest that the chosen reforms were always wise. On the contrary, we have attempted to show, alongside the achievements, that some of the measures had unintended drawbacks. Moreover, it is unhelpful to view the change agents as always being right and those resisting change as always being wrong. The maintenance of a certain amount of stability is 'the condition of any change which can hope to be welcome and enduring' (Vickers, 1972, p. 127).

As a broad generalisation we can say that, of the four themes discussed here, localisation has met with least resistance. Creating a decentralised system of multiservice neighbourhood offices is no easy task – it is a substantial achievement by any standards. But the evidence from our research is that the other dimensions of decentralisation are the ones that are more difficult to put into effect. Strategies for developing new kinds of flexibility, devolving budgets and bringing about cultural change will, almost certainly, encounter more opposition from established interests. It follows that they should be given more attention by those concerned to succeed with public reform strategies of this kind.

The resistance arises because these measures lay down a more fundamental challenge to established practice than localisation.

They represent significant shifts towards a new kind of post-bureaucratic organisation and, as such, are bound to face opposition from many of those who have become comfortable with or, perhaps powerful under, the previous regime.

Decentralised management: lessons from experience

In spite of intrusive central government controls, both Islington and Tower Hamlets have been successful in introducing radical changes in their internal organisation. Their success in developing and implementing new forms of decentralised management disproves claims that local authorities are incapable of developing new forms of public service delivery which are much more welcoming to the public than traditional approaches.

Using the four-part framework described in Chapter 4, we can record, first, that localisation seems to be easier to achieve than the other changes we have associated with decentralisation. Localisation can, in itself, improve public access to services and, if well managed, can lead to a range of improvements in service quality. However, major improvements in service delivery require significant changes along the other three dimensions of decentralisation we have identified. The more flexible forms of working that can be developed within decentralised structures can bring substantial benefits to service users, staff and councillors, but they are likely to be resisted by entrenched, departmental interests. The devolution of budgets inevitably creates tensions between the centre and the neighbourhoods. However, if an authority is unwilling to introduce a significant amount of devolved management *and* accept that this will lead to some diversity in service standards between neighbourhoods, then decentralised management is not a reform strategy it should pursue. While changes in the culture of an organisation are notoriously difficult to measure they can, in many ways, be the most important. We argue that such changes should affect the whole organisation, not just those parts that are decentralised. Indeed, risk-taking and a commitment to service quality in the decentralised units can only be sustained if the centre of the organisation reshapes its own stance to one which puts providing support to decentralised management at the top of its list of priorities.

The evaluation of experience with decentralised management in Islington and Tower Hamlets suggests that there are pitfalls to be avoided as well as possibilities to explore. There is, for example, a tension between a very high level of localisation and the extent to which the local service can be comprehensive. Islington's approach is much more localised than Tower Hamlets', and while this has led to an outstanding level of public access, it has also created problems of staff cover in the neighbourhood offices.

In both authorities the decentralised arrangements have made staff more available to the public. This is a big step forward when compared with the situation where staff work in closed and secretive bureaucracies, but it can create problems. There is a danger of stretching front-line services too far and putting unreasonable pressure on those key staff who serve the public day in and day out at neighbourhood level.

In relation to the tension between central control and local autonomy it can be claimed that Islington has not done enough to liberate its neighbourhood managers, while Tower Hamlets may have gone too far. This is a difficult equation to balance correctly but, given the history of highly centralised management in UK local government, the tendency in most local authorities is towards uniformity. In an era when public services are expected to be more entrepreneurial, local authorities may find it helpful to use the principle of subsidiarity when considering their centre/local balance. This would start from the position that responsibility should be carried locally unless there are persuasive arguments to the contrary.

This creates new challenges for senior managers – success with decentralised management requires a clear and confident centre. Moreover, guidelines about certain key values – for example, a commitment to equal opportunities – need to be set down and monitored by the centre.

A sound local government system needs to combine good management with democratic accountability. We turn to this theme in the next part of the book.

PART III

DECENTRALISED DEMOCRACY

6 Citizen Participation: Theory and Practice

Introduction

In Chapter 2 we argued that local authorities need to concern themselves as much with improving the quality of government as with improving the quality of local public services. In fact, these are not separate tasks because, ultimately, the quality of public services depends on there being a set of pressures for service improvement which reside *outside the state*. A cursory glance at the failed communist regimes in Eastern Europe and the Soviet Union reveals how the absence of such pressure resulted, amongst other things, in poor service performance and ineffective public planning. Václav Havel, president of Czechoslovakia from 1989 to 1992, spoke for millions when he argued that vigorous efforts need to be made to widen citizen involvement in public affairs:

> The schools must lead young people to become self-confident, participating citizens; if everyone doesn't take an interest in politics, it will become the domain of those least suited to it'. (Havel, 1991, p. 118)

Clearly, the problems confronting East European countries are on an altogether different scale, but Havel's desire to promote the development of an active, participating citizenry resonates with current political debates in the UK.

Participation, choice and control

As we noted in Chapter 1, the idea of public participation in local services has been pursued with varying degrees of vigour since the mid-1960s. When one considers how closed and secretive local authorities were then, the shifts towards more open and accountable local government appear to be substantial. However, when one examines the track record on local citizen empowerment in more detail, the results are less impressive. A major study of the many participation initiatives of the 1960s and 1970s concluded that:

> though there have been great moves towards public involvement in local service provision in recent years, little has been achieved by way of a fundamental shift in power, a shift which implicitly underlay the ideas of radical proponents of participation in the late 1960s. In the end, elite perspectives have won out, and participation has served the purposes of building up a consensus for the proposals of those in power, thereby legitimating them. (Boaden *et al.*, 1982, p. 179)

Despite this somewhat gloomy conclusion, it can be claimed that these early experiments with participation helped to pave the way for the rather more radical programmes of the early 1980s. As we noted in Chapter 2, some of these initiatives – for example, those of the Greater London Council – involved a rapid expansion of funding for grass-roots organisations and community groups. These developments and the political strategy which guided them proved to be very unpopular with central government and this is one of the main reasons why the Greater London Council was abolished in 1986.

In recent years, central government constraints on local authority spending, including the capping of local tax levels and the threat of capping, have reduced the funds available to support voluntary organisations and community groups (Chanan, 1991). But these constraints have not extinguished the desire to develop new ways of involving people in the decisions that shape their lives at local level. Empowerment – what it means and how to develop it – remains a key theme for local government in the 1990s. Indeed, a recent paper circulated to all local authorities by the Local Government Management Board argues that empowerment is 'a major theme of our times' and urges every authority to develop strategies which increase public influence and control over the activities of the council (Clarke and Stewart, 1992). To develop effective approaches to local citizen empowerment, we feel it is important to reflect carefully on the notions of choice, participation and control.

The rhetoric of 'control' is used across the political spectrum and is generally perceived to be a desirable outcome of a local democratic process. Arguably, however, neither the political left or right actually offers 'control'. Rather, the right offers the extension of *individual choice* (largely by undermining the political system and placing greater emphasis on the economic system) and the left offers the extension of *collective choice* (by attempting to increase participation in the system of representation). The distinction between choice, participation and control can be illustrated by the analogy of a theatre performance.

A traditional play will be written by an author (read this to be the majority political party) and performed by a group of actors (council officers) to the audience (the public). The audience is not involved in either the writing or the performance, except as the viewer. A more creative approach introduces audience participation. Here there is still a script, but the actors have a certain amount of freedom, and the audience is encouraged to participate. However, if there is any danger of the script being undermined, the involvement of the audience is diminished or withdrawn. The audience can complain, but the most probable result of their complaint is that they will be excluded from the theatre in the future. This is managed participation. Alternatively, the dissatisfied audience could go to another theatre but they would still have no involvement in writing the script. This is what we mean by choice. If the choice the audience wants is not available, the exercise of choice does little to empower the audience.

The attempt to equate choice and participation with control is, then, flawed. The apparent control offered by the 'right to buy' housing legislation, for example, is at best partial as it opens up the participant to a whole range of unknowns dictated by national economic policy. An individual may have control over what colour s/he paints his/her front door, but has no control over how much his/her mortgage payment will be every month. The apparent control offered by neighbourhood committees can also be an illusion. For not only is that control usually tightly bounded by central targets and policies but, as with the audience participation scenario, the risk is that as soon as the local committees start to deviate from the script, they are made impotent. Indeed, this is precisely what Cockburn (1977) observed in her study of neighbourhood participation in Lambeth.

Control means the power of directing. It requires participation in the process of production (writing the script), not only in the process of consumption (watching or participating in someone else's script). Thus one might conclude that citizen control can only be achieved once the citizen can 'get behind the scenes'. Present political arrangements keep the citizen in front of the stage and offer only a passive role. We have a binary political system in which, at root, the voter is able to say only yes or no – 'we no longer like party X so we will vote for party Y'. The products (or policies) are packaged differently so that they appear to offer choice, but it is a heavily constrained choice. The role of the citizen is almost entirely reactive. Thus, while it is possible to argue that Thatcherism has 'commodified' politics to a greater extent than ever before, the system of representation itself has for the vast majority always been a process of consuming others' politics. The citizens *choose* political leaders periodically at elections, but they are rarely involved in producing the values and policies to be pursued by the parties.

It is, of course, possible to claim that citizens do not want control – that limited choice and limited participation are perfectly acceptable because people are too busy doing other things. Indeed, many individuals have been discouraged from participating because they have found, through bitter experience, that their voice is often ignored. A key question for political leaders emerges from this discussion. If a public institution wishes to pursue a strategy for empowering local people, it needs to decide whether or not, in our analogy, it really wants to invite citizens 'behind the scenes'. If it does not want to move in this direction, it should not pretend that it does. As Sherry Arnstein argued in her classic article on participation over twenty years ago: 'There is a critical difference between going through the empty ritual of participation and having the real power needed to affect the outcome of the process' (Arnstein, 1971, p. 176). Arnstein, in an effort 'to encourage a more enlightened dialogue', set out a typology, or ladder, of citizen participation which we reproduce as Figure 6.1. Her typology identifies eight levels of participation, with each rung on the ladder corresponding to the extent of citizens' power in determining the end product.

At the bottom of the ladder are two rungs of non-participation. The objective here is not to enable people to participate in planning or conducting programmes, but to enable power-holders to 'educate' or 'cure' the participants. The next three rungs involve dialogue with the public. Citizens, to varying degrees, have the right to be heard even if they do not take a direct part in decision-making. In this zone of the ladder we find one-way communication from the authority (for example, announcements, pamphlets, posters, local authority annual reports); two-way exchanges (for example, attitude surveys, neighbourhood meetings and public hearings); and co-option (for example, citizens sitting on committees but with power-holders retaining the right to decide). Further up the ladder are three rungs which give citizens increasing degrees of decision-making

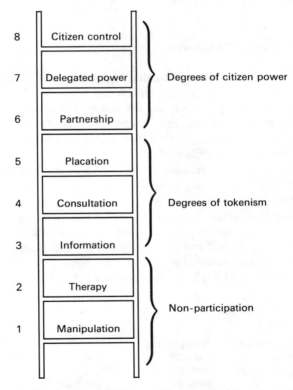

Source: Sherry Arnstein. Reprinted by permission of the *Journal of the American Institute of Planners*, 35, 4 July 1969. Taken from Arnstein (1971).

FIGURE 6.1   Arnstein's ladder of citizen participation

clout. In this top part of the ladder citizens share directly in the process of policy-making and service provision. Arnstein is at pains to point out that the ladder is a simplification, but, twenty years on, it still provides a helpful starting point for discussion of citizen empowerment.

In the following pages we attempt to relate some of the most interesting participation initiatives in local government to this ladder. However, before doing so, we want to update and refine Arnstein's concept. Her ladder was put forward with specific reference to her analysis of federal social programmes in the USA in the 1960s with their aspirations for 'maximum feasible participation' (Marris and Rein, 1974).

Spheres of citizen power

One of the problems with the Arnstein model of empowerment is that it focuses upon the relationship between citizens and specific governmental programmes. To adapt this model to local government as a whole requires a change in some of the assumptions implicit in Arnstein's model. Specifically, we need to understand the existence of a number of spheres of influence – an individual or group may gain a relatively high degree of power within one and yet still have little or no control over the next. Figure 6.2 illustrates this point.

The first sphere refers to the individual person or household. To what extent do they have power to determine the nature of the services they receive and, if they are ill, old, disabled or otherwise deemed 'dependent', the care or treatment plans that are designed for them? Although not the focus of this book, we regard these

(1)	(2)	(3)	(4)
The individual sphere.	The sphere of the estate, neighbourhood, programme, site or facility.	The sphere of local government and administration.	The sphere of national governance.

FIGURE 6.2 Spheres of citizen power

issues as crucial. Together with colleagues at the School for Advanced Urban Studies we have developed various models for understanding individual empowerment and disempowerment (Taylor *et al.*, 1991; Hoggett, 1992).

The second sphere, which is very much the focus for neighbourhood decentralisation, is the sphere within which individuals use public goods, programmes and services in common. This was also the focus for Arnstein's model. A point we wish to stress is that one may be denied power in the first sphere but be able to claim it in the second, or vice versa. Thus a teenager with severe physical disabilities may be completely powerless at home but may attend a day centre where, along with others, she enjoys real influence over the design of activities and the way staff and volunteers work. Devolved management is inextricably linked to empowerment in this second sphere. The users of a local service are more likely to enjoy power within this sphere if the staff running the estate, library, residential centre, swimming pool and so on themselves enjoy delegated powers.

However, it is quite possible for citizens to enjoy a high degree of power within the second sphere yet comparatively little within the third. This may be for one of two reasons. It may be that a local authority or other local public institution delegates operational control to participatory bodies within 'sphere 2' yet jealously maintains centralised control over all matters of strategy and policy making. On the other hand, citizens may be denied power within the third sphere because the local strategic powers which should reside here have been absorbed by the fourth sphere. Clearly, this is what is happening to the education service in Britain in the 1990s. The curriculum is determined nationally. School governing bodies, unable to shape the content of education, are left to struggle with the management of expenditure cuts.

Whoever controls strategy controls the script, because resources and operational practices tend to flow from the former and not the other way around. If a person does not have any influence over the script, it still may be possible to interpret it in a particular way, creatively subvert it or even challenge it. It is only by pushing at the boundaries of a situation that a group can test the limits of its power. The opportunity to create strategy and policy is therefore not an all-or-nothing issue (i.e. either you have it or you do not). Rather, there is a constant negotiation and renegotiation of power relationships during the process of policy implementation (Barrett and Fudge, 1981).

A ladder of citizen empowerment

A strategy for genuine empowerment would seek to maximise the power of citizens as opposed to non-elected élites within all four spheres. This book is primarily concerned with the second and third spheres. It follows that we need to envisage the possible existence of *two adjacent* ladders of citizen empowerment, one for each sphere. Indeed, we would stress the importance of making changes within sphere 3 in order to develop successful approaches to citizen participation within sphere 2. In thinking about the power that citizens can assert within these spheres, it is useful to distinguish between three areas of decision-making:

1. *Operational practices.* The behaviour and performance of staff within public institutions; issues concerning other aspects of the quality of public services being provided – such as the design, heating, opening hours of public buildings; reliability and regularity of service, facilities for service users with particular needs and so on.
2. *Expenditure decisions.* These may relate to delegated budgets, such as small 'good neighbour' budgets or 'environmental improvement' budgets, to major capital budgets (for example, for the modernisation of an estate) or to devolved comprehensive revenue budgets which cover all staff salaries and routine running costs of a particular office or facility. Alternatively (or as well as) citizens' organisations (for example, urban parish councils) may have the independent power to generate their own income by raising local taxes.
3. *Policy-making.* The strategic objectives of a particular service; a strategic plan for the development of an estate, facility (for example, arts centre), neighbourhood or district; spending priorities and resource allocation decisions.

These levels are interconnected – ultimately the power of citizens to effect changes in operational practices will depend increasingly on their power over expenditure decisions. Operational practices and expenditure decisions are themselves strongly influenced by the overall policy framework characterising a service. We can envisage degrees of citizen power within each area. Thus it is quite possible for a participatory body to enjoy considerable power in the second area, slightly less in the first and very little in the third – the new school governing bodies being an example.

Urban parish councils are one of the few participatory bodies to enjoy limited independent revenue-raising powers yet their influence over the operational practices of public institutions is negligible. A problem with the metaphor of the ladder is that it does not allow for such anachronisms as it subsumes these three discrete areas of decision-making into a single continuum. This limitation needs to be borne in mind.

Our experience with participation initiatives in the UK suggests that there are some further reasons why the Arnstein typology needs modification to fit the UK context in the 1990s (Burns, 1991a). First, given our previous discussion, it is necessary to distinguish between participation and control more precisely than they are represented on the Arnstein ladder. Second, in our experience several additional forms of empowerment can be envisaged in the upper half of the ladder. Third, and more important, the rungs of the ladder should not be considered to be equidistant. The experience of the last twenty years shows that it is far easier to climb the lower rungs of the ladder than to scale the higher ones. These factors may have encouraged some organisations to believe that they have gone further with citizen empowerment than, in fact, they have.

In Figure 6.3 we put forward a new ladder of citizen empowerment which we think is more tuned to the needs of the public sphere in the 1990s. To the left of the ladder we note some of the changes that would be needed in sphere 3 (at the level of the local authority, health authority, etc.). To the right of the ladder we identify some of the changes needed within sphere 2 (at the sub-local authority level) and provide some examples.

Three qualifications need to be made. First, by introducing more rungs we run the risk of making the model over-elaborate. This is certainly not our intention. Rather, we aim to stimulate clearer thinking about the nature of empowerment. We would encourage readers to delete rungs and/or add rungs to suit their own situation. Second, as with all models, the diagram simplifies a much more

162

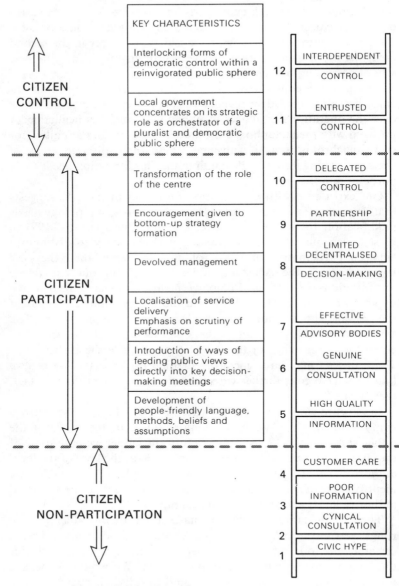

FIGURE 6.3 A ladder of citizen empowerment

SPHERE 2 – THE 'SUB-LOCAL'*

KEY CHARACTERISTICS	Neighbourhood-based	Service- or facility-based
Maximum legal and financial autonomy from institutions in sphere 3. Co-ordination through networking	Neighbourhood governments	Housing ownership co-operatives
Legally autonomous organisations which are financially dependent on institutions in sphere 3. Grant aid and/or relational contracts.	Community associations Community development corporations (USA)	User-controlled community organisations
Substantial control delegated within a centrally prescribed framework, e.g. a management agreement, or legal contract	Neighbourhood trust	Tenant management co-operatives
Power shared between the service institution and citizens' groups within a specific framework	Neighbourhood forum with power sharing	Estate management boards Jointly managed facilities
Limited but real control over operations and/or resources within a specified framework	Community council	Estate committee Residents' forum (in a residential home)
Influence possible over operational, resource and even strategic decisions, but actual control over none	Area advisory committees	Housing, social services and leisure advisory committees
Welcoming procedures encouraging citizens to make their views known	Public meetings at neighbourhood level	Consultation with neighbours affected by planning proposals
Systems developed for effective communication, listening and responding	Citizens' charters	Customer contracts

Note: *The 'local' refers to the level of the local authority, health authority, etc. The 'sub-local' refers to anything below this level. See Figure 6.2 on page 158.

complex reality. Thus some public institutions will have their 'feet' on several rungs at once. Indeed, different departments and different committees may be many rungs apart in their approaches to empowerment. This may be intentional or accidental. In any event, the ladder may help local authorities to compare and contrast different practices within their organisation. Figure 6.3 can also be used to appraise the level of citizen empowerment in the growing number of non-elected institutions of the local state (such as health authorities, training and enterprise councils, and urban development corporations) and privatised public services (such as water, gas and electricity).

The third qualification is that there is a danger that the model may take on a prescriptive tone, implying that all councils should climb to the very top of the ladder as quickly as possible. The logic of the argument we introduced in Chapter 2 is that all public institutions should, indeed, be climbing further up the ladder. However, we are well aware of some of the potential problems associated with the very high rungs. We are aware of the reactionary parochialism which can exist in some communities and clearly there are limits to the neighbourhood government concept. For example, the American Neighbourhood Government Act of 1975, which was never passed into law, would have resulted in 'a massive transfer of funds from higher levels of government to neighbourhood corporations in the order of tens of billions of dollars a year' (Hambleton, 1978, pp. 158–9). Total neighbourhood control, involving the recycling of local wealth, would make rich neighbourhoods even richer and make poor neighbourhoods poorer. It follows that, if equity is considered to be a key value, strategies to increase citizen control need to be coupled with policies of redistribution carried out by higher levels of government.

Citizen non-participation

At the bottom of Figure 6.3 are four rungs, all fairly close together, of citizen non-participation. These approaches, while they should not detain us for too long, cannot be ignored. Manipulation of information and image have become so common in public life it is easy to overlook the corrosive effect of these developments. In Chapter 1 we described how many cities are struggling to present themselves as attractive locations in a competitive national and/or global market place for capital investment. Place wars of this kind have a long history in the USA. For example, real estate interests in Los Angeles had already developed the technique of 'civic boosterism' – to a fairly advanced level in the 1920s (Davis, 1992). During the past decade or so this idea of promoting inward investment, almost at all costs, been imported into the UK. There is nothing wrong with providing high-quality information about a city and its people to potential investors. However, our research on American practice and our review of place marketing in the UK suggest that initiatives to promote economic growth often spill over into civic hype (Hambleton 1990 and 1991). Extravagant publicity campaigns usually attempt to mask the problems associated with urban regeneration and may drift into outright deception. Clearly, hype of this kind provides no basis for participation – information is distorted, gloss takes over from content and the communication is all one way. The government's *Action for Cities* brochure, launched with great publicity by Margaret Thatcher in March 1988, provides an example of this genre (Cabinet Office, 1988).

Turning to the second rung of the ladder, we note that some organisations engage in cynical consultation. This can take the form either of treating participation as a charade or limiting it to trivial matters. Examples of the former can be found in transport planning. County highway authorities, with statutory responsibility for public participation in structure planning, have sometimes left themselves open to the criticism that they are inviting comments on road proposals which have already been decided by central government (Boaden *et al.*, 1982, pp. 79–80). Hospital and school closures provide other examples of situations where the responsible authority may have already determined its policy in advance of a so-called consultation exercise. An example of trivialising participation is provided by the council which, in the context of a massive urban renewal scheme for its town centre, invited comments not on the strengths and weaknesses of the plans, but on what the names of the new streets should be!

Some local authorities and urban development corporations have spent considerable resources on producing flashy brochures which lack substance and authority – they are stuck on rung 1. From the point of view of citizen empowerment a more common problem, however, is that the information made available to the public is often dense and inaccessible – a problem encountered at rung 3. Take a look at a set of papers for a typical council committee meeting. They are likely to be voluminous and off-putting. It is a common experience in committees to see councillors and officers, let alone members of the public, struggling to understand the content and identify the key policy choices. If inaccessible papers are undesirable in main council committees, they are totally unacceptable in meetings designed to involve the public. We have sat in on many area committees in different local authorities where it has been clear that members of the public were unable to follow the agenda because of problems associated with the design, layout and content of the papers. For example, the area committees in Birmingham in the period 1984/5 suffered from this problem, with councillors and officers often lapsing into 'forms of indecipherable shorthand and jargon' (Hambleton and Hoggett, 1987, p. 62). Thus, even when a council has good intentions, poor quality information can undermine the process of participation.

Some readers will feel it is unjust to bracket most customer-care programmes with these unsatisfactory forms of pseudo-consultation at the bottom of the ladder. To be fair, some customer-care initiatives could be located on rungs 5 or 6. For example, where customer-care programmes take complaints monitoring seriously *and* act to rectify the problems highlighted by these expressions of user dissatisfaction, it can be claimed that they offer a modicum of citizen influence. However, as we suggested in Chapter 2, many customer-care programmes are dominated by the 'charm school' approach. Training front-line staff to be courteous, friendly and helpful is an essential step towards providing a high-quality service, but it does nothing to empower the citizen. Indeed, some customer care techniques – for example, those relating to how to deal with extremely angry residents – can be viewed as ways of reducing the forcefulness of the citizen.

Citizen participation

Within the zone of the ladder concerned with citizen participation, it is helpful to distinguish between informing and consulting; decentralised decision-making; and partnership and delegated control.

Informing and consulting

Rung 5 of our ladder is where a genuine citizen input begins. Progressive local authorities have recognised for many years that sound approaches to public involvement need to be supported by high-quality information. There has been a great deal of innovation in this area over the years. A recent review by Gyford highlights the impact of legislation, like the Local Government (Access to Information) Act 1985, the value of 'one-stop shops' providing a wide range of information at a single service point, and the importance of thoughtful public relations (Gyford, 1991, pp. 106–24). High-quality information is seen as crucial by those councils pursuing a citizens' charter approach to citizen empowerment. Harlow Council, one of the authorities which pioneered the citizens' charter concept long before Whitehall had even heard of the idea, stressed the importance of giving citizens rights to clear and unambiguous information:

> Citizens need to have clear, understandable information about decisions and policies and the reasons for these, as well as information about services offered or to which they are entitled. (Harlow Council, 1990)

York City Council delivered its first citizens' charter to every household in the city in April 1989. The specific targets set out in the charter change each year and each charter provides a progress report on the previous year's promises. John Cairns, the chief executive, believes that the York approach is fundamentally different from John Major's initiative because:

> ours articulates the democratic relationship between the council and the community it services. It is a statement made by the council of what it is trying to achieve on behalf of the community, how it is going to achieve these goals and what people should see happening in the city during the year as a result of our action. (John Cairns, quoted in Wills, 1991)

The York Charter is clear, concise and specific. It provides clear information which citizens can use to appraise the performance of their council.

Many councils are now actively developing ways of spelling out clear performance targets – through citizens' charters, service standards, customer contracts, service level agreements and the development of explicit quality programmes. Some councils recognise the importance of drawing citizens into the process of setting targets, on the grounds that there are inextricable links between good quality information, sound consultation mechanisms and high-quality services: 'if quality is to be assessed, complained about, improved through citizens' charters or any other means, then an open, multi-stakeholder process of specifying objectives . . . must be developed' (Gaster, 1992, p. 63).

The mid-1970s saw local authorities embark on a wide range of genuine consultation initiatives. Some of these took the form of one-off exercises – for example, in relation to the preparation of statutory land use plans – while others involved the creation of more lasting advisory arrangements. Some councils increased the frequency of opinion polls and many introduced consultative meetings of different kinds. The first structural shifts came with the development of area advisory committees in Stockport (1974), Middlesbrough (1974) and Newcastle (1976) (Harrop *et al.*, 1978). With the exception of Middlesbrough, the main problems with these structures were that they were not very well plugged into the main council committees. Not only did they not have many formal powers, they also had little influence. Many would argue that they often functioned as a mechanism for channelling people's anger away from the heart of the council.

One example of this marginalisation, which was revealed to us when we carried out a series of training days with neighbourhood staff in the London Borough of Haringey in 1988, was the setting-up of neighbourhood committees on the Broadwater Farm and Tiverton estates after the Tottenham riots. The committees were theoretically set up to give people a greater say in their communities and to stop such a situation recurring. In fact, they received few resources and, as sub-committees of the housing committee, they had no effective route to the decision makers. Another example of a fairly weak area committee system is the one set up by Birmingham City Council in 1984. We monitored this initiative in its early period and, while it was a remarkable step forward for a highly centralised and highly departmentalised local authority, we concluded that the areas were too large and that the council gave insufficient attention to public involvement (Hambleton and Hoggett, 1987, pp. 59–64). More recently, some local authorities, such as Bradford and South Somerset, have developed area committee structures which have overcome some of the weaknesses we discerned in the Birmingham initiative.

It would be quite wrong to suggest that efforts to extend citizen influence through consultative and advisory mechanisms have been unsuccessful. On the contrary, the right of citizens to be heard is now widely recognised in local government. Moreover, some local councillors, in our experience, are now increasingly likely to see themselves as catalysts, encouraging citizens to make their views known. The days of the 'we know best, leave it to us' councillors may be numbered, even in the local government backwaters. Local authorities are experimenting with a wide diversity of consultative mechanisms to 'learn from the public' – many of them small scale and unsung (Local Government Management Board, 1988). Community development workers have played a crucial and successful role in encouraging people to get involved and have their say. While many initiatives have been based on housing – for example, the wide range of innovations with tenant involvement in local housing management (Power, 1984) – other services have witnessed widespread experiment. Imaginative use has been made of community councils in rural areas and in some cities – for example, Middlesbrough and Glasgow (Duncan, 1988). Recent efforts to develop community empowerment strategies on peripheral estates using a highly localised approach have also proved to be effective (Holmes, 1992).

Decentralised decision-making

Some of the initiatives we have just mentioned, depending on the degree of influence exercised by citizens, could be located on rung 8 or above of our ladder. We are making the following distinction between 'limited' and 'significant' citizen influence. On rung 7 and below the local authority (or other service organisation) may commit itself to taking into account the views of citizens before decisions are made, but will not necessarily make a commitment to act on them. The views of citizens may carry great weight but there is no acceptance on the part of those in power that they should be decisive. Arrangements located on rung 8 and above involve a transfer of at least some power – citizens acquire genuine bargaining influence. We suggest that the gap between rungs 7 and rung 8 is a significant one for citizen empowerment – hence it is a wide one on the ladder.

Some of the most successful examples of partnership working have involved user groups. These tend to focus on small areas such as the management of a sports facility. The fact that there is already an active group of users who are in the habit of making the journey to the facility helps the process of participation. One of the most interesting user-group experiments is the Quality Action Group which has attempted to involve people with learning difficulties in decisions about their lives (Burns, 1991b). They are particularly interesting because they have broken away from the committee meeting/reports format. Instead of bombarding residents with weighty papers, groups are formed in residential and day-care establishments and typically involve between seven and fifteen people (Milner, Ash and Ritchie, 1991). The groups go through a process of prioritisation over a number of weeks, deciding what is most important to them, and what they think it is possible to change. They work through a six-stage process:

1. Bringing people together.
2. Agreeing how the service should operate.
3. Looking at what is happening now.
4. Choosing something that can and should be made better.
5. Deciding on and putting a plan into action.
6. Seeing how things have changed and deciding what to do next.

Sometimes a group takes a whole meeting to go through just one of these steps. Each is important. This contrasts sharply with many neighbourhood forums, who lose new members very rapidly because they do not make the time to allow people to get to know each other. In many forums the people who attend meetings are rarely given time to develop a vision of what they would ideally like. They are often flooded with too much information, and asked to do so much that they cannot see the wood for the trees. Good managers and politicians will regularly spend a day or more developing ideas and visions, they will undergo training and carry out regular brainstorming. It is very unusual to find this even in the most advanced participatory forum. The debate is almost entirely reactive and the participants rarely have a clear sense of direction on which to base their reactive judgements.

When most people are asked what sort of service they want, they find it difficult to answer. They have little comparative information and they are not used to working creatively in groups. One exercise in the Quality Action Group resource pack asks users to think about what sort of service they would expect if they were staying in a five-star hotel. Then, using that as a base line, they assess their own service. Visits to other users and services are encouraged. The Quality Action Groups also suggest new ways of organising meetings. It is our view that replacing meetings based on agendas, reports and resolutions with a training format can radically enhance the ability of groups to sustain themselves.

These informal user groups, although small in their sphere of influence, could be an important model for the more formal neighbourhood committees – those which are advisory as well as those with formal powers. Despite the fact that they had limited but real delegated powers, our research into the pre-1989 Rochdale Estate Committees and Community Based Action Area Committees showed that they suffered from the lack of broader cultural change within the local authority (Burns, 1990b). One Rochdale housing officer describing the relationship of the housing department to the local committees said:

> Obviously we are dominating them because we are imposing one boring report down their throats after another. Information is presented so that it is meaningless, we don't provide any contextual information. (Burns, 1990b)

In an earlier publication we quoted a similar assessment of the Newcastle Priority Area Team Forums:

> The fact that team meetings are structured in a manner of council committees, ie with lengthy agendas, formal reports and more than half the time given over to applications for grants, militates against discussion in depth of issues affecting the area. (Newcastle Inner City Forum, quoted in Hambleton and Hoggett, 1987, p. 58)

In the area structures developed in Rochdale this problem was reinforced by the procedures that were adopted and the resources which were available to particular groups. For example, there was a

clear difference in status between officer reports, which were usually
typewritten, and tenants' reports, which were verbal and thus easier
to dismiss, misinterpret and not refer on to other decision-making
forums. Most of the meetings we attended were dominated by
reports, resolutions and 20 page agendas. Even in the most
advanced committees, jargon and gobbledegook was still a big
problem. Also, the way in which council officers pre-empted the
ideas of local people was revealing. In one local meeting which we
attended, residents were told by officers that there was a local
budget. They were told that they would be able to bring forward
their own proposals on how to spend it, but were then immediately
confronted with a detailed report by officers on how they thought
most of the money should be allocated. In our view, if officers
wanted to make helpful suggestions, they should have presented
them for consideration at the same time as proposals from tenants.
This would have helped to create an atmosphere of trust and
fairness.

Despite these criticisms, which are by no means confined to
Rochdale, there were some interesting innovations. In some areas of
Rochdale the agendas were divided into two – tenants' items and
council items – and the tenants' items were always taken first on the
agenda. Many of the committees introduced an 'open forum' – a
session of between half an hour and an hour in which tenants could
raise their individual grievances. This stopped the rest of the meeting
from becoming dominated by personal cases. One area introduced a
'market stall' at the beginning of each meeting, where people from
council departments would deal with public queries. Also, some
local areas had developed theme meetings on issues such as local
play facilities. These seemed generally to be more successful ways of
drawing people in.

Partnership and delegated control

The importance of improving the process of decision-making in
meetings and groups becomes even more important as we step up to
rungs 9 and 10 of the ladder. When a council moves to these levels, it
delegates more substantial powers to the community level.

Estate Management Boards can provide examples of effective
partnership. These are committees of local tenants based on an

estate who take on the day-to-day management of the estate. An Estate Management Board is an autonomous local management organisation with its own legal identity. Responsibilities are delegated to the board under the provision of Section 10 of the Housing and Planning Act 1986. The model separates the local authority's responsibilities for overall housing policy from the day-to-day management of an estate. Local tenants have a majority of representatives on the committee but have no direct say in strategic housing policy.

Tenant management co-operatives provide an example of delegated control, and Rochdale's Cloverhall Co-operative illustrates the approach. In 1985 the Cloverhall Tenants' Association Co-operative, as agents of the housing department, took over the management of 240 properties. This involved undertaking the management tasks of collecting rent and chasing arrears, rehousing, repairs and environmental maintenance. The Cloverhall agreement does not grant full citizen control because the co-operative still retains obligations to the centre and has to work to agreed performance targets. Nevertheless, it does have complete control over how to achieve those targets and has control over any surplus made over and above agreed income levels.

A second example of an organisation combining independence and delegated control is the parish council which, in law, is a local authority with a similar status to a district council, but with fewer obligations. It may take on any of the functions of a local authority (provided they are delegated to it) and it has the power to levy its own rate. It also has the power to call referenda. In the words of Section 101 of the Local Government Act 1972, 'A local authority may arrange for the discharge of any of their functions: (a) by a committee, a sub-committee or an officer of the authority; or (b) by any other local authority.' A parish council is technically an 'other local authority', which means that the powers which could be delegated to it are quite significant. There has been a long-standing campaign to widen the use of neighbourhood councils in cities (Young, 1970). In the mid-1980s Birmingham City Council mounted an ambitious programme to introduce ninety-four formally constituted local parish councils into the city, but the council was unable to persuade the Boundary Commission of the merits of its case. A strength of the urban parish (or community) council is that it is elected by local people. Parish councils are, of course, active in many rural areas (Elcock, 1982, pp. 35–7), but their potential in the urban context has yet to be explored.

Local authorities wishing to develop a high level of citizen empowerment will need to restructure their committees and departments and shift the culture of the organisation towards one which welcomes citizen participation. Citizen participation cannot be added on 'at the edge'. As Chapter 3 explained, Tower Hamlets and Islington are examples of local authorities which have engaged in major organisational change and we explore their experiences further in Chapters 7 and 8. As they strive to widen access to the policy-making process, many members and officers recognise the importance of holding on to core values which the 'centre' will insist upon – relating to fairness of treatment, for example – regardless of neighbourhood views. This is a difficult balance to strike, but is familiar enough to politicians and managers concerned to develop the kind of 'freedom within boundaries' organisation we described in Chapter 4. These initiatives, symbolised by a fundamental change in the main decision-making and service delivery structures of the council, do not add up to citizen control. But, as we discuss in more detail later, they do open up real opportunities for local people to create local policies and mark the first steps into the production of policies.

So far, this discussion has been couched in terms of increasing citizen 'influence' over decision-making although we are now beginning, in the context of local budgets, to talk about the possibility of creating citizen 'authority'. Influence implies the ability to have an effect on decisions which have an impact on local communities. Authority carries with it the ability to take action without prior confirmation from a higher level. This idea of shifting the locus of authority is an extremely underdeveloped area in the UK.

Citizen control

The top two rungs on the ladder (11 and 12) in Figure 6.3 involve citizens having the power to govern a programme, area or institution more or less independently of local government or other parts of the local welfare state. The rung below (10) also refers to a model of citizen control but one which in some respects is highly ambiguous.

Opted-out schools, for example, have a high degree of control over management and, to a lesser extent, finance, but their control over educational policy matters is highly circumscribed given the way central government has exerted control not only over what schools teach but, increasingly, over how they can teach it. Where such forms of delegated control occur it is rare to find matters of policy and strategy included in what has been delegated – in such instances it is not at all clear whether the citizen is the object or agent of control.

The development of more pluralistic patterns of public service provision does not necessarily enhance citizen control even slightly. As we indicate in Chapter 10, many of the non-profit organisations to which service provision is being transferred are not themselves at all democratic. It is not even obvious that such a transfer will generate a greater degree of pluralism. Some see the growth of the 'contract culture' as a process which will turn voluntary organisations into clones of the state (Gutch, 1992; Taylor and Hoggett, 1993).

The contracting-out of public services to non-statutory organisations poses a number of other questions. There are various ways in which sphere 3 can exercise control over sphere 2. Thus control can be delegated on the basis of a legal contract subject to detailed specification. Alternatively, control can be entrusted to a non-statutory organisation, either through a grant-aid relationship or through the development of more informal, non-legalistic forms of relational or co-contracting (Childs, 1987). As the work of Fox (1974), Ouchi (1980) and Powell (1990) demonstrates, the resort to detailed and legalistic forms of contractual relationship corresponds to the breakdown of trust between parties engaged in social or economic transactions. This resonates with the experience of much of the independent community sector in the 1980s, perhaps particularly that part which emerged through the efforts of those such as women, black and ethnic minorities who were usually excluded from local decision-making. The resourcing of such organisations by the GLC and other Labour local authorities in the 1980s was a constant source of irritation both to successive Conservative governments and to the conservative press.

The resort to contractual control not only corresponds to the expression of distrust, it can also severely curtail the independence of contractor organisations – the more detailed the specification, the more the contractor is 'pinned down', even at the operational level. This kind of contractual relationship prevents the contractor from having any influence, let alone control, over the policy framework, as the policies of the client organisation are written into the specification the contractor undertakes to abide by.

Under conditions of delegated control, local government can transfer the delivery of services to a range of non-statutory or quasi-statutory bodies while retaining authority over such inter-organisational systems. However, under conditions of entrusted control, the public institution relies primarily upon its influence rather than its authority (de Ste. Croix, 1992). Relational contracting assumes the existence of trust between parties – a trust primarily built upon a shared commitment to common values, familiarity, the exchange of information and personnel between parties and so on. Current private-sector management theory (Pascale, 1991) resorts to the metaphor of the conductor and the orchestra to visualise relationships between the core firm and its subsidiaries and subcontractors under highly decentralised conditions.

But it is possible to imagine a still more radical set of arrangements. Assuming a much greater degree of democracy than exists today, local government could be supplemented by directly-elected, single-purpose authorities such as health boards, energy authorities etc., and by elected regional authorities. Under these arrangements non-statutory organisations could enjoy considerable or even total legal and financial autonomy from local state institutions. Probably the majority of forms of citizen control correspond to community organisations which are user-led. Some interesting contemporary examples would include day and resource centres run by and for people with disabilities (for example, Centres for Independent Living), black and ethnic minority housing co-operatives and community housing associations, independent membership-based community associations, cultural clubs, and so on.

While it is certainly desirable that such groups have direct control over the work in which they are engaged, they would not, on their own, provide a model for a democratic society because they would be small and fragmented, and each would be free to pursue its own sectional interests in the same way as a selfish individual in the market place. Such conditions would require a new conception of the collective whole (to which organisations and individuals are responsible, and vice versa). This can no longer be conceived of in terms of a single unified state but rather would have to be founded on the concept of interlocking communities which network, federate and debate with each other. These would be dependent on a thriving civil society operating outside the state.

We develop such themes further in Chapter 10, but if, as we suggest, a genuine participatory democracy must go beyond the level of control over organisations to a notion of participation in and control over *communities*, then the idea of community development must be central to our concerns. Indeed, it is not only central to the pluralistic future of service provision we have outlined, but is also critical to any progressive council commited to developing even a minimum of genuine participation:

> It is those with the least confidence and resources, often those seen by outsiders as problem areas, or apathetic, which most need to develop the strength that community organisations can provide. Here community development can help people develop the confidence and skills to get community activities going and to build the networks which will give them more control over the quality of their life and environment (Taylor, 1992, p. 5).

Rethinking the boundaries of citizen control

We have suggested that citizen empowerment is a central task for local authorities – particularly at a time when local democracy is under attack. The new ladder of citizen empowerment we have set out in this chapter is intended to provide a conceptual framework which can help local authorities and others think through their empowerment strategies. Each council needs to develop its own multifaceted strategy. We have suggested, however, that decentralisation can play a major role in empowerment strategies once councils recognise the amount of change that is needed. In the next two chapters we examine how two inner city local authorities have used decentralisation to strengthen local democracy.

In closing this chapter we refocus attention on the top three rungs of our ladder. We would like to extend the metaphor of the orchestra and the orchestrating role of government to which we have previously alluded. For three possible models of an orchestra exist and, in the sphere of jazz music, are put into practice every day.

First, consider *delegated control*. Here operational decisions are devolved to a range of internal and external units but within a set of highly-defined boundaries which may assume a variety of forms such as the commercial specification (that is, contracting out); the management agreement (as occurs, for instance, with housing management co-operatives); or the framework document (for example, the 'Next Steps' or executive agencies within central government). Here, the government can be seen as a kind of composer/conductor. The players may be allowed some licence to interpret the conductor's requirements, and they may well influence the conductor considerably, but there is no doubt who is in control.

Now consider *entrusted control*. Here the boundaries within which devolved units can operate are much looser, and within these boundaries they also have freedom to innovate, to develop their own policies and to influence the development of local government policies. Here government can still be seen as a composer/conductor but what is offered are a few basic themes or structures around which the players improvise. The final performance is determined collectively by both composer and players – indeed, more often than not, the composer will also be a player. A much greater degree of equality therefore exists.

Finally, consider *interdependent control*. Here there is no pre-existing structure whatsoever. There is neither composer nor conductor, simply a set of free-standing representative and participatory organisations, none of which can claim authority over the other. In the context of modern jazz, this is equivalent to free improvisation in which rhythmic or melodic structures may emerge but are not pre-decided. But such improvisation cannot occur unless the players have acquired a demonstrable and acknowledged competence plus confidence and trust in each other, obtained either by deep familiarity over time or by the recommendation of trusted colleagues. These last two models are equivalent to what the psychoanalyst, Donald Winnicott, termed 'shared playing' – the highest form of cultural endeavour (Winnicott, 1974).

As we move towards the second and third models and away from the first, so the governance of relationships between players becomes increasingly founded upon trust and interdependence rather than upon control by either hierarchy or market. It may be that a genuinely pluralistic local public sphere begins at the point where the contemporary visions of both radical right and left stop, that is, at the furthest limits of delegated control, because our models of entrusted and interdependent control envisage a fundamental transformation in the boundaries between state and market economy on the one hand, and civil society on the other. We have lived according to the dull maxims of traditional representative democracy for too long. Empowerment cannot lie with a market whose shiny allure conceals vast concentrations of unaccountable private power, but with the broadening and deepening of all forms of democracy in all areas of life. Some readers may feel that parts of this discussion verge on the Utopian. We would ask such readers to ask themselves, if they consider themselves to be democrats, why are their expectations so low?

7   Enhancing Participatory Democracy: Islington

Introduction

In this chapter we examine the experience of the London Borough of Islington in developing a network of neighbourhood forums. It can be claimed that the council has gone further than any other local authority in the UK in attempting to improve the quality of public involvement in local government. While the bold steps taken by Islington are clearly tuned to the local environment, the innovations developed there will be of wider interest to the local government community because they offer practical insights about how to strengthen the democratic roots of local government.

Following a discussion of the political background we outline the terms of reference and constitution of the neighbourhood forums. Our evaluative commentary on the forums examines the degree to which they can be said to be 'representative' of the local population, considers the process of public involvement in decision making which the forums exemplify, and reflects on the main strengths and weaknesses of the forum model as viewed from different perspectives.

The development of proposals for neighbourhood participation

As discussed in Chapter 3, the Labour leadership on Islington Council always envisaged that decentralisation should go well beyond the improvement of public services to stimulate public involvement – that it should be concerned to improve the quality of government as well as the quality of services. While the localisation of services was sweeping forward in the 1982–7 period, the council was exploring ways of democratising council services. In 1984 the council produced a consultation paper entitled *Setting up Advisory Councils in Decentralised Neighbourhood Areas*. This reaffirmed the council's desire 'to involve people in decision making in the neighbourhood through the establishment, initially, of a variety of advisory forums, some of which, in time, could evolve into decision making Neighbourhood Councils' (London Borough of Islington, 1984).

These proposals were subject to consultation at numerous public meetings in the period 1984/5. The debate culminated in a major conference in October 1985 attended by nearly 300 people. Following the conference the Decentralisation Co-ordination Unit developed a set of public guidelines on neighbourhood forums and a model constitution for neighbourhood forums (London Borough of Islington, 1986).

In developing its strategy for neighbourhood democracy, the council was confronted with multiple tensions:

> The council was determined that the constitution, power and terms of reference of each neighbourhood forum should be decided by the public in the neighbourhood. It nevertheless had to ensure that the forums were organised in a democratic, legal and workable way to ensure that all members of the community had access to them. In particular, the council was concerned to involve people who had previously been under-represented in local democracy. In addition, the council was concerned that existing channels of involvement – like tenants' joint consultative bodies – should be preserved. (London Borough of Islington, 1986)

Reconciling these tensions is no easy task. The public need convincing that they will have real influence and that their views will be taken seriously. Black and ethnic minority people were particularly sceptical as to how much involvement they would have. While some tenants' groups thought that the new arrangements would be an improvement, some tenants' associations were fearful that their established consultation procedures would be overtaken by the forums. The council was concerned about the legitimacy of transferring powers from councillors, elected on a party political manifesto, to bodies which might not have been elected and with no attachment to a manifesto. Some officers were anxious about yet more meetings and more than a few feared being put on the spot in public. Despite these potential obstacles, in 1986 the council decided to stick with its original view that public support for public services could only be won by extending real influence to neighbourhood forums. Accordingly, the Labour Party manifesto for the 1986 local elections stated clearly that:

> Neighbourhood forums will be the bodies responsible for deciding on and monitoring the structure and delivery of services to all sections of the community in the local neighbourhood area. . . The 1986–90 Labour Council will make every effort to encourage local people to participate. (Islington Labour Party, 1986)

In the next four-year period the council did, indeed, put a great deal of effort into the creation of a properly constituted network of twenty-four neighbourhood forums – one for each neighbourhood office area. The 1986 public guidelines made it clear that the twenty-four neighbourhood forums would be composed of local people and that they would 'have the ability to determine how services are provided and money spent in their area' (London Borough of Islington, 1986). The first meeting of a constituted neighbourhood forum took place in July 1986, and by November 1988 all twenty-four neighbourhood forums had had their constitutions approved by the central Neighbourhood Services Sub-Committee. By the spring of 1990 the local Labour Party was able to claim that most neighbourhood forums had been in existence either as steering groups or as fully recognised forums for almost four years:

> They have served a useful purpose in acting as a local sounding board on a wide range of issues, both local and borough wide. They have also made important decisions on funding local environmental schemes. (Islington Labour Party, 1990)

The creation of this network of neighbourhood forums is, by any standards, a significant achievement.

The neighbourhood forums: scope and purpose

The objectives of the forums can be summarised as follows:

1. To help determine neighbourhood office priorities and monitor the quality of service being provided in the neighbourhood;

2. To require relevant neighbourhood office staff, and to invite staff from central departments, to attend forum meetings and to report on actions taken on its behalf;
3. To draw up programmes for the spending of budgets allocated to the neighbourhood office;
4. To help integrate the community and act as a sounding board for local views;
5. To comment on planning and licensing applications; and
6. To operate within an equal opportunities framework.

While there is some local variation in relation to these terms of reference, reflecting local preferences and circumstances, it should be stressed that all the forums are formally *advisory* committees to the council – they are not council committees or sub-committees exercising a statutory role. They have rights to be consulted and they are able to express their views through the formal mechanisms of the council, with the expectation that their views will be taken into account when decisions are taken. But they do not have formal decision-making powers.

This model differs markedly from the system of neighbourhood committees in Tower Hamlets, described in the next chapter, where the local councillors serving on the neighbourhood committees exercise a wide range of powers. If the forums were to be given formal powers they would have to comply with the Local Government Act 1972, section 102(3), which states that membership of council committees with spending powers must be a minimum of two-thirds elected councillors. Islington has, ever since its consultation exercise of 1985, taken the view that the primary purpose of the forums is to enable local people to express their views to the council and to other authorities and organisations. The council therefore decided against the idea of creating a system of area committees comprising local ward councillors. Instead, ward members are non-voting members of the forum covering their ward – at meetings they sit with the public, not at the table with the chair of the forum.

In research interviews various respondents inside and outside the council outlined two sets of arguments in favour of this model. On the one hand several forum members, and some councillors, thought that councillors would dominate if they were voting members of the forum. Several respondents suggested that while it was a good thing for local councillors to attend forum meetings to answer questions and give advice, it was right that they did not occupy a central role. As the chair of one neighbourhood forum explained: 'They have their chance to put their views at the committee meetings in the town hall. We get a lot of help from our local councillors, but this forum meeting is our meeting.'

On the other hand it was also suggested to us that going for an advisory model meant that power remained within the council. Senior officers and the local authority unions have, from the outset of the decentralisation initiative, expressed concern about the dangers of devolving, as they see it, too much control in sensitive areas of decision-making, such as staff recruitment. This view was shared by almost all the councillors we spoke to. One councillor put it in rather vivid terms when he asserted that, regardless of the legal arguments, it was essential to limit the powers of the forums particularly in relation to staff management: 'We would be stark raving mad if we handed over operational management responsibilities to the forums. If the forums were allowed to control staff it would be like throwing people to the lions.'

This is not to suggest that the forums are powerless. As we shall see, many of the forums, and particularly the better-organised ones, are extremely effective in lobbying council committees, in taking officers to task when service performance has been unsatisfactory, and in generally influencing decisions that affect their area. Over the years the influence of the forums has increased. For example, while legislation prevents the council from giving spending powers to the forums, an arrangement was developed whereby those budgets that were locally controlled and delegated to the Neighbourhood Officer (Chief Executive) (now the Neighbourhood Manager) were exercised in a way which directly reflects the wishes of the forum. In this context the officer would only override the forum if its wishes were contrary to council policy or against the law.

Another good example of the way in which the powers of forums have been progressively increased relates to public involvement in land-use planning. In July 1989 the council decided to introduce a pilot scheme whereby four selected neighbourhood forums would consider and comment on all planning applications affecting their neighbourhood. The main aims of the scheme were to:

1. Enable neighbourhood forum consideration of significant planning applications;
2. Ensure that neighbourhood considerations are taken into account while maintaining consistency of application of the council's policies throughout the borough;
3. Establish a scheme which can be operated in every neighbourhood; and
4. Establish a scheme which is no less efficient in terms of the time taken to reach decisions.

In Finsbury, applications are considered by the Planning, Environment and Transport Sub-Group of the forum. This group, which consists of local councillors and local residents and is chaired by the chairman of the neighbourhood forum, meets regularly in the community room at the neighbourhood office. At a typical meeting there are around seven forum members and three officers seated around a table with an 'audience' of between ten and fifteen people – some of them developers and some local people.

The atmosphere of the meetings is businesslike but informal. The local planning officer introduces the applications and outlines the planning issues involved. The developers, if they are present, are invited to offer their views. The discussions about the applications are well-informed, not least because forum members have incredibly good local knowledge and find it easy to picture the sites proposed for development. Finsbury is on the borders of the City of London and is under immense development pressure. A significant number of the applications are fairly large scale and involve sophisticated discussion of, for example, plot ratio policy and principles of planning gain.

If the Sub-Group agrees with the recommendation of the planning officer the decision becomes a delegated decision, that is, the decision of the council. If the neighbourhood disagrees with the officer the decision is referred to the main Development Control Sub-Committee of the council. In the period of operation of the scheme few decisions have been taken over the heads of the neighbourhood. This suggests that the arrangement involves a real degree of neighbourhood empowerment. The local planning officer points to two advantages of the system:

Firstly, there is direct involvement of people in the locality. The traditional approach to consultation usually only reaches those who are very near, if not on the doorstep of, the development. This approach reaches others. Secondly, involving the neighbourhood improves the quality of decision making. We get more sensitive decisions because of the fact that there is local, public processing of the application.

In relation to the discussion of empowerment, the success of the scheme suggests that it is perfectly possible to involve local people in decision-making about issues affecting their area, even when this involves the exercise of regulatory functions.

Despite these developments, councillors have tended to retain a fairly paternalistic view of the forums, which may be a block to their development. One councillor drew an illuminating parallel with parenting:

> The only serious political issue in decentralisation is how much power do you give to the forums? In some ways the council is a bit like a parent handing over jobs to the forums. But we won't let them make the important decisions because they're not quite grown up yet. To be honest I wouldn't like to give my forum the power of decision on the location of a home for mentally handicapped people.

The neighbourhood forums: membership and organisation

The council lays down certain minimum conditions in relation to both the membership and the organisation of the forums. Reference has already been made to the fact that ward councillors can only be non-voting members of the forum. The general aim of the membership requirements is to ensure, not only that the forums are rooted in the population of each neighbourhood, but also that they promote better understanding of the needs of underrepresented sections of the community. Notable features of the membership requirements are that:

1. Staff who work in, or supervise the work of, a neighbourhood office cannot be on the forum;

2. All voting members must live in the neighbourhood;
3. The following sections of the community are guaranteed representation on each forum:

   (i)   young people under 21;
   (ii) ethnic minorities;
   (iii) people with disabilities (defined as including mental illness and learning disability as well as physical disability);
   (iv) women whose caring responsibilities tend to result in their underrepresentation in community activities; and
   (v)   people of pensionable age.

There is also an expectation that each forum will try to involve housebound people and those in residential care; people who work in the neighbourhood; representatives of established groups in the area; and representatives of newly-formed groups in the neighbourhood. All groups recognised by a forum have to satisfy criteria laid down by the council to ensure that the groups are properly representative and democratic.

The recommended constitution allows for three methods of determining the main body of the membership – by election, by nomination from local organised groups, or by a mixture of the two. The size of the membership and any electoral boundaries are arrived at locally. Two forums have opted for an elected body, six for group representation and the other sixteen for a combination of the two.

In relation to the way forum meetings are organised the requirements imposed by the council are intended to encourage open government and a welcoming environment to those who are unused to public meetings. The organisational requirements include the following:

1. Agendas, minutes and meetings of the forum shall be open to the public;
2. Forums must meet regularly and at least six times a year;
3. Forums will have a quorum of fifteen people or one third of the membership, whichever is the lower;
4. Inquorate meetings can still discuss urgent business and have their views considered by the council;
5. Neighbourhood officers are expected to attend forum meetings; and

6. Meetings should be held in buildings with access for people with disabilities; crèche and/or babysitting facilities should be available; meetings should not clash with religious festivals; and translations of agendas and minutes should be available.

From the outset, an emphasis was placed upon designing a participatory system which would encourage involvement by usually-excluded groups. The Federation of Islington Tenants' Association co-ordinated a vigorous campaign of opposition to the proposal for forums throughout the 1984/5 period of public consultation. Tenants' representatives were particularly hostile to the idea that forums should contain 'reserved places' for members of underrepresented groups. One officer who was involved in most of the initial consultative meetings noted:

The debate on section places, and hence about representation and discrimination, dominated the public meetings. It was perhaps the first time in this authority that there had been a clear public confrontation around such issues and in that respect it was highly significant . . . the language used was very basic and raw. The tone of forum meetings now, with many of the same people involved, is very different. The point I'm making is that at worst forums have modified the language of such people, moved us forward on what is and what is not acceptable, and at best actually changed some people's attitudes.

In 1989 the council carried out a major review of the effectiveness of the forums and this led to a number of measures designed to bring about improvements (London Borough of Islington, 1989). This review concluded that no formal changes should be made to the established arrangements for determining forum membership. However, the review did lead to a number of suggestions on how to maximise representativeness and encourage greater understanding between sections of the community. These proposals concerned, for example, improved publicity in different languages, a strengthening of equal opportunities objectives in local community work, open days and cultural evenings targeted at particular sections of the community, a more appealing approach to the preparation of agendas, renewed attention to the tone and style of meetings to help generate popular attendance, and training programmes for forum members and officers on a variety of topics.

One finding that emerged from the 1989 review, which was confirmed by our own research, was the discovery of a fairly widespread feeling within the forums that too many officers did not take the forums seriously enough. Many forums reported problems in getting central department staff, and even some staff based in the neighbourhoods, to attend forum meetings and report on defined topics.

The council responded to this problem by requiring all neighbourhood officers to report regularly to their forum and to attend forum meetings to answer questions, and by requiring all other departments to introduce a system for reporting to all the forums on a quarterly basis. Our research suggests that these changes have improved officer attendance and helped to strengthen officer accountability to the forums. As we shall see many of the forums have created subgroups to deal with particular topics or services and these have led, in our view, to many examples of high-quality working between forum members, officers and local councillors. Having sketched the main features of the neighbourhood forum system in Islington, we now consider in more detail how the system has worked in practice. First, we examine the composition of the forums.

The composition of the forums

Over the years since 1986, Islington Council has sought to strengthen the role of the forums. The more forums gain influence in planning and decision-making the more important it becomes to ensure that they are representative of local communities and of those who use or need council services. With this concern in mind, as mentioned earlier, the council carried out a detailed survey of the composition of the forums in June 1990 (London Borough of Islington, 1991).

The data collected covers the forum membership in June 1990 and attendance at forum meetings over the previous three meetings – mainly in the period March to June. While all twenty-four Neighbourhood Officers (Chief Executive) completed survey forms only twenty-two returns were included in the survey as two forums were at that time unconstituted steering groups. A total of 667 people were members of the twenty-two forums in 1990 and, on average, 558 (84 per cent) attended meetings – the average attendance per meeting was twenty-five people. This is a significant level of local involvement. It is important to stress that there is, as with the other figures referred to below, considerable variation across the borough – thus some forums have over forty members while others have less than twenty.

Local variations aside, consider for a moment the fact that the average workloads of local politicians in general are nearly twice those in official estimates (Barron, Crawley and Wood, 1991). It is clear that many councillors carry enormous burdens and it is not surprising that many experience considerable stress. In the face of evidence of this kind few would dispute the fact that our existing representative structures in local government are under great strain. Although it would be quite wrong to imply that forum members carry the same roles and responsibilities as councillors, it can be suggested that the existence in the borough of around 650 other people, who are committed to taking an active interest in local affairs, enlarges the democratic voice of the electorate considerably. Islington, with fifty-two elected councillors, has an average population per councillor of just over 3000, which is similar to other inner London boroughs. The average population per forum member is around 250. This level of democratic involvement is probably without precedent in the UK.

It is, however, not just the numbers that are significant. Because the council has sought to draw in groups who are often excluded from local government decision-making, the forums are, in a statistical sense, far more 'representative' of the local population than, say, the elected members of a typical city council. Take gender. According to the Widdicombe Committee, 19 per cent of councillors in England and Wales in 1985 were women. Islington Council has a far better gender balance than the average for councils in the country as a whole – around 35 per cent of Islington councillors are women. However, even this relatively high level of female participation does not compare with the forums. The survey shows that, in both membership and attendance, the male/female split of the forums is roughly 50/50.

In relation to age, while there is considerable variation, the forums tend to attract a slightly older group of people than the adult age profile of the borough as a whole. The main area where there is underrepresentation concerns people who are under 21. We note, however, that the age profile of the forums probably matches the local population more closely than the age profile of the typical city council. The data on disability is less reliable, reflecting a reluctance on the part of staff in the neighbourhoods to define others as being disabled. The survey suggests that 7 per cent of forum members and 4.6 per cent of those attending meetings were disabled.

In relation to ethnic minority composition the survey suggests that, while considerable progress has been made, there is more to do to enhance representativeness. Returns from the twenty-one forums that could give an ethnic breakdown of forum membership show that 18.5 per cent of members are from a black or ethnic minority community. This compares with an estimated ethnic population for Islington of 19 per cent. A higher proportion of ethnic minority members become members of forums through 'section' places and co-options. While the overall proportion of ethnic minority people who are members of the forums is very close to the estimated proportion in the borough population as a whole, the attendance figures show that black and ethnic minority members are only half as likely to attend forum meetings as white members.

In summary, it can be suggested that the composition of the forums is more 'representative' of the local population than the typical city council. While the council is keen to extend public involvement in the forums, and has launched a number of imaginative approaches aimed towards widening participation, it is important to record that the existing forums, even as they stand, have created an opportunity for a large number of people, from a wide range of backgrounds, to have a say in what happens in their neighbourhood. But how do the forums work? And what sort of influence do the forums wield? In the rest of this chapter we examine the operation of the forums in more detail and offer an assessment of the degree to which the forums enhance local democracy by considering three criteria: the way in which the forums improve the responsiveness of organisations which make decisions affecting the neighbourhood; the role of the forums in political education; and the performance of the forums in terms of empowerment.

The operation of the forums

Given that there are twenty-four different forums it is difficult to generalise about the way the forums work in practice. However, using the 1991 survey and our attendance at several forums, we offer some overall comments on the way they operate, and follow this with some detailed comments on one particular forum to fill out the picture.

As mentioned earlier, all forums must meet regularly and most meet around once every six weeks. There has been much argument about dates for forum meetings. Some councillors have tried to push forums into meeting on a fairly small number of particular dates when there are no committees. In contrast, some forums have held out for their right to choose when to meet, particularly if this enables them to meet regularly on the same day of the week or month. Typically, they meet in the evening at 7.00 or 7.30. Almost all forums offer refreshments – usually tea and biscuits at the beginning of the meeting. All the forums meet in a building in their neighbourhood – often in a local leisure centre or community building. The rooms are able to accommodate between 25 and 200 people. Several forums provide a crèche facility, all are accessible by wheelchair, and some have interpreters present.

Many neighbourhood offices produce a local newsletter covering issues relevant to the neighbourhood and these are used to publicise forthcoming meetings. Other methods used to attract public interest include posters, leaflets, advertisements and mailing lists as well as, of course, word-of-mouth communication by forum members. Several forums produce publicity material in more than one language. All of these measures are important, not only in giving people reasonably easy access to the meetings, but also in making them feel welcome when they arrive. Our experience of attending forum meetings is that they are far more welcoming than a typical public meeting or council committee meeting. This is partly because they are very local, and people tend to know each other, and partly because of the care and attention given to the way the meetings are organised.

In addition to the main meeting nearly all of the forums also have subgroups meeting separately and reporting to the main forum. In 1991 six forums had one subgroup, eight had two, two had three, and one had four. Forums decide for themselves what subgroups to have: thirteen have subgroups dealing with traffic, planning, and environmental matters and eight have subgroups focusing on housing and tenant issues. Other subgroups are concerned with disabled people, women, education, employment, crime prevention and forum development. One advantage of the subgroups is that they focus on key issues in depth – the groups are much smaller than the main forum and the people attending get more fully involved in discussing and working on the issues. The subgroups have therefore become a further way of tackling the tendency for public meetings, including forum meetings, to become dominated by particular groups. The arrangement also responds creatively to the enthusiasms of local people, because individuals work on groups that interest them most. Many of the subgroups can, if they so wish, link into other council structures, such as the tenants' Liaison Forum. To give more of a feel of how the forums operate in practice we provide a brief description of one meeting concentrating on the atmosphere rather than the substance of the discussion.

Cameo 7.1   The Finsbury Forum

The Finsbury Forum meets in the St Luke's Leisure Centre which is a modern building owned by a private trust. The meeting on 10 July 1990 started at 7.30 p.m. and tea was available from 7.00. Between 40 and 50 people arrived – about twenty of them women. The meeting room, which has around 70 seats, has no platform. The chair of the forum and people who had been invited to address the meeting sat behind a table at one end. All three councillors representing this area were present and sat in the body of the meeting at the back. Various officers were grouped to one side, although some of the officers were sitting in the audience.

The chair, who has lived in Finsbury all his life and is well known to many residents, welcomed everyone to the meeting and made sure they had agenda papers. Each different item was printed on different coloured paper and throughout the meeting the chair referred to the colours to help everyone keep abreast of the discussion.

This particular agenda had eleven items. The minutes of the last meeting attracted considerable attention as participants used these to check progress on decisions made previously. The chair was able, with the willing assistance of the Neighbourhood Officer (Chief Executive), to deal with most of these issues, but the councillors also helped to inform the meeting on the progress of items going through main council committees. Interestingly, several of the topics discussed related to the performance of organisations other than the council – for example, London Transport's management of the subways at the Old Street underground station, and police action, or rather perceived inaction, in relation to flyposting in the neighbourhood.

Three regular items on the agenda were reports from the Planning, Environment and Transport Sub-Group; the Housing Sub-Group; and the Neighbourhood Officers (covering housing, environmental health, social services, support services, advice and community work). Major items dealt with at this meeting related to the local library (threatened with closure because of poll tax capping); the future of decentralisation (as the council elected in May was at that stage developing proposals to strengthen neighbourhood management); and various consultation papers concerning education (relating to, for example, primary school admissions). By the time the meeting closed at just before 10 p.m. a large number of people had expressed their views on these topics – all of which had aroused a considerable amount of local interest. There is no doubt that while many of the speakers from the floor were the leaders of local tenants' associations, a considerable number of people who would not otherwise have a voice were able to make their views known.

Forums and organisational responsiveness

At first the forums were not that successful in improving responsiveness. It is clear that, in the period 1987–9, many forums became frustrated with their inability to bring about what they saw as comparatively minor adjustments and improvements in local service delivery. Thus, the review of neighbourhood forums in 1989 concluded that:

A general problem is the lack of accountability of the officers to forums. Forums complain of buck-passing, letters being ignored, responses being delayed, advice being given to the council that is contrary to the wishes of the forum and the absence of information necessary for them to play a proper part in decision making. Despite this, there is no mechanism by which forums can take offending officers to task. (London Borough of Islington, 1989, p. 9)

Perhaps it is inevitable that, in the early years, the forums would encounter resistances; they were forced to concentrate on establishing their legitimacy and asserting a role for themselves. Certainly, the forums, in pressing for officers to be accountable in some way to the neighbourhoods, were seeking a significant departure from the highly-centralised model of accountability the council had built up in previous years. Clearly, some officers were cynical about the role and potential of the forums. As one councillor put it to us: 'Some of the chief and senior officers thought that the enthusiasm of the new councillors for the forums, indeed for decentralisation as a whole, would fizzle out. It didn't.' The forums have, over the years, become increasingly successful in acting as a check on the performance of organisations operating in the neighbourhoods. Indeed, following the council decision of 1989 to require relevant officers to attend forum meetings, the forums have become much better at holding officers to account. In a typical local authority there is often no contest in a conflict between the officers and the public. The officers have professional and managerial expertise on their side, tend to possess most of the information that is deemed to be relevant, and public discussion is usually held in a committee room deep inside the town hall.

Our observation of neighbourhood forums in action suggests that the power relationship can be shifted. In a neighbourhood forum the legitimate focus of debate is the impact of decisions on the neighbourhood – local knowledge matters and, to some extent, it is the officers, certainly those from central departments, who are off-territory. We have seen officers taken to task in forum meetings and we have spoken to officers who have been extremely anxious about how well their reports will go down at forum meetings. Slowly the forums are bringing about improvements in service responsiveness by asserting the neighbourhood view and we will amplify this point in the discussion of empowerment below. But first it is important to look at the role of the forums in relation to political education.

Forums and political education

One of the main arguments put forward by the Widdicombe Committee in favour of local government is that it contributes to political education (Widdicombe Report, 1986, pp. 45–52). The Committee argued that local government is a school in which democratic habits are acquired and practised and the infrastructure of democracy laid down. By extension it can be argued that the neighbourhood forums contribute to local democracy by providing accessible opportunities for local people to engage in local politics – to learn about the powers and responsibilities of local and central government, and other agencies, to explore the relationship between policy statements and the impact of policy on the ground, and to debate the pros and cons of alternative courses of action.

There can be no doubt that many of the neighbourhood forums in Islington have performed very well against this criterion. We have already referred to the comparatively large numbers of people who have become actively engaged in the work of the forums. We know from direct observation and research interviews that many of the people involved are new to public life and have found the experience rewarding. The chairman of one forum put it to us this way:

> My father was a good trade unionist. He always said 'If you've got something to say, say it'. This is what our forum is about – helping you to get your view across. People are coming because they can air their views . . . get at the officers . . . argue with the reports. More people are learning what's going on. The more you get involved the better it is. There's great satisfaction when you walk round the area and see the achievements.

There is evidence to suggest, therefore, that the forums are having some effect in diminishing feelings of powerlessness – at least for some participants.

The forums have also been successful in raising the quality of debate about the policies not just of local government, but also of central government and the private sector. Officers underestimate the understanding of forum members at their peril. As one councillor put it to us: 'Some officers are a bit arrogant. They like to think they can have their bit of fun against local ignorance. But they often come unstuck.' We witnessed many high-quality debates, not just in the main forum meetings but also in forum subgroup meetings. The following example, drawn from the Finsbury Neighbourhood Forum meeting referred to earlier, will illustrate the point. The debate about the possible closure of the local library was sophisticated. Forum members were clearly united in their desire to save 'their' library but the discussion went well beyond straightforward protest at a possible spending cut. First, there was a high level of understanding of the nature of local government finance and of the conflict between local and central government. As one forum member put it:

What people must understand is that there is a war going on between central and local government. Mrs Thatcher is using the salami method – a slice at a time so you don't realise what you've lost. Never forget that the St Luke's library is threatened because of poll tax capping.

Second, the tactics to save the library which emerged from the discussion were imaginative – a 'use it or lose it' campaign to boost borrowing figures, a delegation to the council's Recreation Committee to pressure the relevant councillors, and a public campaign to raise awareness of the potential threat to the library.

It can be claimed, then, that the neighbourhood forums have been successful in spreading information about political choices affecting the future quality of life in the neighbourhoods. The newsletters, the local presence, the energy invested in community and outreach work, the risks taken by local councillors in exposing decisions to local scrutiny, the high quality of many of the reports submitted by officers to forum meetings – all these factors – have contributed to local political education. Forum members are remarkably well informed about proposals affecting their neighbourhood and are, as their experience grows, developing increasingly sophisticated political skills.

Forums and empowerment

In the previous chapter we considered aspects of representative and participative democracy and put forward a new ladder of citizen empowerment. Even a cursory examination of the issues suggests that there are widely varying definitions of empowerment. For example, those on the political right stress the importance of trying to extend market mechanisms into public service provision as a means of empowering individuals in their dealings with the state. In recent years, at the behest of central government, an enormous amount of time and energy has been spent trying to introduce competition into local government. Meanwhile, those on the political left have attempted to develop forms of representative, participatory and direct democracy by empowering groups of citizens – particularly those groups who normally lose out in the battle to influence events.

An important point, which proponents in the argument about empowerment tend to overlook, is that empowering one individual or group can often be disempowering for another. This is because there are widespread conflicts of interest. To take a simple example, a decision on a planning application may please one interest group and horrify another. At a deeper level, as we argue in more detail in Chapter 9, there are, particularly in multiracial communities, substantial misunderstandings and conflicts between different groups within civil society. Our conclusion is that a key task for area based participatory structures in urban neighbourhoods is to assemble the preconditions from which genuine forms of empowerment can proceed. This involves not only developing the ability of local people to engage in social action, but also furthering the community's capacity to understand different points of view, contain anxiety and rise above sectionalism. These are, by any standards, challenging tasks.

Another important point which must be borne in mind in any discussion of empowerment concerns the fact that government – whether central, local or quango – fulfils many roles. These include providing services, enabling other organisations to provide services and, just as important, regulating the behaviour of individuals, groups and organisations. Some argue that while it may be possible to empower people in relation to the first two of these roles, it is much more difficult in relation to the governmental role of regulation.

Thus it can be argued that impartial professionals should be the key actors in relation to a decision to, for example, prosecute a restaurant for insanitary conditions, evict a family from a council house for racial harassment, or decide on a planning application. The neighbourhood forums in Islington have pushed at the frontiers of this argument and, as discussed earlier in the chapter, have had some success in relation to public involvement in regulation – notably through neighbourhood participation in development control.

Before considering some of Islington's achievements in relation to forum empowerment we should record two problems with the forums uncovered by our research. First, while in recent years the council has devolved more budgets to neighbourhood level, it remains the case that the forums are essentially consultative bodies. Put bluntly, they lack power. Certainly, forum members complained to us that they are not that influential in relation to major decisions. This finding can be supported by evidence from a small-scale survey of forum members carried out in 1988 which found that less than one in five respondents felt that forums had 'a great deal' or 'quite a lot' of influence on Islington Council's local policy development (Khan, 1989).

Since this survey was carried out, steps have been taken, as described earlier, to strengthen the role of the forums in policy formulation – by, for example, involving them in the preparation of neighbourhood action plans. Since May 1992, two neighbourhood Forum Chairs have been co-opted on to the new Neighbourhood Services Committee as non-voting advisers (as we noted in Chapter 2, the Conservative's Local Government and Housing Act 1989 abolished the rights of co-optees to enjoy voting rights on main council committees). Forum chairs also meet on a regular basis with the chair of the Neighbourhood Services Committee. This enables them to share experience across different neighbourhoods and thus learn from each other.

In spite of these developments, however, the legal position is that the forums have no formal powers. It should be noted that, unlike other urban areas in the UK, there are no legal powers to underpin the setting up of urban parish councils in London. It is possible that this illogical legal obstacle has acted as a barrier to greater devolution of powers to neighbourhood level.

A second concern relates to the fact that forum meetings can be dominated by a few confident people. For example, we witnessed forum meetings where the leaders of the local tenants' associations held sway while other forum members said little. It is not unknown for racist attitudes to be displayed at forum meetings and while the council has clamped down vigorously on this kind of behaviour, tensions remain between local white people and members of black and ethnic minority groups within at least some of the neighbourhoods. The council is, of course, well aware of these problems and has developed a 'code of conduct' to assist forum chairs and officers to deal with racist and other unacceptable types of behaviour. Staff in the neighbourhood offices put a good deal of energy into neighbourhood community work to bring in new people. The tone and style of meetings is under more or less constant review and, in many neighbourhoods, there is increasing use of informal subgroups which many people find less threatening.

Notwithstanding these two main drawbacks it can be claimed that the neighbourhood forums have begun to create the preconditions from which effective forms of empowerment can develop. As explained earlier, the forums give access to the policy making process, expose participants to different points of view, and many have been successful in bringing about a wide range of local improvements – notably in relation to environmental projects (Barnard, 1991). It is particularly important to note the success of the forums in standing for collective concerns. There is no question that the forums have brought local people together and helped them to identify shared concerns and priorities for action.

Conclusion

In the period since 1986, Islington Council has facilitated the creation and development of a network of twenty-four neighbour-hood forums designed to act as sounding boards in relation to a wide range of issues affecting their areas. We have suggested that this bold initiative is an experiment in neighbourhood democracy which has national significance. Indeed, it can be claimed with justification that Islington has gone further than any other council in the UK in establishing reasonably stable arrangements for widening public involvement in local government decision-making.

The neighbourhood forums have been successful in drawing a comparatively large number of people from a wide range of backgrounds into the process of decision making about the areas in which they live. They have improved communication between councillors, officers and members of the public; increased the responsiveness of council services; contributed to local political education; and given at least some of their members a feeling that they can influence events. In a statistical sense the forums are more 'representative' of the population than is the typical city council. Even so there are still certain groups – for example, people aged under 21 – who are underrepresented. The forums do not have formal authority to make decisions, but they are undoubtedly becoming increasingly influential.

8 Extending Representative Democracy: Tower Hamlets

Introduction

In examining the forms of local democracy to have emerged in Islington and Tower Hamlets it is important to discern the particular meaning given to local democracy by the political groups in control of each borough – then we can examine the formal arrangements developed for participation and the functions they have performed. In the previous chapter we discussed the Islington approach to neighbourhood participation. In this chapter we examine the neighbourhood committee system developed in Tower Hamlets. We will examine specifically the extent to which a greater level of representation has been generated and the extent to which this participation has included the variety of different communities and groups residing in the locality. We consider some of the costs associated with the extension of democracy and examine whether the model may put too much power in the hands of small groups of local councillors.

Giving power back to local representatives

In Chapter 3 we suggested that the Liberal Party in Tower Hamlets needs to be understood as a maverick organisation containing within it an enormous range of political opinion. As a consequence one should be wary of making too many generalisations concerning this local party, particularly since the in 'Principle of neighbourhood autonomy' has allowed different local forms of Liberalism to obtain their expression within the various neighbourhoods under Liberal control. One hears, for instance, that in inner party debates before 1990 at least one Stepney Liberal councillor would sometimes insist that the Liberals in Globe Town did not deserve the title 'Liberal' but should be considered as Labour instead. So the conclusions we draw should be considered with caution, more as general tendencies rather than iron laws of Liberalism in the area.

Perhaps the one thing we can say with certainty about the sublocal democratic structures created in Tower Hamlets is that their primary purpose appears to be the extension and strengthening of local representative democracy. In other words, the structures are designed primarily to empower local neighbourhood councillors by creating a situation in which local decisions are made by local representatives who have good local knowledge and who are locally accountable. Tower Hamlets Liberals have always insisted that orthodox models of local government are ridiculous because they make real political accountability impossible to achieve. A *Liberal Focus* newsletter in March 1986 sets out this position clearly. Speaking of their proposals for creating the seven neighbourhoods, they argue:

> everything will be run from there, so if you want to see anyone about any Council matter you simply go to your neighbourhood office. And your councillors, instead of sitting on big Borough-wide committees making decisions about areas they know nothing about, will instead sit on their Neighbourhood Committee and will make all the decisions only about the area that elected them. So, *you* will know *who* made all the decisions affecting the Neighbourhood you live in and you'll know where to find the officers who are supposed to carry those decisions out!

Implicit in this model of neighbourhood democracy is a belief in the power of democratic accountability – that if structures are created in which local representatives are visibly responsible for the decisions made in the area then the electors will judge the efficacy of their performance through the ballot. This belief in the possibility of real accountability also encouraged local Liberals to see 'the community' and its elected representatives as being more or less synonymous. According to Eric Flounders, a leading Liberal activist, 'the important thing was to take power from the officers and give it back to the people, and in a representative democracy the only sensible way to do this is to give it to the councillors'. Although, as we shall see, many of the neighbourhoods have subsequently experimented with developing participatory forms of democracy, the linchpin of the Tower Hamlets model rests upon extending the existing representative forms of government to neighbourhood levels.

The neighbourhood committees

When the Liberal regime in Tower Hamlets was first launched upon an unsuspecting local government world in 1986 there was a widespread belief that the model was unworkable and that in any case the Liberals would not have the courage to implement it. The Liberals proved everyone wrong on both counts. As we explained in Chapter 3, the neighbourhood committees were established almost immediately and soon demonstrated that a single committee was capable of taking decisions on a wide range of service matters without being snowed under by appallingly long agendas. With the exception of the Isle of Dogs where, for a time, Labour councillors boycotted the neighbourhood system, the neighbourhood committees have all continued to meet on a monthly basis. They have largely been able to get through business without having to go on until unsociable hours of the night and the majority have been able to do this without having to establish an elaborate subcommittee structure. In other words, contrary to prevailing wisdom, the neighbourhood committees have not encountered problems in managing the volume of business facing them.

More surprising, however, was the fact that the Liberals implemented their plan for radical political devolution even though this meant that when they gained power in 1986 they controlled only four of the seven neighbourhoods. Moreover, in a subsequent by-election the Liberals lost control of Poplar neighbourhood. As they continually pointed out, what other political party would gain control of a local authority which had been in the hands of an opposing group for decades only to place the biggest slice of the service budget in the hands of the group that had just been defeated? While, as we saw in Chapter 5, the autonomy granted to Labour-controlled neighbourhoods was not unequivocal, there can be no gainsaying the unprecedented degree of political devolution the new system introduced. Although Labour politicians in the borough have continued to deny that any real devolution has occurred, their view was not shared by any of the senior officers that we interviewed in the Labour controlled neighbourhoods. Clearly, the Liberals believe that their principles have been politically vindicated because, in the 1990 local government elections, they took Poplar and then gained control of Stepney (though as we shall see the Liberal victory in 1990 involved electoral practices which were widely perceived as being fraudulent).

While the neighbourhood committees constitute the main plank of local democracy in Tower Hamlets, other kinds of participatory structures have also been developed. Most of the neighbourhoods have neighbourhood consultative bodies which operate alongside the neighbourhood committees. Some of these, such as the one in Bow, seek to draw upon the views of all residents in the area. Indeed, Bow's consultative body is based upon direct elections using proportional representation within eighteen 'blocks' in the neighbourhood. This 'Canton' style of democracy has found its furthest expression in Poplar, where the Liberals have introduced a network of directly-elected 'tenants forums' to deal with very local issues at a sub-neighbourhood level. By using the model of 'block elections' both Bow and Poplar have sought to find ways of giving direct representation to local areas, representation which is unmediated by tenants or other community organisations. While tenants' associations and other community organisations are active in all the Liberal-controlled neighbourhoods and relations are sometimes constructive and cordial, the Liberals have not always drawn an equation between the strength of such organisations and the power of the local community. If anything, Liberal activists have often seen local community organisations as potential competitors for political loyalty and neighbourhood identification.

The five other neighbourhoods have also developed forms of consultation, but in this case they have been built upon the existing fabric of local community organisations rather than apart from it. In Globe Town, for example, the consultative forum consists of a number of representatives nominated by the Neighbourhood Tenants' Forum (which itself consists of representatives from local tenants' associations) together with nominees from the neighbourhood's youth and pensioners' forums. In Stepney, when it was under Labour control, consultation occurred primarily through the 'Housing Advisory' (a body consisting of representatives from all neighbourhood tenants associations) but also through several small working groups dealing with social welfare issues which co-opted representatives of local community organisations. The neighbourhood consultative bodies clearly varied according to the degree of autonomy they enjoyed from the formal neighbourhood structures themselves. Whereas the consultative forums in Bow and Stepney were chaired by local councillors and tended to follow the agendas of local councillors and officers, the Globe Town Forum was chaired by a tenants' leader.

Participation: whose voices are heard?

Attendances at the various committees and forums throughout the neighbourhoods varied considerably according to the issues being dealt with. All meetings were open to the public. In Bow, where local Liberal councillors kept a very firm grip on all aspects of decision-making, public attendance at neighbourhood committee meetings was often negligible and, while councillors conscientiously attended all committee meetings, 'lay representatives' on the consultative forum attended irregularly. In Stepney under Labour control the neighbourhood committee experienced quite poor attendances, even from Labour councillors. However, the Housing Advisory was consistently well attended by local tenants' representatives and there were usually twenty or more members of the public present as well. On major issues the public tended to turn out in large numbers – nearly 200 crammed into one meeting of the Globe Town consultative forum which was dealing with tenants' fears about asbestos and complaints about the behaviour of contractors on local estates. In Stepney, particularly after the Liberals took control in 1990, the public gallery was often packed with supporters and opponents of the controversial decisions being made by the new ruling Liberal group.

Unlike Islington, no figures are available detailing attendances at local meetings within the neighbourhoods. Our experience was one of considerable variation. Nevertheless, participation by representatives of tenant and community groups on a consistent and regular basis was much higher than would be normal for a traditonally structured local authority. A conservative estimate would suggest that at least 150 local representatives were involved in this way, but if we were to include those involved in estate-based, rather than neighbourhood-based, committees and forums then the figure would be much higher. But perhaps more striking was the number of members of the public drawn to neighbourhood meetings. This contrasts strongly with the traditional experience of local authorities in Britain, where public attendances at central council committee meetings are negligible unless a deliberate political mobilisation has been orchestrated around a particular issue. In Tower Hamlets, although activists did sometimes mobilise politically around neighbourhood issues, we found that public attendance at neighbourhood meetings was less orchestrated and based more upon spontaneity of interest built around local knowledge, networks and associations.

If the purpose of democratic structures is, as we suggested in Chapter 2, to establish accountability via 'voice' strategies, then the question remains of whether all parts of a given spatial community find their voice through the particular democratic arrangements that have been constructed? In reality, any given arrangement will tend to amplify the voices of some groups within a spatial community while muting the voices of others. The task of creating a single form of participation within which all voices can be heard to equal effect is immensely difficult and possibly unrealisable. What is required, therefore, is a plurality of structures through which different voices may be heard rather than a single, dominant medium. Within Tower Hamlets two forms of democratic structure dominate – the neighbourhood committees and the consultative forums. Our experience suggests that although a certain form of representation of the Bangladeshi community does occur through the neighbour-hood committee structure the consultative forums are dominated by the interests of the white working-class community, specifically through tenant representatives.

A form of representation of the Bangladeshi community occurs through the neighbourhood committee system by virtue of the fact that by 1990 ten local councillors in the borough came from the Bangladeshi community, five more than in 1986. Four of these, all Labour, represented the Wapping neighbourhood, including the Chair of the Wapping Neighbourhood Committee. Four, three of which were Liberal, were also returned among the nine councillors elected to the the Bethnal Green neighbourhood. One Bangladeshi Liberal councillor was returned in Globe Town and one Bangladeshi Labour councillor was returned in Stepney. No Bangladeshi councillors were returned in Bow, Poplar or the Isle of Dogs neighbourhoods, indeed only one stood for election in these areas (a Labour candidate who was defeated in Limehouse). To a considerable extent these figures represent the distribution of the Bangladeshi community within the borough as a whole and specifically the spatial concentration of this community at the western end of the borough. Bangladeshi councillors now constitute one-fifth of all Tower Hamlets' elected representatives, which means that the community is only slightly under-represented at the formal political level – the Bangladeshi population is estimated to be 22.9 per cent of the population.

The problem is, however, that given the dominance of the white working class within the consultative forums, the Bangladeshi community has little alternative but to seek representation through the formal system of competitive party politics as it is fought out at neighbourhood level. There are few other participatory structures through which the general interests of the Bangladeshi community can find expression. This means that the elected Bangladeshi councillors must place the needs of a particular party or spatial community before the needs of the Bangladeshi community in general.

But there is a further complication. The Bangladeshi community has itself traditionally been divided, both on political lines (according to allegiances to existing political formations in Bangladesh) and on religious ones (specifically between 'fundamentalist' and secular forms of Islam). For a while, in the late 1970s and the early 1980s, forms of unity transcending such divisions were realised, particularly through the Bengali Youth Organisation, but this unity tended to fracture as competition emerged between different groups for grant-aided community resources in the area. The neighbourhood system has certainly politicised the Bangladeshi community but through the prism of an anglicised competitive party politics, a form of politics which has drawn upon brokerage and patronage systems within the Bangladeshi community and which has tended to exacerbate the political divisions traditionally present within it.

Some attempts have been made, however, to find alternative and, perhaps, indirect means of giving voice to Bangladeshi interests and experiences. Some neighbourhoods, particularly those under Labour control, have sought to represent the needs of minority communities in a mediated way at the policy level through the creation of specific posts such as race or women's officers. While such strategies can be effective, the problem remains of translating policy into practice. The danger is that the creation of 'right sounding' policy statements and monitoring systems becomes a substitute for small but real and practical changes.

An alternative strategy is one which prioritises work on an everyday basis within the spatial community itself, primarily through community development. On a number of estates, such as Ocean in Stepney, effective strategies for encouraging Bangladeshi participation in housing issues were developed as part of Priority Estates Project work. Globe Town adopted a community development approach on all the estates in the neighbourhood. By 1990 it had a community development capacity equivalent to ten posts, four of which were dedicated to ethnic minority outreach work. While recognising the particular experience and needs of Bangladeshi tenants in the area, the community development team has tended to work with local tenants on the basis of what unites them rather than on the basis of what makes them different. On the Bancroft Estate the development of a tenants' management co-operative provided the means for bringing together polarised groups of white and Bangladeshi tenants. On the Digby/Greenways Estate, community development workers managed to convince white tenants of the need to create a Bangladeshi tenants' forum as a subgroup of the tenants' association. In both cases the neighbourhood offered the prospect of much greater control by tenants over local management issues as an inducement to improve race relations on the estate.

The Globe Town approach, though not without its failures, was overall a demonstrable success. Relations between whites and Bangladeshis on some estates in the neighbourhood became virtually unrecognisable when compared with the tensions that existed before. But the success of the strategy depended upon several factors: the availability of capital to bring about major estate improvements; the political willingness of Liberal councillors in Globe Town to put resources into community development (for example, on the Bancroft Estate) rather than administration or direct service delivery; a vision of local control shared by councillors, officers and tenants alike; and the skills, commitment, courage and patience of the community development workers themselves. However, even in Globe Town, competitive party politics began to contaminate developments on the ground: it is this problem of political opportunism to which we will now turn.

The politicisation of community

It is important to remember that the degree of managerial and political devolution in Tower Hamlets means that the neighbourhoods effectively handle most of the major decisions that central committees would handle within traditional local authorities. A survey of the two main local newspapers (the *Docklands Recorder* and the *East London Advertiser*) throughout the period 1989–90 demonstrates the way in which the local media were forced to respond to this shift in the locus of political decision-making – most striking was the fact that the number of reports concerning decisions taken at neighbourhood level far outweighed those concerning Tower Hamlets as a whole.

A random sample of fifteen issues of the *Docklands Recorder* in the period between February and November of 1990 revealed that 44 out of the 69 articles on politics in the borough referred to neighbourhood issues. Our research suggested that far from the neighbourhoods only being involved in peripheral issues while the 'real action' went on elsewhere, the neighbourhood system in Tower Hamlets had brought about an extraordinary degree of politicisation of local issues. As we shall see later this led to a number of retrograde developments but what cannot be doubted is the success of the Liberals in bringing political debate down to the level of everyday life – 'the politics of dropped kerbstones and streetlighting', as one Labour councillor cynically put it.

This picture of the neighbourhoods as the focus of politics in the borough is reinforced by the public interest and participation in local meetings that we have already noted. We therefore feel it is reasonable to infer the existence, in an embryonic form, of a local political culture in the borough, one based upon a reawakened interest in local affairs, a gradual increase in local political knowledge (particularly within some sections of the tenants' movement) and a sense that it may just be possible for local people to begin to have some influence over events in their immediate neighbourhood.

One index of the degree of interest in local political life is obviously turnout at local government elections. Table 8.1 compares voter turnout in all London boroughs between 1982 and 1990. The increase in turnout in local government elections in Tower Hamlets is unparalleled (we should also note that Islington recorded the

TABLE 8.1 Voter turnout in London Borough elections, 1982–90, per cent

London borough	1982	1986	1990	Percentage difference between 1982 and 1990
Barking & Dagenham	33.7	34.9	38.6	+4.9
Barnet	48.8	42.0	50.0	+1.2
Bexley	45.4	46.4	50.1	+4.7
Bromley	47.8	46.8	49.8	+2.0
Brent	43.3	44.1	42.9	−0.4
Camden	45.1	46.7	46.2	+1.1
Croydon	40.3	42.7	45.8	+5.5
Ealing	49.5	47.9	49.0	−0.5
Enfield	43.4	46.7	48.0	+4.6
Greenwich	45.5	47.8	51.1	+4.6
Hackney	*34.2*	*36.1*	*36.1*	*+1.9*
Hammersmith & Fulham	50.0	51.8	53.2	+3.2
Haringey	45.2	50.7	46.6	+1.4
Harrow	48.6	46.7	51.1	+2.5
Havering	44.4	43.3	49.1	+4.7
Hillingdon	42.4	48.1	52.9	+10.5
Hounslow	46.4	46.8	48.9	+2.5
Islington	**40.1**	**47.1**	**46.2**	**+6.1**
Kensington & Chelsea	38.7	39.4	42.2	+3.5
Kingston-on-Thames	46.5	51.3	56.4	+9.9
Lambeth	44.7	47.7	45.9	+1.2
Lewisham	41.5	45.6	45.2	+3.7
Merton	47.5	49.8	53.7	+6.2
Newham	*31.4*	*34.9*	*36.5*	*+5.1*
Redbridge	44.6	43.9	48.5	+3.9
Richmond-on-Thames	59.4	58.9	59.7	+0.3
Southwark	*34.3*	*40.8*	*39.6*	*+5.3*
Sutton	52.1	51.1	55.4	+2.3
Tower Hamlets	**31.1**	**38.9**	**46.1**	**+15.0**
Waltham Forest	42.8	44.9	50.8	+8.0
Wandsworth	48.7	51.4	56.5	+7.9
Westminster	37.4	39.6	51.5	+14.1
London (all)	**43.8**	**45.4**	**48.2**	**+4.4**

eighth largest increase of the thirty-two boroughs during this period). In 1982 Tower Hamlets had the lowest voter turnout figures in the whole of London at 31.1 per cent. The increase to 46.1 per cent in 1990 is equivalent to a further 17 200 adult residents participating in the later elections. We would highlight figures for the London Boroughs of Hackney, Newham and Southwark, which surround Tower Hamlets to the north, east and south respectively. Demographically these four boroughs are very similar, the only difference being that the other three have no comparable recent history of political or administrative innovation. With the exception of Tower Hamlets, electoral turnout in these boroughs remained more or less the lowest in all of London. The change in Tower Hamlets should therefore be recognised as being dramatic.

Figure 8.1 reveals the process of change within Tower Hamlets itself. With the exception of the Blackwall ward in the Isle of Dogs neighbourhood and the Shadwell ward in the Wapping neighbourhood there have been major increases in electoral turnout between 1982 and 1990. In some wards turnout has more than doubled. What is also striking is the variation between neighbourhoods. The increase in electoral activity has been smallest in Wapping and the Isle of Dogs, the last remaining bastions of Labour control. The increases have been most dramatic in Poplar and Stepney, where the Liberals gained control from Labour between 1986 and 1990.

These figures surely confirm our contention that the development of neighbourhood democracy in Tower Hamlets has contributed to a reawakening of a local political culture. This does not, of course, mean that the political and administrative innovations in themselves have brought this about, rather we need to understand how such innovations have both given expression to and reinforced the form of politics (Liberal community activism) that inspired them. Liberal activists have consistently outflanked their political opponents through their systematic and intensive campaigning at the very local level. Interestingly, the creation of the neighbourhood structures tended to weaken some aspects of Liberal grass-roots politics as many of the key Liberal activists became absorbed in the running of neighbourhood administrations. But by and large the innovations which developed in Bow, Globe Town or Bethnal Green have given expression to this activism, although in an altered form. Thus, for example, the well-known ritual in which the Liberal Leader in Bow undertook a 'neighbourhood inspection' by marching around

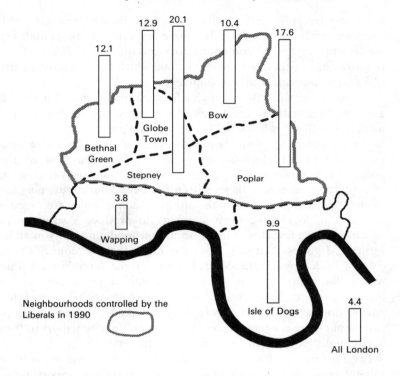

FIGURE 8.1   Tower Hamlets: percentage increase in voter turnout by neighbourhood, 1982–90

'his' area every Saturday morning with a bevy of senior neighbourhood managers struggling to keep up behind him.

Old wine in new bottles?

The Tower Hamlets model seeks to extend traditonal forms of representative party politics to the neighbourhood and ward level. It seeks to give meaning to the notion of 'local accountability' which is implicit in the role of the local councillor but which has rarely been given organisation or substance in British local government. Our experience of Tower Hamlets in 1989–90 certainly suggests that a much greater politicisation of everyday affairs has been achieved, together with an increase in some aspects of accountability concerning neighbourhood councillors and officers. However, there is a downside to these achievements, one which became most clearly revealed in our case study of Stepney.

The problem with the borough's 'councillor-led' model is that, if anything, it invests too much power in the hands of small groups of local councillors who would normally expect to govern their neighbourhoods for four years (the interval between succeeding local government elections in London). The weakness of the political and administrative 'centre' in Tower Hamlets, the absence of a plurality of power bases within the neighbourhoods, plus the intense distrust of professionals and bureaucrats which was such a hallmark of local Liberalism, combine to produce a situation in which there are few checks upon neighbourhood autonomy in all its forms and guises. Not only does this mean that the councillors in control of a neighbourhood lack some of the boundaries within which ill-conceived ideas could be contained (as occurred, for instance, when Bow councillors proceeded with an ill-fated partnership scheme with a private firm called Assured Developments) but there is a temptation for unscrupulous councillors to turn a neighbourhood into their own private fiefdom.

Even before they had gained control of Stepney some of the local Liberal councillors had developed a reputation for opportunism. Front-line officers in both housing and social services had been subject to 'political approaches'. One team leader in Stepney social services (who has since left) was approached on a couple of occasions (once after having given a professional presentation) by a local Liberal councillor who intimated 'you could be very useful to us'. Other officers who had the misfortune to disagree with these councillors remarked upon the atmosphere of revenge and intimidation that surrounded them. As one put it, 'I had an argument with "X" a year ago, he's just waiting for me to make a mistake.' According to another:

> The two Liberal councillors here are very eager to throw mud at officers, it looks good in front of the tenants. Standing orders hold no sway here in terms of how member's and officers relate. Members enquiries are often rude and abusive, you get no protection from higher up . . . everyone's vulnerable.

Once the Liberals gained control of Stepney in May 1990 they began a systematic clear-out of the senior officers whom they regarded as being either incompetent or 'Labour appointees'. On more than one occasion we witnessed this process at work as the new Liberal councillors in control in Stepney singled out an officer for treatment at the Neighbourhood Committee. It was an ugly sight, indeed, the humiliation doled out to an officer at one of these meetings was such that even some of the Liberal's supporters in the packed audience were heard to cry 'shame'.

Within a few months the new Liberal administration in Stepney appeared to be embarking upon policies which came close to transgressing the necessary boundary between the sphere of politics and administration. Funds from the capital programme within the neighbourhood appeared to have been diverted to estates within the electoral wards under Liberal control and away from the St Dunstan's ward, which had returned three Labour councillors. Paradoxically, this meant that estates such as the Limehouse Fields estate, whose tenant association leaders were staunch Liberal supporters, suddenly found that there was no money available for capital works which had been agreed under the previous Labour administration. Perhaps even more worryingly, the Liberal group decided that housing officers had been exercising too much discretion in rehousing families considered to be 'emergency transfer' cases. They clearly felt that too many 'undeserving cases' were being rehoused through this channel and decided to set up a panel of local Liberal councillors to examine all future cases being considered for rehousing in this way. Once elected politicians intervene in the personal affairs of their constituents they are entering into murky waters indeed!

The paradox about Liberalism in Tower Hamlets is that despite its grass-roots activism it is intensely competitive and in some ways quite manipulative and autocratic. This particular form of competitive politics came close to digging its own grave, and once again the problem arose because conventional boundaries governing fairness in local politics were seen by some to have been transgressed. The issue concerned the use by some Liberal activists of a bogus electoral leaflet in the 1990 local elections. The leaflet was very skilful in the way in which it sought to exploit the fears of local voters. It was a credible collage of some of Labour's policy intentions, but one which represented Labour as a high-spending local party, soft on squatters and homeless families, biased against the local white population and bent on confrontation with the Conservative government rather than working for the everyday needs of the local populace. The local Labour Party appealed to the Electoral Court, accusing the Liberals of malpractice. The appeal was dismissed but when it was taken to the High Court Labour's case was upheld and the Electoral Court was ordered to undertake action against a number of offending Liberal councillors. As a consequence, up to thirteen Liberal councillors came close to being banned from office for five years. However, a further Liberal appeal against the High Court ruling eventually proved successful the Liberals had come within a whisker of destroying their own power base through their own intense competitiveness!

We can understand this form of politics better by considering its strongly populist emphasis, one peculiarly suited to certain aspects of the traditional culture of the East End. Many of the local Liberal leaders are forthright and dominant figures who rule 'their' neighbourhoods with a very strong grip indeed. In some neighbourhoods, such as Bow, this approach has led to the creation of a strong partnership with local officers who clearly identify with many of the policies, for instance concerning efficiency in housing management, which the political leadership have put into practice. In other neighbourhoods there is much less identification and much more fear within the officer ranks and, as we have noted in Stepney, this has enabled some Liberal councillors to step well beyond the boundary of fairness and propriety.

Liberalism and racism in Tower Hamlets

Given the impoverishment of the borough and the rapid recent growth of the Bangladeshi community the conditions for the growth of racism have been present for some time as the struggle for scarce housing and educational resources has assumed the character of a competition between the white and Bangladeshi communities. As early at 1986 a House of Commons Select Committee chaired by Sir Edward Gardner QC warned the government that, unless Tower Hamlets was given more money for housing, race relations in the borough could be seriously damaged. The committee added that Tower Hamlets was unique among local authorities because of the scale of immigration and its impact upon housing. Despite such warnings no significant increase in government allocations was forthcoming. But nor, for its part, did the Liberal Party in Tower Hamlets organise any campaign which might have led it to confront the government over housing issues. Indeed, to the contrary, Liberals in some neighbourhoods such as Bow have been vigorous proponents of the 'right to buy' strategy the outcome of which has been further reductions in the size and quality of an already inadequate public housing stock.

One of the distinctive characteristics of Liberal populism in Tower Hamlets has therefore been its introversion. Political energies have been focused upon enemies within – bureaucracy, professionalism, local labourism – rather than upon the more powerful enemies outside. But what of the Bangladeshi community itself? Has this also become a convenient 'enemy within' against which the Liberals have been able to whip up white electoral support by playing the 'race card'? The question has become particularly pertinent since the success of the fascist British National Party (BNP) in the Millwall ward by-election on the Isle of Dogs in September 1993, the first success for a fascist party in a British local government election since the mid-1970s. In the aftermath of this shock victory for the BNP local Liberals stood accused once more of using race scare tactics in their electoral campaign, accusations which led Paddy Ashdown, the leader of the Liberal Party, to order an internal enquiry into the activities of the Tower Hamlets party.

Our own research suggests that the Tower Hamlets Liberal Party is a complex and contradictory phenomenon combining both liberal and illiberal characteristics. The party certainly contains some councillors and an unknown number of activists who are overtly racist. On the other hand, prominent members have also included Christian radicals, greens and a not insignificant number of local Bangladeshis. At times the 'principle of neighbourhood autonomy' has provided the means by which such different interests could find safe expression, thus avoiding the conflict which would have ensued if all such interests had been forced to converge around a single borough-wide political strategy. But it is also the case that despite this variety certain persistent themes have emerged which constitute a kind of background rhythm upon which different neighbourhood patterns have been constructed.

As we have seen in Chapter 3, the populism of Tower Hamlets Liberals has been linked to a set of strongly naturalistic notions of community which linked a sense of place to tradition, kinship and family. Such ideas suggested the existence of a number of geographically concentrated communities in the local area which could be reawakened by a local council bold enough to seek to harness the social forces thus aroused. It should therefore come as no surprise that the particular strategy which has most consistently brought Liberal populism in the borough to the edge of downright racism has been the pursuit of 'sons and daughters' schemes as an element of the process of allocating scarce housing resources by local neighbourhoods. In reality, of course, this strategy has been largely symbolic as the acuteness of the housing crisis in the borough has been such that, even where such schemes have been implemented, the number of allocations which have been possible on this basis have been marginal in relation to the degree of housing need of young white households in the borough. The British National Party demonstrated a shrewd awareness of this in the run-up to the Isle of Dogs by-election and were able to represent themselves as the true upholders of 'right for whites' in the borough, thus outflanking the Liberals and beating them at their own game. The Liberals have been playing with fire and the danger is that they have now awakened social forces which, given the introverted nature of their populism, they have neither the ability nor commitment to control.

Decentralised democracy: lessons from experience

It will by now be apparent that the two democracy projects we have described are quite different. At a surface level we can contrast Tower Hamlets' concern to strengthen the representative role of the councillor with Islington's desire to stimulate public participation. But the differences are more profound and contain a paradox which centres around Islington's paternalism and Tower Hamlets, populism. Central to this paradox are political values. Critically it is the values of the political parties and not the organisational structures of decentralisation (although these are, of course, shaped by the values) that have determined the political outcomes which decentralisation produces.

The two local authorities we have examined have different conceptions of justice. The Labour Party in Islington has a universalistic conception of social justice (Rawls, 1972). Hence their stress upon equal opportunities and anti-poverty strategies as well as decentralisation. The Liberals in Tower Hamlets, on the other hand, have a conception of rights founded on historical relationships to territory and property – one which would not be uncomfortable with the radical libertarian philosophy of Robert Nozick (1974). Thus their stress on 'sons and daughters schemes' and endorsement of council house sales alongside their enthusiasm for decentralisation.

Islington's conception of personal identity is based on culture, oppression, interest and spatial identity, Tower Hamlets' on territorial constructions of community and class. Islington conceives of freedom as part of a 'social contract' between the individual and the state. Citizens have a right to a 'voice' but only with the acknowledgement that it is ultimately the state which guarantees our liberty (council housing, for example, is a guarantor of freedom for the poorest part of the community). For the Liberals in Tower Hamlets the state mediates against freedom and should be

219

kept to a minimum; thus they see no conflict between decentralisation and privatisation.

So for Islington the outcome of its decentralisation/ democratisation project is a sort of progressive paternalism which emphasises equality, but fears to slacken the reins of power. For Tower Hamlets the outcome is their institutional embodiment of a populist philosophy which stresses the views of the majority (and is, in this respect, quintessentially conservative). At the same time, however, it offers real local control because the political leadership is not afraid of what it might unleash. In some cases this has endorsed overtly racist behaviour (as we document more fully in Chapter 9), and can be inferred from the borough-wide effects of 'sons and daughters' schemes for council house allocation which privilege the white working-class community. In others it provides a force for progressive change enabling relations between communities to be radically improved (as on the Bancroft Estate).

PART IV
BEYOND DECENTRALISATION

9 Fragmented Communities and the Challenge to Democracy

Introduction

In Chapter 6 we sought to extend and develop existing models of citizen participation and control to provide a framework from which to consider how, in practice, the balance between citizens and the local state could be shifted in favour of the former. Although the framework we offered may, to many readers, have seemed quite complex, in one crucial way it was too simple. For in counterposing the power of 'the citizens' or 'the people' with that of 'the state', we draw attention away from the fact that 'the people' themselves are not a homogenous block, but highly differentiated. Within the context of local civil society, these differences find expression in the patterns of interaction occurring between the many communities which are contained in a given locality, communities which are not only diverse but often in conflict.

One of the objections most commonly voiced to the idea of extending participatory forms of democracy is that only some people participate, they are often quite unrepresentative of those they purport to speak for and may also be dominated by sectional interests. Moreover, as civil society becomes progressively less homogeneous, in what sense can we continue to speak of 'community participation' when communities themselves are increasingly diverse, fragmented or polarised?

This chapter seeks to address such objections squarely. It focuses upon our experience of participation in Tower Hamlets during the period (1989–90) when racial tensions within the borough were extremely strong. By using a number of case studies we reflect upon a series of questions which are crucial to the development, in practice as well as in theory, of a democratic alternative to the market principle. What is the nature of 'community', and of the civil

society of which 'community' is a part? What are the implications of
a non-idealised concept of 'community' for our understanding of
citizenship and of the public sphere? Has the state a role to play in
facilitating the development of a civil society which has the capacity
to contain difference and handle conflict? What kind of relationship
between representation and participation best provides for an
effective balance between majority and minority interests?

We begin our analysis with an exploration of the concept of
'community' itself and then, through a cameo of participation in
Tower Hamlets, proceed to examine the nature of community
identities in Stepney.

Concepts of community

Willmott has provided a useful review of 'community initiatives'
which shows clearly that the word has multiple meanings:

> Those advocating a new initiative, or those attaching or defining a
> particular point of view, may invoke the community in support of
> their case, without making it clear which community they mean,
> in what sense they refer to it or how far they have established
> what its opinions or interests are. (Willmott, 1989, p. 5)

Different interpretations of the word 'community' and the
implications for local government are explored in a paper for the
Local Government Management Board (Hambleton, Stewart and
Taylor, 1991) and we draw directly on this source in the following
discussion. On the one hand, community is a unifying concept, the
expression of common interest, solidarity, integration and
consensus (*Gemeinschaft* in sociological theory). On the other,
community is not a singular concept but in reality represents a
mere umbrella under which shelter a multitude of varying,
competing and often conflicting interests. The politics of
community in this second model are pluralistic rather than
consensual, with the role of the authority in the community one
of mediation of interest and the management of complexity rather
than representative of a single 'community'. Public institutions
need to be clear as to which meaning they are basing their policies

upon. In some areas of policy the former definition may be dominant. But more often than not public institutions need to apply the complex rather than the simple model.

The term 'community' has been attached to a wide range of services, programmes and occupations in recent years and can refer to an astonishing diversity of activities. Consider the following small selection of usages: community care, community projects, community business, community architecture, community social work, community relations councils, community action, community policing, even community charge! To penetrate this confusion it may be helpful to distinguish between different meanings of the concept of community as follows:

1. Community as *heritage* – the expression of a common cultural tradition or identity – a sense of continuity and belonging – a concept of community drawing its legitimacy from history.
2. Community as *social relationships* – the patterns of interrelationship reflected in kinship, neighbouring, mutuality, support and social interaction often deriving from the residential base – a concept of community drawing its legitimacy from sociological and anthropological traditions.
3. Community as the basis of collective *consumption* – an appropriate aggregation of the needs or demands of groups or neighbourhoods for local public goods (libraries, transport, environmental quality and so on) – a concept of community which draws its legitimacy from economics.
4. Community as the basis for the most effective production and *provision* of local public goods, whether these be provided by private, public or voluntary sectors (including the community itself) – a concept of community drawing its legitimacy again from economics and from the technologies of service provision.
5. Community as the source of influence and *power* from which is derived empowerment and representation, whether these be through formal or informal, representative or participative channels of political action – conversely a shared sense of powerlessness or alienation – a concept of community drawing its legitimacy from political science.

It is important to stress that, in practice, these various meanings overlap in complex and subtle ways. In general, the more of these factors that apply the stronger the sense of community is likely to be:

> An ethnic community in a particular town may draw on a common heritage, a common experience of powerlessness, kinship networks and face-to-face contact, especially if they live in the same part of town – all of which reinforce each other. (Stewart and Taylor, 1993)

Conversely, if fewer factors apply, the sense of community is likely to be more fragile.

It is also important to emphasise that the sense of community is not necessarily a force for good. Sometimes it can take on an extremely defensive, even selfish, form and be used as a means of excluding unwanted groups. This process can often be seen in the definition of residential areas in towns and cities. A vivid example is provided by Mike Davis in his incisive analysis of the affluent homeowners' associations in Los Angeles (Davis, 1992). He argues that 'community' in Los Angeles means homogeneity of race, class and, especially, home values. He describes how a city council member from the west San Fernando Valley was put under siege day and night by angry residents when she renamed a residential area. This tampering with the 'community's' imaginary boundaries sparked waves of protest from homeowners who argued that redesignation eroded their house values. Needless to say, there were racial connotations too. When, in an attempt to reach a compromise, she revised her decision, she was almost 'ground to bits' by 'the incessant conflict of microscopically parochial interests'. His analysis led Davis to conclude that decentralisation of, for example, land-use decision-making to the neighbourhood level in Los Angeles was an extremely difficult business because:

> The most powerful 'social movement' in contemporary Southern California is that of affluent homeowners, organised by notional community designations or tract names, engaged in the defence of home values and neighbourhood exclusivity. (Davis, 1992, p. 153)

It would, of course, be quite wrong to imagine that this is a peculiarly American phenomenon. The local sense of place has been mobilised by reactionary forces in UK cities and we explore this later in this chapter.

In applying the five concepts of community mentioned above, it is useful to distinguish between two different but often related types of community – communities of interest and imagined communities. Both draw on elements of heritage, social relationships, consumption, provision and power and, in both cases, people 'have something in common'.

Communities of interest reflect the common material concerns or characteristics of their members and/or the issues of common interest around which they group. Thus, within any local authority area, but not necessarily relating in any clear way to spatial patterns or boundaries, will be found communities drawing their strength from their economic position (small firms, traders, major employers, trade unions, the unemployed), from the activities with which they are involved (leisure and recreation, arts and culture, voluntary local support), or from their shared use of services (as tenants, patients, passengers, users).

Following Anderson (1983) we can see how many communities are formed on the basis not of common interests but of common identities – they are *imagined communities*. Here the basis of the social bond concerns likeness or similarity. Durkheim (1984) spoke of such forms of social bond in terms of 'mechanical solidarity' in contrast to the forms of 'organic solidarity' which emerge when people organise to pursue material interests. Such imagined communities may form around identities based upon ethnicity, religion or other shared characteristics.

Communities of place can be thought of as a particular kind of imagined community. In Chapter 1 we referred to the 'locality debate' and 'spatial coalitions' which can be mobilised to defend local interests. Such territorial communities can vary widely in size although it is probably the case that the commonest scale is relatively small and local. As we have seen, neighbourhood decentralisation initiatives often try to key into this local sense of place. Area-based communities may be identifiable in terms of administrative service boundaries, and/or in terms of socioeconomic or political characteristics and status. Elements of heritage and actual or perceived social relationships may, however, suggest communities of place which are barely recognisable in terms of administrative geography but mean a lot to residents – for example, streets, blocks, estates, neighbourhoods, parishes, former small boroughs. For others, the community of place will be more clearly related to functional areas – for example, the local economy, the travel to work area, the industrial estates, particular commercial quarters, heritage or tourist areas.

In closing this discussion of concepts of community, we would stress that people have multiple identities and linkages. While much of this book concentrates on neighbourhood decentralisation and therefore inevitably on communities of place, we agree with Deakin when he observes that 'neighbourhood' is just one of many sources of identity:

> As citizens, most people have a variety of cross-cutting allegiances, some to locality, some explicitly to neighbours or friends, some to relations, some to peer groups, some to ethnic or gender groupings, others deriving from occupation or work place. These allegiances co-exist and assume different levels of importance at different times. (Deakin, 1984, p. 20)

It follows that, if local authorities wish to develop a leadership role for the communities in their area, they will need to develop a multidimensional strategy which is responsive to the range of communities within their boundaries. They need to recognise that some communities are better organised and more powerful than others and that they need to redress the imbalances created by these disparities in power and position.

As our reflections on decentralised democracy in Islington and Tower Hamlets revealed, a limitation of the neighbourhood model in these two boroughs was that it gave insufficient attention to such non-spatial identities and communities. This was particularly pronounced in Tower Hamlets, where the embrace of neighbourhood was extreme. At times it was not just that the Liberals in the borough seemed unaware of the disparities in power between the different communities, they also opportunistically sought to give expression to what they perceived as 'the majority interest'. The following detailed cameo of participation at the Tenants' Advisory Forum in Stepney in early 1990 illustrates that the participation process is not always a pretty sight!

Cameo 9.1   Polarised communities and public participation

The scene

The meeting occurred in the conference room at Cheviot House, Stepney. Tenants' representatives, officers and councillors were seated around a series of tables arranged in a horseshoe shape at one end of the conference room. The meeting, which is open to the public, was an extraordinary meeting called to discuss Stepney's procedures on racial harassment (Stepney neighbourhood was at this time under Labour control). There were about six officers, sixteen tenant representatives and two councillors present as well as about seventeen people in the audience. The tenants representatives were nearly all aged over 50, eleven were male, five female; virtually everyone present was white. The audience was arranged in tiered seating at one end of the conference room. The meeting was led by a local Liberal councillor who was the Chair of the Advisory Forum.

The style of the meeting

Stepney's Policy Officer gave a brief presentation. This was followed by a prolonged period of discussion which was quite tightly chaired. The meeting lasted for over two hours in all and included a brief cooling-off period and a final structured session which dealt with proposals and recommendations from the floor. The dynamic of the meeting can be divided into four phases.

Phase 1

This phase lasted about twenty minutes, during which time the Policy Officer gave a brief factual presentation which was followed by a number of statements from tenants' representatives. The officer attempted to provide a factual account of statistical information available indicating the level of racial harassment in the East End. One only had to hear the first few contributions from tenants' representatives to realise that statistics cut no ice with the people present.

As soon as the officer sat down a tenants' representative raised the issue of harassment of whites by blacks. Although no one said as much, many contributions pointed to the feelings of frustration of white tenants and their children which may be fuelling the harassment that the officer talked about. For example, one tenant from the Sydney Estate talked of 'White people who'd had their names down for years but keep getting pushed to the back', an obvious reference to problems in the allocation of council properties. The tenant proceeded to raise issues about 'immigrants' unhealthy habits'. He went into great detail about one particular case of an Asian family who kept spitting from the balcony of their flat. 'They can do what they like, but we can't do anything,' he continued, 'When we put in a complaint about them, nothing gets done.'

Another tenants' representative raised a case of two old ladies whose life was being made unbearable by the foul language of local children. He argued that harassment assumed all forms in the area and yet the council only seemed to be interested in one kind. Another representative returned to the issue of the unfair allocation of vacant flats and argued that he had figures concerning his block of flats on the Clichy Estate which showed that of twenty-nine vacant flats, twenty-eight went to Asian families.

A tenant from Siege House suggested that new tenants should be informed of 'our standards of hygiene and social behaviour'. She complained that anyone who talked about standards of hygiene was accused of racial prejudice. Finally, a representative (who, as we shall see, is a key actor in all of this) from the Limehouse Fields Estate raised a number of issues. First, he noted from the draft document, those found guilty of racial harassment could have their security of tenure threatened or withdrawn. He clearly felt this to be very threatening and questioned its legality. Implying that the introduction of such a policy would not be without cost he asked 'Whose repairs are not going to be done?' (loud applause from the audience). He went on, 'We're on about harassment (of all kinds) why do we have to have "racial" included?' He added that he would like a resolution put to the meeting to this effect.

Phase 2

At this point Stepney's Policy Officer replied to a number of the contributions that had been made. He pointed out that the document focused specifically on racial harassment, but the council recognised that lots of other forms of harassment existed: sexual harassment, for example. The Limehouse Fields representative retorted, 'If you phone up the council and say it's "racial", it's given top priority, but if an old lady rings up about harassment by youths it's not given priority' (this process of constantly alluding to the desperate need of hypothetical old ladies was a tactic used by tenants' representatives throughout the meeting). At this point an officer from the local law centre made a contribution in terms of the legal status of the document. He provided a definition of race which was quite useful for the meeting in that it suggested that the category 'race' could include any race, including English, Irish, Scottish, etc. The implication being that racial harassment could therefore include harassment of, say, Welsh by black Afro-Caribbean. The Limehouse Fields representative replied 'Why can't we therefore cut out the "race business" and just call it harassment?'

At this point the chair mentioned that a Labour councillor present wanted to speak (someone in the audience next to me said 'Let's see if X does a little crying act'). There are only two councillors present at the meeting; the Chair who is Liberal, and X, who is Labour. Many officers had already suggested to us that the Liberal councillor deliberately chairs meetings of the Advisory Forum in a way to gain electoral kudos. It is also suggested that he is adept at playing to the blatant racism of the audience.

This is the most rowdy and aggressive part of the meeting. It begins with Stepney's Policy Officer, in a quietly assertive manner, replying to the various comments with the statement 'Our intention is to make quite clear to tenants where they stand.' A number of other officers are quizzed by the tenants' representatives, including the Principal Housing Officer for the neighbourhood, who was asked by the chair about whether the document included references to harassment by age. The officer tried very hard to give a clear analysis of a very complex issue but by now, it seemed, the audience was in no mood to listen to such forms of explanation (someone in the audience said 'Listen to him, we'll never get a straight (i.e. simple) answer).'

Phase 3

This phase of the meeting revolved around a long contribution made by the Labour councillor, the only contribution which attempted to defend the racial harassment document. She was clearly nervous and spoke in a very defensive and rambling fashion to begin with. Not long into her contribution the audience began to heckle her, a process orchestrated by the representative from the Limehouse Fields Estate. She tried to talk openly and honestly about some very difficult issues facing the meeting. She began by saying that she did not feel easy in talking about race (audience – 'We're not allowed to'). She rebutted accusations that Bangladeshis were responsible for bringing about infestation by cockroaches by attributing the problem to the council's central heating systems (the Limehouse Fields representative was scornful and sarcastic at this point and openly displayed his feelings towards the audience).

The Labour councillor acknowledged people's reservations on this issue (her antagonist used this as an opportunity to say to the audience 'They ought to be on reservations'). The councillor then made what turned out to be a fatal mistake by saying, 'We do have in Stepney still to this day some all-white estates.' At this point there was uproar both within the audience, within the group of tenants' representatives, and everyone (including the chair) started shouting 'Where?' The chair went so far as to say that the Labour councillor's remark was offensive and demanded that she withdraw it (this she refused to do).

She continued even more nervously by saying that everyone had to talk through these issues and 'the Advisory' needed further opportunities to discuss such issues without people feeling accused. At times she teetered on the brink of paternalism, referring, for example, to the need for meetings with 'a more educational format' (she was clearly referring to the need for small-group-type discussion meetings here). The chair eventually intervened by saying to her, 'You have called me a racist on innumerable occasions, it's a bit rich for you to talk about the fact that people often feel uneasy in talking about race.'

At this point a worker from the Tower Hamlets Tenants' Federation attempted to pour oil on troubled waters. In a contribution which tried to appeal to the better side of the tenants in Stepney he said 'Tenants are not bigots, they do want fair play.' He nevertheless tended to side with all previous contributions by suggesting that council officers 'need more education in dealing with other forms of harassment; he added that it was not taken seriously enough. At this point the chair chimed in, 'It takes a strong kind of officer to take this kind of action when you run the risk of being accused of racial harassment.'

By now the meeting had been going on for over an hour and a half and a number of similar contributions were made by tenants' representatives. The representative from the Sydney Estate returned to the theme of the way in which immigrants 'got special treatment'. Another tenants' representative gave a story of a beating and a rape perpetrated by Asian youths which never got into the press (applause from the audience). A third representative talked about St Bernard's school, which had to close early because of attacks on pupils by Asian youths, 'Do the press know about this?' he continued, 'It's all one-sided, we never hear of the other side.' By this time the chair was really starting to stir things up and was systematically attacking the Labour councillor whenever possible. The mildest intervention of the entire evening from the floor came from another representative from Siege House who made an interesting distinction between different groups of ethnic minorities, 'West Indians have conformed to our way of life, it's the Asians who haven't.' However, she then proceeded to make some rather sweeping generalisations about the uncleanliness of Asians which eventually caused the chair to intervene and ask her to withdraw some of her remarks.

Phase 4

This was the final phase of the meeting in which the Chair made a number of summary contributions and a few resolutions were put from the floor. The Chair commented, 'There is a widespread belief (by whites) that they are being discriminated against because of their colour.' He continued that he hoped officers in Stepney would confront the problem by allowing open discussion and not by driving the issue underground. He suggested a small tenants' representative/officer working group should go through the report in detail, line by line. The Labour councillor asked for non-white tenants to be represented. This again caused a stir (audience: 'Bengalis just don't want to be involved. We've begged and pleaded with them').

The Limehouse Fields representative marked his own closing statement by saying 'If you ask them to join in anything you get "no"; but if you tell them there's a coach outing then it's "yes".' He mentioned a Limehouse Fields/Ocean Estate initiative undertaken some six or seven years before, which was designed to bring about better racial understanding between the two groups. He added 'But once it was over they all went back to their own little groups. What they want is to be on their own, in their own little areas, in their own little blocks. Why should I break my back being nice to them when they don't stop to say hello in the street?'

Finally, a representative from the Clichy Estate proposed that the racial harassment document should have the word 'racial' deleted from it. This vote was carried eight for, one against, with several abstentions.

Reflections on a public meeting

Only two Bangladeshis were present at the meeting, one was the race adviser to Stepney neighbourhood the other was a council officer who happened to live on the Ocean Estate. Each remained quiet throughout the meeting, there was no one therefore, to speak of the Bengalis' own experience.

This meeting demonstrated real racism, a mixture of hatred, aggressive humour, and some honesty. It was chaired in a less than helpful way. Clearly it did not constitute the right context for an open discussion of very sensitive issues. What was most striking was the class divide. 'The goodies' – the Labour councillor and assorted officers – were all obviously middle-class in dress and language. 'The baddies' were all working-class. We really got the feeling of an almost unbridgeable gulf between two different worlds.

Three distinct social groups influenced the discussion at the Stepney Tenants' Advisory meeting – council officers and politicians, local white working-class tenants and local Bangladeshis – but the latter was influential only in its absence. Within an area like Stepney a number of tremendously strong popular sentiments exist within the white population – a finely tuned sense of 'outsiderism' (i.e. is this person 'one of them' or 'one of us'?) a strong feeling that no one, particularly officialdom, wants to listen to 'us'; a belief, bordering on unshakeable conviction, that 'incomers', particularly Bangladeshis, are systematically favoured by these same 'powers-that-be'. All these sentiments found expression at the Advisory meeting. The racist sentiments expressed by those who saw themselves as representatives of the interests of local white people had other elements. They clearly felt themselves to be the 'silent majority' governed by an officialdom who did not live in the area and therefore 'didn't know what it was like'. Moreover, in Stepney under Labour control, these white tenants clearly felt that free expression was being denied to them because of the fear that those that spoke their mind would be accused of racism.

Let us consider some further complexities in the picture. Virtually all of the tenants' leaders were 40 years old or more; the majority were probably pensioners. Several of the representatives who were present, particularly from the Sydney and Clichy estates, were 'outsiders' themselves once. For example, a large number of elderly Jews live on the Sydney Estate in particular. There is only one estate in Stepney where the tenants' leadership is much younger; this is the Ocean Estate, the largest in the area, the one with the lowest-quality accommodation and the largest number of Bangladeshi tenants. Many of the tenants' leaders on the Ocean are ex-squatters and radicalised incomers, they are seen as being 'different' by the other Stepney tenants' leaders. No representatives from the Ocean were present at the meeting.

Imagined communities

The age profile of the tenants' leaders, though striking, is probably not exceptional. We noted a roughly similar age profile at tenants' meetings throughout Tower Hamlets and in Finsbury, Islington. Although it does not appear to have been formally researched, our experience suggests that the majority of active tenants' organisers throughout the country tend to be older, and are often pensioners. Clearly, such people are more likely to have the time, and they may also have the length of experience as a local resident which gives them a certain legitimacy. It is also likely that they are at the stage in the life-cycle to experience a strong internal need to preserve things from 'decline' irrespective of whether this refers to the physical body, the body of the family or of the community.

We have found Anderson's notion of 'the imagined community' (1983) to be very helpful in understanding the way in which identity, history and physical place interlink to bring about a strongly ethnicised sense of 'local neighbourhood'. Although Anderson uses this concept as a means of understanding the emergence of the modern nationalist community it seems to us that the essential principle is generalisable to a set of more micro-level and, at times, subcultural phenomena where it is possible to perceive the existence of what could be called a 'collective community in the mind'. Such imagined communities, no less real for being imagined, resemble a kind of collage of elements drawn from material of the group's history and present experience. There is a parallel in many psychoanalytic notions of personal identity where the self is seen as being a representation of the individual's history and experience constructed through a process of recollection and forgetting, a weaving together of phantasy and reality via mechanisms of idealisation, splitting and repression (Baranger, Baranger and Mon, 1988).

Few studies exist of the development of such imagined communities at a micro-level though, interestingly enough, one of the few examples concerns an analysis of the Bangladeshi community in the East End (Eade, 1989, 1990). Eade's study, which is based upon an analysis of the development of this community in the 1970s and 1980s, suggests the way in which key local actors were at first instrumental in articulating a secular nationalist identity, one which was challenged in the late 1980s by a more universalist, Islamic identity. His analysis suggests that those activists within the community who facilitated its organisation around material interests overlapped with, and were often identical to, those most engaged with the articulation of the community's collective identity.

We would hazard a guess that something similar occurs within the white working class in the area. In this case it seems that the layer of local activists, disproportionately drawn from older, long-standing residents within the borough (East End matriarchs and patriarchs, as we came to think of them) not only act as the vehicle through which the material interests of the local white working class are mobilised, but also act as an important vehicle for the articulation of this group's collective identity. We conducted a number of detailed interviews with tenants' leaders on the Limehouse Fields Estate in Stepney, virtually all of whom were white, and middle-aged or elderly. Most had lived on this estate since it was built just after the Second World War. The estate has suffered from neglect for years and is located very much on the lower rings of the ladder of desirable estates in the Stepney area.

One could not fail to be struck by the warm feeling that virtually all of those interviewed displayed when asked what it was like in the 'old days'. We were tempted to believe that this was just a romanticisation of a past which was as ordinary and messy as the present, but the tenants were so uniform and so insistent in their pictures of the past that one could not help but wonder whether this was pure nostalgia or actually rooted in a lost reality. According to all of those interviewed, the physical and social environment was far better in the early days of the estate. One tenant, pointing to the ground below her balcony which was a tarmacked waste interspersed with abandoned buildings and fenced off, overgrown, grassland, said, 'This area used to be one big playground. Waterview (a tower block) was a woodyard and there were small, terraced houses all down the road, by the canal.' She pointed to a piece of rat-infested wasteland, saying, 'I've reported it and reported it [that is, to the authorities] but nothing happens. I've been round to the local office no end of times.' Another tenant who had lived on the estate for over twenty years added, 'Look at the grounds, there's lumps and holes everywhere. In the old days, everyone cleaned and took their turn. The people were nicer then. Now, we've got the whole league of nations here.'

The tenant who said, 'Years ago you knew everyone but now half of them, you don't know who they are' was speaking for virtually everyone interviewed. There was a unanimous view that in the old days you did not have to keep your doors locked, old people could go out at night, gardens were left as gardens without being vandalised, people helped each other out . . . the list goes on endlessly. Without being able to say whether these perceptions of the past are accurate or not, it is fairly clear that none of these things exist in the present. Not even the friendly East End pub is very much in evidence on the ground. Most of the pubs we visited in the Stepney area were as desolate during the evening as the estates were that surrounded them. One woman we interviewed echoed this point when saying that as a family they had long ago stopped going to local pubs. However, the old network still remained alive. She referred to a couple of clubs – the Dockers' Club and the Vaughan Club – saying that here 'You're with your own. You feel like a family.'

Many of those interviewed, particularly pensioners, have experienced great isolation. As one woman put it, 'Upstairs they're mostly coloured . . . boat people, you know. I haven't got any friends on the landing, except the man at the end, and I've got a friend down in a flat below.' These two friends, therefore, were all that seemed to be left of this perceived network of neighbours from the past.

After a while we began to wonder to what extent the past as portrayed by these tenants was a construction based upon forms of forgetting. For example, when interviewing two old ladies in their seventies, one said, 'There was more children then.' Her friend quickly corrected her and said, 'I wouldn't say that with all the Pakis, Lil.' Many of those we interviewed who complained about the size of the Bangladeshi families had previously told us that they themselves were one child of many, six or seven brothers or sisters being not uncommon. Another tenant, who had lived in the area even before the Limehouse Fields Estate was built, pointed to an area and said, 'This used to be Carr Street. Down there, they'd nick your shoelace while you're talking. You would never go down there alone.' Little episodes like this sometimes felt like chinks or gaps in an otherwise perfect picture. Of course, we have got no way of knowing what the past was actually like. Nor can we be sure to wha extent the meaning of the past is determined by the meaning of the present.

In these passages we have traced one line of imaginative construction of 'community' which contributes to what is virtually a kind of micro-ethnic identity among many of the white working-class residents of London's East End. There will undoubtedly be other paths traversed by the collective imagination which contribute to other aspects of this identity, paths which, for instance, contribute to the class as opposed to the ethnic basis of this sense of community. Although this ethnic consciousness is strong, and for much of the time dominant, we do not want to imply that the sense of community and forms of political consciousness underlying it are homogeneous and without contradictory elements. As we shall see in the following section, class interests also often came to the surface. Indeed, during the period of our study there were occasions in some parts of Tower Hamlets when all sections of the local population united against the imposition of government policies concerning, for example, the introduction of Housing Action Trusts and the poll tax.

So far we have examined the way in which particular spatially-defined neighbourhoods, considered as forms of local civil society, contain a number of powerful imagined communities. Such imagined communities will often not be coterminous with the administratively defined boundaries of local government. However, there will often be considerable overlap, particularly where these administrative boundaries have themselves drawn upon notions of historically-existent settlements such as Stepney, Poplar or Finsbury. Ethnic-minority communities may also be spatially concentrated within particular areas or neighbourhoods. The Bengali community, centred in the Spitalfields area, is an obvious case in point. Here the contrast with Islington, which, as we explained in Chapter 3, contains a much greater diversity of ethnic minorities more spatially dispersed throughout the borough, is striking. However, our hypothesis is that while an imagined community may or may not coincide with the existence of what is sometimes described as an ecological or demographic community, it will coincide closely with a third sense of community, one that is often referred to in terms of 'community of interest'. For the latter notion draws us towards a consideration of civil society as the site for the mobilisation of groups on the basis of collective material interests.

Communities of interest

What are the key material resources that contribute to the quality of life locally? The answer is not hard to find – jobs, homes, schools, places to meet and leisure facilities, accessible means of transportation and a cared-for environment are the ones most frequently mentioned. Clearly, particular groups, such as the frail elderly or people with learning difficulties, will have particular needs, but in any local area there will exist a set of resources that most people will have need of at some time in their lives. Following Wallmann (1982) and others we have found it useful to think of a particular locality, such as Tower Hamlets, as the location of a number of private, public and communal resources around which local groups will sometimes compete for access and control and on other occasions unite to preserve or enlarge. In Tower Hamlets, indigenous white-working-class control of local labour markets in the docks and printing industry is now a thing of the past. Competition between this group and others for public housing, education and community resources is, however, still very strong.

Such complicated patterns of competition and co-operation, overlaying local markets for scarce housing and other resources, contributes to the richness of community action. Tenants' associations which, through effective forms of direct action and mass campaigning, vigorously fought off the Conservative governments' attempt to impose Housing Action Trusts will, in another context, be just as vigorous in their advocacy of 'sons and daughters' lettings schemes which have the effect of discriminating against the housing needs of ethnic minority groups. Such experiences should remind us that social and political consciousness, far from being homogeneous, is a complex and dynamic construction within which conflicting and contradictory ideas and sentiments wrestle for attention. Several of the members of the audience at the Stepney Tenants' Advisory meeting who were engaged in heckling the solitary Labour councillor were themselves sporting stick-on badges in support of local ambulance workers who were engaged in the National Ambulance Workers' Strike at the time. Some, as we have already noted, were themselves elderly Jews who had no doubt experienced in the 1930s the same kind of hostility that they were now involved in visiting upon the Bangladeshi 'incomers'.

Our experience would therefore suggest that groups mobilise around both identity and interest either to obtain access and control to local resources or to defend control which has already been established. In this sense it is not simply a question of distinguishing between local social movements which are progressive and those which are reactionary (Pickvance, 1985); rather it is a question of understanding such movements in their dynamic sense as ones which often combine both progressive and reactionary moments. This is particularly the case for areas or groups which have a history of social and political volatility.

Stedman Jones (1976) has argued that the white working class of inner East London, lacking the historical experience of the factory system which characterised their counterparts in the North and Midlands, have long constituted a combustible mass ripe for political exploitation. In his analysis of racism and vigilantism in East London, Husbands (1982) develops a similar analysis and notes that Stepney in particular has acted as the locus for vigilantist forms of racism since the end of the nineteenth century. Husbands argues that Stepney cannot simply be seen as a 'defended neighbourhood' in Suttles' (1972) sense, as this is a more contingent phenomenon referring to processes of inter-ethnic accommodation rather than to persistent and unremitting forms of racial hostility. Instead, Husbands proposes that 'the concentration of racial attacks in the Stepney area and in northerly and westerly adjacent locations can be explained only by suggesting the existence of some form of very locally based and socially transmitted vigilantist culture whose origins go back at least to the anti-Semitic agitation that occurred at the turn of the century' (p. 21).

Husband's notion of a local vigilantist culture is an interesting hypothesis. However, his survey of the area finished in the late 1970s. The wave of racist incidents in the late 1980s/early 1990s affecting East London seemed more dispersed than his analysis would lead us to presume. Overt racial harassment seemed to be highest in the Poplar and Isle of Dogs neighbourhoods, traditionally all-white areas which have only recently been subject to immigration as Bangladeshi families spread eastwards through the borough from the Spitalfields heartland. Here the concept of 'defended neighbour-hoods' appears to have more explanatory value for understanding white hostility. On the other hand, the incident which in 1990 led to the mobilisation of many local people in a 'rights for whites campaign' (a campaign which has provided the opportunity for the re-emergence of organised Fascism in the area through the British National Party) concerned the alleged stabbing of a white youth by Asian youths at the Stepney Green School.

There can be no doubt that decentralisation within Tower Hamlets has given expression to and reinforced parochial tendencies within the local civil society. Many officers and councillors in the area seemed very conscious of the way in which the struggle for scarce community resources exacerbated tensions between local whites and other groups. For decades the borough has suffered from a declining local economy, from central government neglect and from the complacency of the old, right wing local Labour administrations. The Liberals, particularly through their Advanced Leasing Scheme which has funded a massive, borough-wide estate modernisation programme, have certainly begun to address some of the bad conditions in the area. Nevertheless, the material conditions for white racism remain. The paradox is, then, that parts of the local white population see themselves in a way that is very reminiscent of an ethnic minority view – systematically neglected, and faced with an officialdom which consists almost entirely of 'outsiders'.

The idea of civil society: a plea for realism

It should be clear from this discussion of civil society in London's East End that, far from existing in some natural state of grace, the structure of civil society is itself influenced by the distribution of economic and state resources around which different local groups compete. Moreover, the basic building block of civil society, the family, is itself hardly uninfluenced by the mode of production. The very form of the modern family and the division of labour upon which it rests is clearly influenced by quite contingent developments within the labour market, which vary through time, from region to region, and so on. And yet we also know that this division of labour, and the patriarchal relations of which it is an expression, long pre-existed the rise of the capitalist mode of production.

The basic social forms – family, kinship, social networks, communities – which make up civil society, long pre-date the emergence of modern capitalism and are more biographically determinant than the social forms to be found within either economy or state. In this sense civil society seems formative, both because it is constitutive *of* our subjectivity and constituted *by* our subjectivity. But it is not just the site of the private sphere, of our private lives, it is also, crucially, the everyday locus of our unmediated social and public nature. It is the site for the most basic forms of association (Hirst, 1992) – of clubs and pubs, voluntary and community organisations, mutual aid groups (both class- and ethnic-based), cultural, political and religious organisations. In other words, civil society constitutes that part of life within which people attempt freely to interact, care for each other and enjoy each other's company, as well as organise to protect their social and physical environment. This is important, because if we only ever see civil society in terms of 'actions' and 'movements', we forget that it is the seedbed from which new approaches to producing things, new forms of recreation, enjoyment and culture, new ways of caring for each other, all spring. Within civil society we react against the state and economy but we also seek to reproduce ourselves as imaginative, sensitive and transformative beings, albeit within the constraints set by the pincers of the state, workplace and market.

It would seem, then, that civil society is a Janus-headed phenomenon, a site for conflict, division and domination as well as conviviality, solidarity and mutuality. It would be reassuring to attribute the former to the impact of external forces located within the economy and the state, as if these basic social structures are responsible for the contamination of what would otherwise be a natural state of sociability. Keane (1988, pp. 42–6) traces such myopic attitudes back to the work of Tom Paine, who construed the state as the locus of interference in a civil society which would otherwise exist in a natural condition of freedom. The issue at stake here concerns the character of civil society and the need to maintain a non-idealised conception of that subjectivity of ours to which civil society has such an intimate relationship. In this light the work of the influential group psychoanalyst, Wilfred Bion, appears to get much closer to providing the understanding we require, for Bion insists that if we are 'group animals' then we are also group animals at war with our 'groupishness' (Bion, 1961). We explore this and related themes in greater depth elsewhere (Hoggett, 1992a).

Viewed from a psychoanalytical perspective, all social forms are multidetermined. A particular institution not only performs a certain set of practical functions but also gives expression to, and works upon, human sentiments and emotions. Specifically, a tradition has emerged within psychoanalysis that examines the way in which human institutions contain both meaning and anxiety (Menzies Lyth, 1988; Hinshelwood, 1987). This containing function serves to keep collective anxiety within boundaries; failure of this containing function is equivalent to the creation of a rent in the social fabric which supports our 'going-on-being', leading to the heightening of anxiety and the onset of paranoid and projective tendencies (Hoggett, 1992b).

With regard to civil society, on the one hand we can see how it is the crucible within which collective needs are formed, dreams are constructed, and 'associationism' flowers. But we also need to consider the containing function of the social forms (family, group, community) within civil society as a kind of organic social fabric which can easily be torn, leading to forms of social demoralisation (that is, collective despondency, apathy and withdrawal on the one hand, and the destruction of social values on the other). In such instances, failure of the containing function unleashes diffuse and malignant forms of social sentiment which tend to transmute social differences into oppositions via those primitive grammars of unconscious fantasy which provide the symbolic material of racism, xenophobia, moral panics and other forms of 'out-grouping'.

Viewed from this perspective, civil society can be the crucible for both emancipation and reaction. For Tom Paine, in a manner reminiscent of some psychoanalytic radicals such as Wilhelm Reich, the project of emancipation was roughly equivalent to pulling the state off the back of civil society so that our natural, sociable, associative nature could shine through. The problem is that for those with a less idealised view of civil society, the project of democratic emancipation seems less straightforward. Do we not need some kind of social agency (perhaps a kind of state which has not yet been created) which can pressurise adults to respect the needs of children, enable silent voices to be heard, restore a group's capacity to resist the temptation to embark upon the process of inferiorising other social groups, and sustain a commitment to the collective interest which is as vibrant as that to one's self-interest? For these are very real and yet immensely difficult tasks which face any project, nationally or locally conceived, which pins its hopes upon the extension of democratic participation as an alternative to government by private interest. And they are tasks which are all the more difficult to accomplish within those parts of civil society such as Islington and Tower Hamlets which are subject to immiseration, neglect and technocratic interference, where the struggle for scarce resources tends to pit family against family and group against group, as often as it leads to solidaristic action.

The democracy project

The tendency to idealise civil society runs deeply within traditions of socialist thought, particularly within libertarian tendencies. But it also finds expression within contemporary forms of liberal and social democracy. While the circumstances in Tower Hamlets are somewhat extreme, they are a microcosmic picture of a civil society which seems remote from that drawn by many advocates of the contemporary citizenship movement.

Both Islington and Tower Hamlets councils were committed to strengthening local democracy. Both believed that neighbourhood planning and management could make local local government more responsive and more accountable. In an important sense, therefore, the following sentiments expressed by Marquand would have enjoyed widespread support among both Labour and Liberal politicians in both boroughs:

Citizenship is nothing if it is not public. The notion of the citizen implies the notion of the city – of the polis, of the public realm, of public purposes, publicly debated and determined. Of course citizens have an obligation to the city; and, of course, that obligation has to be discharged privately as well as publicly. But it springs from participation in, and membership of, a public body, a political community.

To narrow the scope of public power, to take activities out of the
public domain and put them into the private is, by definition, to
narrow the sphere of citizenship. (Marquand, 1989)

These words from a contemporary proponent of the broad
democratic project which has emerged in the UK during the past
few years conjure a number of crucial images, in particular the idea
of the 'public sphere' as a space for democratic debate and decision-
making, as opposed to the closed, private sphere of administrative
dictate and blind market forces. This democratic project argues for
the restoration of 'voice' as opposed to 'exit' (Hirschman, 1970); for
political democracy as opposed to the new right's model of market
democracy; and as a model for conducting human affairs. In doing
so, it re-evokes the faded Aristotelian ideal of 'the polis', of a vibrant
political community through which individual and collective
interests and purposes are publicly debated.

The experiments in local participation and democracy in Islington
and Tower Hamlets provide a crucible within which many of the
claims regarding the possibility of democratic emancipation can be
tested. Indeed, Islington's neighbourhood forums by their very
name conjure associations with political society in Ancient Greece.
The practical experience of these two boroughs throws light upon a
number of crucial questions. Is the creation of a space for open
public dialogue and decision-making possible, or is such a space
mythical, perhaps precluded by the very nature of the state and civil
society themselves? If such a space exists, where is it located – within
part of the state, within civil society, or on the boundary between the
two? Is the state, and the local state, the problem, or can it be part of
the solution? In other words, can the state facilitate democracy or is
its role inevitably one which constrains and inhibits the democratic
impulse? Is there an ideal relationship between representative and
participatory democracy? For example, does one stand for 'the
general interest' and the other for 'particular interests'? The
following sections and Chapter 10 address these questions.

The opportunistic state

To consider civil society as something which is basically flawed is
not to rule out the possibility of its development. The vision of a

vibrant local political culture, of a civil society within which difference is welcomed rather than feared and where the overlaps and conflicts between general and particular interests are addressed openly and creatively remains a viable one. It was this kind of vision which motivated many of the councillors, officers and activists we encountered in the two boroughs. But to recognise civil society as flawed is to admit that, apart from exceptional circumstances, it lacks the internal capacity to transcend its own fragmentation – the divisions of gender, generation and ethnicity as well as the particularism of wants and interests.

Indeed, if we look at many of the things that the state has historically been called upon to do – for example, the institutionalisation of those construed as 'mad', 'infirm', 'crippled' or 'retarded' (we choose these words deliberately) – then we can see how it has taken upon itself the management of 'problems' which civil society lacked the capacity to contain in humane terms. Drawing on Hegel, Keane (1988, pp. 46–8) notes how the constitutional state becomes to be seen as the only agency capable of remedying injustice and synthesising particular interests into a universal political community. But in doing so the institutionalisation of social life develops an inexorable logic of its own, so that by the twentieth century some political ideologies (particularly those on the far left and far right – that is, those most enchanted with the notion of state control) had entirely confused social form with state form.

It goes without saying that the institutions of the state, and the interest groups which inhabit them, have not declined from the invitation proffered. Much of the growth of the state and the well-being of the occupational groups which reside within it has depended upon this willingness to take on board tasks which civil society seemed unwilling or unable to perform for itself. As Keane notes, 'the power invested by civil society in this political apparatus is turned back on civil society itself . . . in the name of democracy, society falls under the sway of a "benevolent", inquisitive and meddlesome state power . . . the state becomes a regulator, inspector, adviser, educator and punisher of social life' (Keane, 1988, p. 49).

The experience of tenants in Tower Hamlets probably spoke for a common experience of many in traditional working-class areas. The repeated encounter with a central and local state apparatus which would not or could not respond, actively discouraged attempts at self-organisation. There was little in the way of a tradition of 'active citizenship' to draw upon and the experience of the 'political community' had been mediated constantly by a complacent and territorial political élite (the old borough Labour Party). Moreover, the opportunism of the state had removed from local civil society the necessity of thinking beyond the needs of one's own group and hence also the responsibility for conceiving of 'the general interest'. If civil society appeared to be inward-looking and parochial, as many councillors and officers around the country who were opposed to the idea of a local participatory democracy often argued, then this was to a large extent a situation of their own creation. The social relations of the opportunist state were deeply ingrained. If such relations were to be transformed then local government had first to understand the many ways in which it was complicit in reproducing them.

The various disabling effects of state intervention in the public sphere have by now been charted thoroughly (Offe, 1984). Among these effects we might list the tendency for state institutions to treat symptoms rather than tackle causes (an approach which typically leads to the individualisation of collective problems); the belief that administrative/technocratic methods can be used to solve social/ political problems; the assumption of the existence of a self-evident body of expertise and experience to which those outside the state are not privy; the tendency to distrust and undermine alternative bases of power within civil society through techniques of divide and rule, incorporation and absorption, and so on.

As a critique of such state power the democratic liberal and socialist project of the early 1980s sought to construct an alternative vision and practice, one which sought to redress the balance between state and communities, between administration and politics, and between individual problems and collective solutions. Critical to this project – as it found implementation through strategies of local authority decentralisation, in new forms of professional practice, in the grant-aid strategies of local governmental organisations such as the Greater London Council, and in a renewed emphasis upon community development – was the notion of 'empowerment', the idea that the state, its institutions and those who worked within them could develop *enabling* rather than *disabling* forms of practice.

A funny thing happened on the way to the forum

Conceived by many as an alternative social vision to that of the radical right, this programme of democratic renewal, necessarily confined to the 'lower reaches' of government and community, nevertheless soon began to encounter a social and political terrain which was in many ways unexpected and different from the experience of the previous decades. The degree of fragmentation of civil society and, the absence of sources of identity which could transcend immediate group affiliations, appeared to contrast strongly with the pre-Thatcher period in which the stable identities of class permitted much easier identification with 'the people' as opposed to the state or private capital.

But by the late 1980s many of the new social movements, particularly those based upon identities of race, sexuality or other differences, appeared to have transmuted into new forms of particularism. Inter-ethnic rivalries (for example, between black Afro-Caribbean and Asian groups), in part fuelled by urban management initiatives, appeared to be growing upon the base of apparently highly essentialist notions of collective identity. Indeed, the left seemed to have been involved in exacerbating such forms of particularism through the very project of empowerment it had adopted (Cain and Yuval-Davis, 1990). Looking back on the 1980s, the editors of the international *Community Development Journal* noted, 'somewhat ironically, the emphasis on separateness, distinctiveness, and even essentialism, has often been promoted in the name of empowerment' (Miller and Bryant, 1990, p. 324).

Such developments have led to a reappraisal of civil society and the social movements which spring from it. It would seem that there is less of a basis for political commonality now than there appeared to be before. Some see this simply as an expression of class defeat and the corresponding decline in traditional class and trade union identities which, whatever may be said against them, tended to draw people together as workers or 'the people' over and above whatever else made them different from one another. As we noted in Chapter 1, others see the decline of such stable identities as the outcome of more deep-seated forms of economic and social restructuring, as indicative of the emergence of a post-modern civil society within a 'post-Fordist' world. Viewed from this perspective it seems as if the locus of social conflict has shifted in some way from the social relations of production to the social relations of consumption and reproduction, from the economy and the corporate state to civil society and the redistributive state. Whatever the causes of this shift the implications for the democratic project are profound. In place of David Marquand's vision of a vibrant public sphere within the city, apathy, withdrawal and resentment often seem to be dominant.

This discussion enables us to reflect upon some of the concepts of citizen participation and empowerment outlined in Chapter 6. Crucially, we need to distinguish between the empowerment of the group and of the local civil society as a whole. The ladder of participation focuses upon the empowerment of the group vis-à-vis the state. Our discussion in this chapter focuses upon power differences between groups within civil society and the way in which the amplification of some voices may lead to the muting of others. A number of important conclusions follow from this. Specifically we need to abandon existing definitions of empowerment which construe this simply in terms of the transfer of powers from the state to groups of local citizens. For example, a body of tenants may have grasped control of their own estate, they may have their own budget and hire and fire their own staff but if, as a collective body, they lack the capacity to tolerate differences within them, or if they contain groups whose voice is unable to find expression, then as collective bodies they are flawed. Given this degree of fragmentation and polarisation within many contemporary urban and rural communities, we would suggest that the democratic project should not take the concept of 'collective empowerment' as its starting point. Rather, the starting point should be to assemble the preconditions from which genuine forms of collective empowerment can proceed. A similar line of analysis has been proposed by Hodgson (1988) in thinking of a strategy for creating a democratically-planned economy.

It follows from this that we do not see the essential task of area-based participatory structures as being collective empowerment because, in most urban neighbourhoods, the preconditions for this kind of empowerment do not exist. Even in the most demographically homogeneous areas we would suggest that the primary role of a local public forum should be to provide a space in which conflicts, misunderstandings and hostilities can be worked through. In multiracial communities this seems to us to be a prerequisite for the democratic project to succeed. We suggest this, not in the belief that this will bring about integration, although it may in some areas, but in the belief that it can facilitate cohabitation between culturally diverse and, at times, incommensurable communities.

10 Local Democracy beyond the Local State

Introduction

Local government in the UK is in deep trouble. In Chapter 1 we outlined the main dimensions of the current crisis and explained how the Thatcher government, elected in 1979, introduced a series of measures designed to undermine the power of local authorities, to slash central government financial support to local government and to introduce market principles into the process of public service management. In this final chapter we revisit some of the key political themes we have discussed earlier in the book and outline a vision of a strong and reinvigorated local democracy. In this vision, locally-elected authorities would have much more power than they have at present, but we want to stress at the outset that we are not advocating a return to a glorious, possibly mythical, municipal past. A vibrant local democracy for the twenty-first century requires a powerful enabling capacity within the local state, but this does not imply a return to state domination of local decision-making and service provision.

Local authorities should be encouraged to see themselves as leading actors in a pluralistic institutional environment. The concern with the provision of a wide range of important public services will continue, but the local authority of the future will put just as much emphasis on its orchestrating role. It will see itself as working not just within the boundaries of the public sector, but also across the boundaries of the public, private and voluntary sectors. Its attention will focus not only on the quality and effectiveness of its own services, but also on the development of outward-looking strategies designed to shape the local social, economic and cultural environment. While we see the orchestrating role of the local authority as being crucial, we envisage the institution of local government as only one part of a transformed public sphere. A truly effective local democracy will involve the extension of public

252

accountability into a wide range of public and private institutions
which have an impact on the lives of local people. Just as important,
it will require the development of the democratic capacity of civil
society itself. Before we explore these possibilities we take stock of
the current position relating to central/local relations in the UK and
we think that the picture we paint is disturbing.

Rolling back the frontiers of local government

A major and highly respected study of the relations between central
and local government, commissioned by the Joseph Rowntree
Foundation, came to the following conclusion:

> We believe that there is undue stress in the relations between
> central and local government in the United Kingdom: that this
> goes beyond the disagreement which is natural between organs of
> government which have different purposes, and causes relations
> which are not as constructive as those found in other countries:
> and that the stress, if it continues, will gravely weaken local
> government, making it a service which is unattractive to men and
> women of goodwill. (Carter and John, 1992, p. 2)

The language in *A New Accord* is diplomatic but the thrust of the
argument is crystal clear – the relations between central and local
government have deteriorated to an unacceptable degree and local
government is on the brink of being completely undermined. The
reasons for the deterioration are largely, but not entirely, the fault of
central government. We would highlight four main failings in the
approach that central government has adopted towards local
government in the years since 1979.

First, there can now be very few dispassionate observers who
would attempt to defend the Conservative government's track
record on local government finance. There are three main flaws in
the government's policy.

1.   The the scale of the cuts in central government financial
     support to local government has been breathtaking. To return
     to the 1980–1 level of funding, central government would need
     to make a massive increase in revenue support grant (by

around 50 per cent). Because of the complete failure to fund local government properly, many councils have been forced to make deep cuts in services. The fact that this is largely the fault of central and not local government is usually missed in media coverage of local decisions on spending cuts.

2.   With the passing of the Rates Act in 1984, the government took the power to limit the rate levels of individual local authorities regardless of the wishes of local voters – a process known as 'rate capping'. This was an astonishing centralisation of power which Whitehall has retained ever since – rate capping was followed by poll tax capping in 1988 which, in turn, has been replaced by council tax capping. By stopping local voters from setting their own local tax levels, the Conservative government has made a mockery of local democracy. Visitors from other Western democracies, when they learn of the capping arrangements, gasp in disbelief.

3.   The government has constantly tampered with the financial regime within which local authorities are expected to operate. Ill-thought-out interventions, switches in revenue and capital controls, and erratic changes in direction have destabilised the system. Intelligent expenditure-based planning in local government is now impossible and as a consequence public confidence in local government's ability to deliver has been weakened.

A second major problem with the government's approach is that it has tried to do too much too fast. More than fifty Acts of Parliament have diminished the powers of local authorities in the period since 1979. Some of this legislation has imposed detailed requirements on particular services – for example, in the fields of housing, education and community care. Other acts have set down detailed requirements in relation to the process of planning and decision-making to be used by local councils – for example, the Local Government and Housing Act 1989. Yet others have sought to introduce and extend the process of compulsory competitive tendering. The volume, penetration and diversity of central government interventions has been startling and has forced local government into a largely reactive mode.

Even if these changes could be justified, which we would strongly challenge, a third drawback is that many of the changes have been designed to reduce local discretion. Shortly after the 1979 election, the government announced its 'determination to reduce substantially the number of bureaucratic controls over local government activities' (Department of the Environment, 1979, p. 1). Michael Heseltine, then Environment Secretary, talked enthusiastically about the need for a 'bonfire of central controls'. Given the actual behaviour of central government in subsequent years, these claims about Whitehall's desire to remove or relax controls on local government now appear far-fetched, if not downright misleading. In practice, local government has been subjected to an increasing number of controls, ranging from the minute specification of what gets taught in the classroom to the intricacies of voting arrangements for certain kinds of council committees. The extension of detailed controls has been driven by a 'Whitehall knows best' attitude which has caused a great deal of resentment in local government.

The fourth retrograde dimension of the government's strategy has been its drive to by-pass and marginalise local government. More and more functions are being taken away from local councils. Take, for example, education – higher education has been hived off to independent corporations and further education is going the same way; schools are being offered financial incentives to opt out of local control and become nationally-financed, independent 'school boards'; City technology colleges, supported by central funds, are being set up to compete with local authority secondary schools; and the curriculum and examination systems are now to a large extent centrally prescribed. In the words of the Rowntree study: 'These changes naturally convey the impression that a committee of local councillors is no longer seen as an appropriate forum for major decisions in education' (Carter and John, 1992, p. 17). For a variety of reasons, central government has sought to by-pass local authorities and wherever possible give powers to non-elected agencies. The result has been a rapid expansion in the number of quasi-governmental organisations that carry responsibility for aspects of local public policy and service provision. Examples include the Training and Enterprise Councils (TECs), Urban Development Corporations (UDCs) and the joint boards set up in 1986 in Greater London and the metropolitan counties to run important services such as public transport, the fire services and police.

Stewart has written graphically about the emergence of a new magistracy in the sense that a non-elected élite is assuming responsibility for a large part of local governance:

> They are found on the boards of health authorities and hospital trusts, Training and Enterprise Councils, the Board of Governors of grant-maintained schools, the governing bodies of colleges of further education and Housing Action Trusts. (Stewart, 1992, p. 7)

He points out that there is no possibility that those appointed can be regarded as locally accountable. The membership of these bodies is largely unknown locally and they are not necessarily subject to the same requirements for open meetings, access to information and external scrutiny that local authorities are subject to. On this analysis, public policy-making at local level seems to be increasingly being taken over by a non-elected, secretive élite of the kind that ran Britain in the 1880s.

Taken together, the cumulative impact of these four features of central government policy is alarming. Leading figures in all the political parties, including some prominent Conservative council leaders, are becoming increasingly concerned that the identity and character of local government as an entity is being irreparably damaged. Fortunately, these four trends can all be reversed.

Re-empowering local government

If local accountability is to be strengthened, the proportion of local authority revenue derived from local taxation needs to be much higher. This implies widening the tax base of local authorities, a feature common in other countries, and, according to the Rowntree study referred to earlier, points to the need for a local income tax. Such an argument finds support in the excellent report prepared by the Layfield Committee on local government finance. This concluded that, if the main responsibility for the level and pattern of expenditure on local services is to be placed on local authorities, they will need to be able to levy a local income tax (Layfield Committee, 1976). There may be some technical problems, but we believe that these can be overcome and we agree with the Rowntree study which concluded that local income tax is by far the most suitable means of restoring financial freedom to local authorities (Carter and John, 1992).

This change would not necessarily mean higher taxes. The introduction of a local income tax would reduce the need for central taxation because central government would provide less in the way of revenue support to local authorities. Naturally, the power of Whitehall to cap local tax levels would be removed as this severely impairs local accountability. The elected councillors must be made fully responsible to their electors for the level of tax set. Finally, reasonably stable arrangements need to be introduced for distributing central government revenue grant support to local government and for handling capital spending by local authorities. The obstacles to introducing these changes in the financial regime are, at root, political rather than technical.

The government has pressed for the use of the principle of subsidiarity in its dealings with the European Community (EC), arguing rightly that political decisions should only be taken at a higher level of government when 'absolutely necessary'. This eminently sound principle is suitable for central–local relations within the EC and we see no reason why it should not also be applied to central–local relations within the UK. It follows that all decisions affecting localities that are taken in Whitehall, including its regional offices, should come under scrutiny. The relevant central government departments should be required to demonstrate why it is 'absolutely necessary' to take particular decisions at central government level. If this necessity could not be demonstrated, the power and responsibility would be switched to local government. Over a period of years the application of the principle of subsidiarity, coupled with the notion that locally elected assemblies (not secretive, appointed élites) should be responsible for local policy-making, would lead to a massive democratisation of public and quasi-public services. Service in these powerful and influential local authorities would, to use the words of the Rowntree study, become extremely attractive to women and men of goodwill because all would recognise the value and importance of the local government role.

As part of the redefinition of the frontiers of local government, local authorities should be granted a general power of competence to provide services and to carry out any function not specifically

258 Beyond Decentralisation

prohibited by law. Such a shift would do away with all the present-day restrictions based on the principle of *ultra vires* and would free the local authority to respond without hindrance to the diverse problems and needs of its area. In advocating this vision for local government, we are reinforcing a view put forward some years ago:

> What is being put forward is a very different conception of a local authority from that of a local authority as a provider of a collection of services congregated together by historical accident or for administrative convenience. It is the conception of a local authority with a wide ranging responsibility and concern for the social, economic and physical well-being of its area and for those who live and work within it. (Jones and Stewart, 1983, p. 149)

Later in the chapter we extend this vision by examining new possibilities for enlarging the public sphere and strengthening local democracy outside the state. First, however, we need to examine the immediate outlook for local government.

Assessing the Conservative proposals for local government

In December 1990, a few weeks after John Major became prime minister, the government announced its intention to put the structure and operation of local government under review. The review was to be led by Michael Heseltine who, having failed to win the Conservative Party leadership contest, was granted a second spell as Secretary of State for the Environment. While the top priority was to sort out the poll tax mess, the review was to be much more wide-ranging. During 1991 the government published three consultation papers as part of the review – on a new tax for local government; on the structure of local government; and on internal management (Department of the Environment, 1991a; 1991b; 1991c). While the first of these related directly to England, Scotland and Wales, different versions of the other two papers were published by the Scottish Office and the Welsh Office. There are some interesting differences between the approach adopted towards local government reorganisation in Wales when compared to England and we have examined these elsewhere (Hambleton and Mills, 1993); Scotland is different again. However, for the purposes of this discussion, we focus on the Department of the Environment proposals for England.

The finance paper outlined proposals to replace the poll tax with a new 'council tax' (Department of the Environment, 1991a). This tax, which comprises a personal and a property element, was rushed into law in the shape of the Local Government Finance Act 1992. This received the Royal Assent on 6 March, five weeks before the General Election. The poll tax was such a vote loser it was essential for the Conservatives to be able to claim they had got rid of it almost regardless of the merits of the replacement tax. The council tax, which is a tax on buildings and not people, only applies to domestic property.

The poll tax was so misguided that, to say that the council tax is an improvement, is far from a ringing endorsement. It ought, for example, to be simpler to collect. However, the council tax fails the crucial test of being related to ability to pay. The features of the present financial system, which we criticised earlier, are all left intact. Business rates remain nationally controlled and the Secretary of State's powers to cap local authority budgets are continued. The council tax manifestly does not strengthen local accountability. The poll tax position, whereby only 15 per cent of local spending in England, 11 per cent in Scotland and 8 per cent in Wales was financed through local taxation, is also continued. Once again the opportunity to develop a progressive basis for the financing of local government has been missed.

If we now turn to the structural proposals, the outlook is also unsettling. In 1969 the Royal Commission on Local Government in England, chaired by Lord Redcliffe-Maud, proposed the creation of unitary local authorities for the whole of the country except for the very large conurbations. The Conservative government, led by Edward Heath, rejected this advice and, through the Local Government Act 1972, saddled the country with the unsatisfactory two-tier system of counties and districts which was to last for over twenty years. In 1991, the government recognised that it would clarify lines of accountability and strengthen local government if citizens could identify one local authority which would take the lead in securing services in their area. It therefore came out broadly in favour of the creation of a single tier of unitary authorities in most, if not all, parts of the country. It anticipated that the new authorities would be smaller than the existing shire counties and it hoped that the structure of local government would be related more closely to communities with which people identify (Department of the Environment, 1991b).

What are the main criticisms of the restructuring proposals? First, it is clear that the structural changes are being taken forward in isolation from financial and other changes. A thorough reappraisal of the role, function and financing of local government is needed before sensible conclusions on structure can be arrived at. Second, the process is being pushed along very quickly in certain parts of the country – for example, in Wales and in the 'first tranche' areas of England, (Avon, Gloucestershire, Somerset; Cleveland, Durham; Derbyshire – Humberside, Lincolnshire, North Yorkshire; Isle of Wight). This is putting unnecessary strain on the governmental system. Third, the approach has provoked an almighty battle between the counties and districts as each camp fights for survival. Cynics argue that the government's strategy has been to ignite a series of squabbles between counties and districts so that many of those involved in local government will be distracted from much more important strategic issues – such as the increasing centralisation of power in Whitehall and the new opportunities opening up for local government in the emerging 'Europe of regions'. Fourth, the proposals seem to be designed to reduce the number of local councillors in UK local government. This is certainly the case in Wales and there is great concern that the changes will weaken the representative structure of local government (Rao, 1993).

Arguably of equal importance to the changes in finance and geographical structure are the emerging proposals for the internal management of local authorities. The consultation paper discusses present arrangements and outlines several options for the future, some of which owe a good deal to the influence of American local government experience – with city managers, the commission form of government, and the mayor-council model – and we explore the transatlantic comparison further elsewhere (Hambleton, 1993).

A key weakness of the consultation paper is that while it is strong on ideas for improving executive action in local government, it is very weak on proposals for strengthening representative and participatory democracy at local level. The paper concentrates almost exclusively on ways of creating a powerful executive. Despite the trumpeting of the Citizen's Charter in the previous twelve months, the consultation paper says nothing about new ways of opening up local government decision-making to create new opportunities for citizen involvement.

The paper makes great play of the importance of developing the enabling role of local government. The government takes the view that the local authorities' role in the provision of services should be to assess the needs of their areas, plan the provision of services and ensure the delivery of those services. Councils, the government believes, should be looking to contract-out work to whoever can deliver services most efficiently and effectively, thus enabling the authority to be more responsive to the wishes of their electorate. Earlier in this chapter we argued that local authorities need to develop an orchestrating role in relation to other public, private, voluntary and community organisations in their area and we explore this theme further below. We are not against developing the enabling role of local councils: on the contrary, we are in favour of it. The crucial question, however, is who is to be enabled to do what?

Before leaving this discussion of the government's management proposals, we would wish to highlight the neglect in the consultation paper of decentralisation. As we have argued elsewhere, the government's proposals envisage a highly centralised form of management (Hambleton and Warburton, 1991a; 1991b). In essence, the proposed model assumes that the centre holds expertise in contract specification and monitoring, and that responsiveness to the consumer is assured by means of competition. However, for many services, the needs and wishes of consumers will vary significantly from area to area. Experience has shown that it is difficult for a centralised bureaucracy to respond to the diversity of such needs, so how can a centralised bureaucracy responsible for contract specifications reflect such diversity? A second major weakness is that, as envisaged by the government, the contract model presumes the needs of the service can be fully specified before the contract is let and will remain the same for the duration of the contract. This denies opportunities for learning and development during the life of the contract.

In contrast to this, we would advocate a model of local government where the role of the centre is to give strategic direction and encourage the creation of a shared culture within all organisations responsible for delivering services that local govern- ment funds. This model recognises that it is unsound to stipulate from the centre precisely how service delivery is to be specified. It is driven by the belief that the periphery of the organisation – the front line – is closer to the customer and citizen and that it is here that invaluable local learning takes place. It is based on a belief that interorganisational and intraorganisational transactions should be based upon trust and the principle of 'social exchange' rather than the distrust which is inherent in 'economic exchange' (Fox, 1974). It is a model of local government which combines strong, confident, strategic guidance with radically decentralised local management. In this model the centre of the organisation is less concerned with specifying courses of action than with developing a role as an initiator, facilitator and goad to local learning:

> The opportunity for learning is primarily in discovered systems at the periphery, not in the nexus of official policies at the centre. Central's role is to detect significant shifts at the periphery, to pay explicit attention to the emergence of ideas in good currency, and to derive themes of policy by induction. The movement of learning is as much from periphery to periphery, or from periphery to centre, as from centre to periphery. (Schon, 1971, p. 177)

In the remainder of this chapter, we move the discussion beyond the role of the town hall. So far we have outlined the case for restructuring the state so that there is a radical decentralisation of power from central to local government and we have offered a critique of central government's proposals for the reform of local government. But a strengthened local government operating a decentralised form of management is only part of our vision for a reinvigorated local democracy.

Varieties of democracy

What we have in mind, is a set of public institutions which contribute to, and are accountable to, a vibrant democratic civil society which surrounds them. Existing within a milieu of decentralised and autonomous provider institutions, such a local society would inevitably develop forms of political organisation which were more diverse in nature than existing ones. Simultaneously, new forms of democratic accountability would have to be developed to regulate the new organisations and the relationships between them.

Some of these would exist within the familiar realm of representation, but increasingly they would need to move down a path towards greater popular participation. We envisage a spectrum where there are three main categories of democracy: representation, participation and direct democracy. Each would be appropriate to different situations, yet each would need to be modified from its present form.

The most familiar of all these forms is, of course, representation. In earlier chapters we explored some of the limitations of representative democracy. The strength of the representative system at the local level is that it is the only mechanism we have devised so far for giving formal expression to the common good. But, in Britain at least, representative democracy at both national and local levels seems tired, if not worn out. In earlier chapters we outlined some ways in which local representative democracy can be extended and rejuvenated. The main limitations of representative systems lie in their mediated and discontinuous nature. The very term 'representation' illustrates the manner by which voice is not directly expressed, rather the perceived needs of a constituency are re-presented in another time and another place by its representative. In other words, a gap in space and time is inherent between the original need or aspiration on the one hand and its representation on the other. This gap is, in many respects, analogous to that which operates within the market between the myriad disaggregated individual choices and the resulting market signal. Such time and space gaps constitute a form of 'resistance' within the dynamic system which inevitably leads to inefficiency within the signalling process. Within representative systems this gap provides the space inside which many well-known elements of democratic failure occur – for example, problems of accountability, the unrepresentativeness of representatives in terms of class, gender or race, and so on.

Second, representative forms are inherently discontinuous. Hence the classic anarchist joke: a card is held up with ten crosses on it, your lifetime share of democracy! While a number of methods have been devised to overcome this discontinuity effect: for example, the introduction of referenda to supplement electoral democracy, holding annual elections, activist involvement in local political

264

The further up you go the more the conduct of democracy is left to a few, and the more the majority are reduced to the role of spectators: consumers of a politics produced by others.

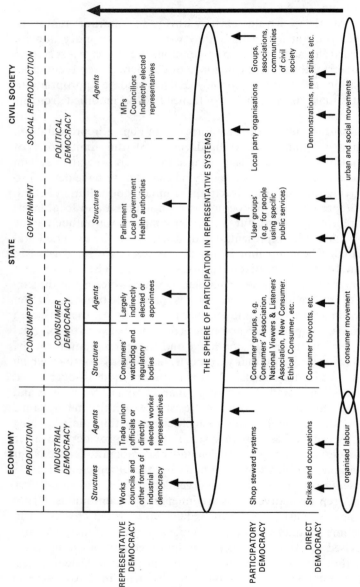

FIGURE 10.1 Varieties of democracy

parties – the basic tendency for a disjuncture to occur between representatives and the represented – expressed long ago by Michels (1959) through his concept of 'the iron law of oligarchy' – appears to be a recurring failure of this system.

Representation is not, however, the only form of democracy that exists in practice. Consider Figure 10.1. In each sphere we can discern a different type of democratic relationship. In the sphere of production (that is, industrial democracy), representative systems are expressed through the election of trade union officials, representatives on works councils and so on who are engaged in formal bargaining procedures with employers. However, this system is typically supplemented by a more directly participatory shop steward system made up of people who are still involved in the job and who are far more accountable to the shop floor. Finally, there is the level of direct democracy – for example, the strike committee – which often consists of every one of the workers making decisions in open meetings, through a show of hands and so on.

In the sphere of consumption, representative bodies of various kinds act as watchdogs on behalf of the consumer. Some of these consumer protection functions are located in local government, others in various appointed quangos (for example, those that are supposed to represent the interests of the consumer in the privatised public utilities including gas, electricity and water). The consumer's voice is also given expression through a variety of consumer organisations such as the Consumers' Association and the National Consumer Council. Such organisations participate actively in the policy process. At the level of direct democracy we are all familiar with the power of consumer boycotts which, interestingly are becoming more widely used – for example, as a mechanism to stop nationwide supermarket chains from building unwanted retail stores.

Similar patterns can be observed within the sphere of local political democracy. Representation is symbolised by the Member of Parliament or councillor, participatory democracy is symbolised by the activities of the countless groups and communities within the local civil society, and direct democracy finds expression in demonstrations, rent-strikes, mass campaigns of poll tax non-payment, and so on.

It is important to distinguish between participatory democracy as a form of self-government – in which local clubs, associations, groups and federations run their own organisations and arrange activities or provide services for their own members – and the participation of such organisations within local government or other public institutions. Many aspects of participatory democracy are proto-political because the majority of activities of, for example, a community association or ramblers club, do not force participants to confront questions of economic or political power. When such questions are raised then such groups may respond by exerting pressure through the representative system, or through direct action, or both. Direct democracy abolishes the gap between the constituency and its representation – the constituency makes its presence felt through action immediately. For this reason, direct democracy tends to be transitory. It also tends to set itself up in opposition to the formal representative mechanisms above. The examples of 'unofficial strikes' and the diverging positions of elected councils and community movements on the poll tax being stark examples of this polarity. Direct democracy does not by definition have to be transitory, however: a campaign or a movement may operate on the basis of plebiscitary democracy for a considerable period of time, as often occurs with factory or student occupations. Indeed the whole city of Barcelona was run on this basis for a time during the Spanish Civil War.

Consuming politics?

Figure 10.1 also indicates another distinction between the three forms of democracy. Within representative systems the conduct of democracy is performed by 'the few' and the danger is that 'the many' are reduced to the status of spectators, consumers of a politics enacted by others. As we explained in Chapter 6, the distinction between the production of politics and the consumption of politics seems to us to be essential. The culture of our society is increasingly becoming a 'choose or exit' one, built, according to Jean Baudrillard, upon the conviction that 'I consume, therefore I am'.

The danger is that when groups or communities choose to participate in representative government, their participation will amount to no more than the ability either to choose between limited options or to reject the options presented to them. They may very rarely be in a position to create. In essence, they are excluded from the production of politics. Even some radical visions of a participatory democracy have tended to be bounded by the same parameters. For example, the advocacy of frequent local referenda commodifies politics to an even greater extent than traditional representation. Here extremely complicated political issues are packaged into a single statement for the consumer to agree or disagree with. This observation by no means undermines the validity of referenda, but it does serve to remind us that it is still only addressing the *consumption* as opposed to the *production* of politics. Other commentators on democracy, such as McLean (1986), have speculated on a future for new technology in which citizens express opinions through interactive television screens – a technology which would actually be feasible at the present time for most modern industrial countries. Such analyses have failed to grasp the importance of participation in the production of politics, what Warren *et al.* (1992) call 'operational citizenship', the right to contribute to the production of policies and the shaping of choices.

One of the key problems of local government is that it tends to provide services that most people are not involved in making decisions about; therefore people remain uninterested. The problem is compounded when local government defines itself as a service provider, not as a centre of government. Thus, some local authorities that have established neighbourhood forums or area committees tend to construe them as a place to discuss council services, yet these form only a fraction of those which are provided within the wider community. The role of the state should be to fill gaps in community provision and to ensure equity, not to substitute itself for relationships which occur naturally within communities.

Let us take the example of community care. There are far more people looking after elderly relatives at home than there are residential care workers or community nurses. And there are more people looking after children at home than there are crèche workers or even teachers. These 'home carers' are not only affected (a passive relationship) by issues relating to care provision, they are involved (an active relationship) in them, and have a huge base of knowledge about the issues – a million and one ideas, thoughts, fears and aspirations – but it is not possible to tap them through a state consultation process, and it is not likely that they will have the time or inclination to discuss council services in official forums unless council services are put into the wider context of care. For example, if voluntary carers were brought together in a self-help forum, while they would probably start talking about practical things like developing shared care and they might broaden their discussion into political issues such as why women do not get paid for working in the home, it is also inevitable that they would talk about the needs that they could not meet themselves, what they want from the state and what they want from the community. This surely would provide the starting point for an analysis of which services a local authority should provide and how to provide them.

The largest, most lively and participative local meetings we have attended have been thematically based. They have discussed a particular traffic plan, play facilities in a neighbourhood, or racism on a particular estate. The state and other bureaucratic institutions are notoriously bad at creating relationships with transitional groups – groups without constitutions, groups which appear fluid, spontaneous and uncontrollable. Yet it is often these groups which are the most dynamic, providing the key triggers for change. When people say to politicians that what they are doing has no relationship to everyday life, politicians often fail to understand. The reason for this is because they often perceive state provision as being the centre of the local universe, whereas the people see it as the periphery.

In Chapter 6 we outlined a model of participation and power. In our view, participation will be meaningless and unsustainable without devolved control over the production of services and the creation of policies, and devolved control will be dangerous if it is not accompanied by substantially extended participation. It is often argued that if participatory systems of democracy were introduced they would be at the expense of liberty and justice – 'if it were left up to the people they would bring back hanging'. But if there is a difference between the 'representative' and the 'general population' it is only that the representative has been exposed to more information, has more knowledge of the process of government, and has participated in the process of decision-making. This implies that if more people are involved in decision-making then more of the decisions they make will reflect values of equity and liberty as well as democracy. In short, we do not need to be protected from ourselves.

Empowering who?

Unfortunately, the experiments with local democracy in the 1970s and 1980s have often mirrored 'development' interventions in the Third World. They have both tended to be symbolised by:

- Development workers offering (and sometimes imposing) 'wisdom/expertise' from outside the culture of the host society.
- The creation of structures and ways of organising which mirror those of the 'developed' country or organisation.
- The professionalising of the process of development – that is, the use of professionals to involve those who, it is believed, need to be involved, thereby often depoliticising a process which should be profoundly political.

The critical question in terms of the relationship between government and civil society is 'Who empowers whom'? This begs a further question: 'Where does power lie?' Surely one of the most important lessons for local government over the past decade is that real power does not lie within it any longer. As we explained earlier in this chapter, successive legislation has weakened local authorities dramatically. We have argued in other forums (Burns, 1992, Hoggett and Burns, 1991) that the defence against the poll tax by local communities in Anti-Poll Tax Unions probably prevented local government from being totally decimated. Ironically, the local state was empowered by a vibrant civil society to which it stood in active opposition.

It is time to rethink the old notion of the state empowering the people. The ideal is a symbiotic process in which they empower each other. But if there is a choice, it is probably more important to think of the people empowering, controlling and giving legitimation to the state, and not the other way around. This brings us full circle. If a non-market-centred vision of public services is to be developed then in the long run the quality of service will hinge upon the quality of local democracy – specifically upon the empowerment of service users and organised groups and communities. A fundamental problem with the exit strategy is that it reduces the social body to an aggregation of atomised individuals within which common and conflicting interests obtain no means of expression. This reduces the local polity to an impoverished rump.

As we noted at the beginning of this chapter, local government can make a vital contribution to local democracy but it should not be confused with it. But what constitutes high-quality local democracy? Inevitably, judgements here will reflect an individual's own values. For our part we see the key lying in the existence of an informed, organised and confident citizenry engaged within a public sphere where no voices are excluded. Crucially, it will provide a space in which differences can be respected and conflicts worked through, a space in which both the common good and particular interests can find expression and where the resulting tension can lead to creative development rather than to disintegration and destructive attack. In a word, a space through which differentiated and increasingly fragmented communities might engage in dialogue and co-operation – 'united they stand, divided they fall'.

We now need to face two important questions which stand as potential obstacles before such a democratic project. Is such a strategy compatible with the bureaucratic institutional form? Also, is it compatible with the monopolisation of public service provision by state institutions? Our answer to each of these questions is 'no'. However, we also believe that the conditions now exist for overcoming each of these limitations to democratic innovation. Let us take the issue of bureaucracy first.

Democracy without bureaucracy

If an essential function of local government is to contribute to the quality of local democracy, then the paradox is that, when one considers traditional forms of local government in the UK, a system less conducive to popular participation would have been difficult to design. Huge departmental structures, remote and complex political decision making procedures, obscure professional and bureaucratic gobbledegook, unclear lines of responsibility and patterns of accountability, and so on. For most service users or members of local communities, local government seems quite impenetrable. But perhaps the conditions for overcoming bureaucracy now exist.

In Chapters 1, 2, 4 and 6 we have suggested that the development of local authority decentralisation strategies can be seen as being connected to wider movements of social change and transformation.

During the past decade there has been a great deal of talk about the development of what are often referred to as 'post-Fordist' approaches to the organisation of production. A critical factor here appears to be the innovations in information technology which have permitted the development of entirely new forms of organisational control. This has had a profound effect upon the nature of complex organisations. Specifically, the new forms of organisation at last provide the possibility for developing, to use Schumacher's phrase (1974), simple ways of managing complex tasks. In other words, size and complexity need no longer mean bureaucracy.

It is important to understand that there is no single model of post-bureaucratic organisation of production emerging; rather, as several theorists (Clegg, 1990; Leborgne and Lipietz, 1987; Lane, 1988) have suggested, we need to think of a new paradigm or template from which a variety of novel choices become possible. In an earlier paper, Hoggett (1990a) suggested that the basic character of this paradigm consisted of 'the progressive decentralisation of production under conditions of rising flexibility and centralised strategic control'. Traditional forms of 'control through hierarchy' within vertically integrated firms (the old Ford Michigan plant is often cited as the exemplar of vertical integration – the entire manufacturing process, from conversion of raw materials to assembly of finished product was done on the one site and, of course, within the same firm) appear to be giving way to forms of contractual control within horizontally integrated systems – for example, networks or 'family groups' of firms, subcontracting or collaborating with each other, often within a market dominated by a single 'core' firm.

In other words, the bureaucratic pyramid is being replaced by the post-bureaucratic federation (Handy, 1990) or solar system – a model often referred to as the core–periphery model (Clegg, 1990; Wood, 1989). In the private sector, the collapse of the pyramid corresponds to processes of both internal devolution and external decentralisation (that is, contracting-out). Where production remains organised within the boundaries of the firm the latter becomes reconstituted into a much flatter form with strong internal devolution. The divisions, units and teams exercise their greater autonomy within a framework of core values and explicit performance targets emanating from the centre. In their by now infamous book Peters and Waterman (1982) describe such organisational forms as 'tight/loose'.

What does this mean for local government? Essentially, it means that the conditions now exist for entirely new forms of service organisation which allow both for much greater degrees of operational freedom and for centralised strategic control. The key question is how these conditions are shaped by political choices and strategies, for it is the struggle around these issues which will decide the relative weight given to internal as opposed to external decentralisation, where strategic command is to be (in local or central government) and so on. Our vision of a reformed public service seeks to replace complex bureaucracies with far more internally devolved structures. Within the context of a local authority, internal devolution gives service managers and staff the power to deliver and simultaneously frees the centre from absorption in administrative detail so that it has the time and space to get on with its strategic function – policy development, priority setting, and so on. In place of departmental hierarchies a new kind of organisation emerges in which there is a strong but lean centre with an outer ring of devolved service delivery units.

In contemporary jargon such units function as 'cost and performance centres' – locality teams in the social services, neighbourhood or estate-based housing teams, libraries, schools, multi-function neighbourhood offices, and so on. Because control over resources has been devolved, the basis now exists for real accountability both to the centre and to the devolved service unit's users and the surrounding community. So long as the organisation of local government was built upon the foundation of large, complex and hierarchical departments there was no way in which they could be adequately opened up to voices from below. It would always be a tiny minority of (usually the most articulate) tenants, library users, parents of pre-school children or local residents who were motivated to become interested in the machinations of large service organisations with multimillion-pound budgets. People participate in public life primarily on the basis of their immediate interests and experiences – what is happening on my estate, in my neighbourhood, in my school, in my local library or sports centre. It is only from this basis – of immediate need or interest – that involvement in wider issues concerning the common interest can be built. On the whole, it is only through engaging locally that people begin to think globally – the movement is almost always from the particular to the general, from the individual or group to the collectivity.

A pluralistic public sphere

We have noted that the new forms of organisational control permit a much greater degree of external decentralisation. Powerful organisations are learning that to control something you no longer have to own it yourself, that it is possible to exert control over networks of less powerful organisations and get the same job done but in a more flexible and more economical manner. Organisations are beginning to realise that they derive their power not from their size but from other sources – this occurs in particular where an organisation dominates the market for a specific good or service. Such dominance gives core organisations tremendous leverage over the interorganisational networks which revolve around them. We can see how the boundary between an organisation which is radically devolved internally and one which commands an external interorganisational network is a fine one indeed. Within each case a core–periphery model has been adopted; the only difference concerns whether the devolved production units are inside or outside the boundaries of the firm. Indeed, given current trends, such conventional models of organisational boundaries are becoming obsolete. For example, it is now quite possible for 'internal trading' to occur within internally-devolved organisations, and many support services, such as personnel and information technology, are operating on this basis within both private and public sectors. Moreover, within some branches and regions of the private sector, core organisations are engaged in forms of detailed collaboration and resource transfer, including technical know-how, with external partners and suppliers (Aoki, 1987).

What does this mean for the public sector? Such new forms of organisational control can be harnessed to a range of political strategies. Successive Conservative governments have promoted decentralisation primarily as a means of undermining the public sphere by breaking up public services and shifting more and more production out to unaccountable private or quasi-public organisations. But our objection is not to the transfer of activities from the state to non-statutory organisations as such. As we shall demonstrate later, it is entirely possible to reduce the size of the state sector while enlarging and strengthening the public sphere. Our vision of the public sphere is one in which a plurality of forms of *democratic* public provision can exist alongside a state which has realised that its power is not dependent upon its size.

In other words, so far we have considered ways of de-bureaucratising local government. But it is possible and necessary to go further than this. A local authority, such as Islington, which was internally highly decentralised and made a real attempt to develop proper forms of democratic accountability and community involvement still constitutes a form of state monopoly, albeit a responsive and democratic one.

We choose our words carefully here – for too long the sphere of the public has been confused with and reduced to the sphere of the state. But what do we mean by 'public'? First, we must understand that while all life is social, concerning patterns of interdependence, only part of it is public. The public sphere stands between the two contrasting elements of the private sphere – the private sphere of personal life on the one hand, and the sphere of private institutions (that is, 'the private sector') on the other. Private institutions operate within the market and while markets may be regulated by the government the institutions themselves cannot be made democratically accountable either to elected representatives of the public at large or to the users of the goods and services that they provide. A supermarket chain which was accountable either to an elected authority or to local committees made up of customers and representatives of local communities is perfectly conceivable but this would be incompatible with the private ownership form as we know it. In Britain the Co-operative Retail Society had its origins in just such a notion of a consumer co-operative but today stands in relation to this inspiration in a dull and bureaucratised form. Such a membership organisation is quite different from a private company whose ownership is restricted to individual or institutional share-holders whose primary interest is to receive a return on their capital. Our position therefore is this – only those organisations which have the potential to be democratically accountable either to the public at large, or to their own members, or to those that use, benefit from or are affected by them, shall be deemed as organisations of the public sphere.

Given this definition it is important to understand that the institutions of the welfare state which comprise much of what we call 'the public sector' are just one part of the public sphere; indeed, they express the idea of 'the public' in its most abstract sense as including everyone and therefore, in a concrete and immediate sense, no one. For example, who owns a social services department or a local authority library? No answer can be given, which directs us towards a living and concretely identifiable entity. 'The public' here, then, exists as a kind of legal abstraction, as a kind of embodiment of the general interest. But the public sphere also includes a huge range of other organisations. We have found it helpful to distinguish three categories: i) membership organisations; ii) voluntary groups; and iii) quasi-public institutions.

Consider an allotments society, for example. Its membership will typically be drawn from allotment holders who share a particular site and who are therefore in a number of ways dependent upon one another. The fact that most membership organisations are built around shared interests or identities does not mean that they have to be exclusive. For example, an independent 'free' school is only exclusive if it denies membership to certain categories of children (for example, the poor) who might otherwise use it. Such organisations therefore belong to their membership in a tangible and concrete way – tenants associations, sports and cultural clubs, mutual aid and self-help organisations, co-operatives, community associations, the cultural associations of majority and minority ethnic groups, trade unions, local or national campaign organisations, and so on. The striking point about all these organisations is that, while they sometimes provide a means for political participation, they are nearly always also engaged in providing services or running activities for their own membership. Such organisations, along with the more informal end of the voluntary sector, constitute the bedrock of civil society and participatory democracy.

Membership organisations can be distinguished from another category of organisation in the public sphere – the informal voluntary organisation. We distinguish such organisations, which operate on the basis of freely-given labour by volunteers, from formal 'voluntary' organisations. The distinction is not a black-and-white one but there is a huge difference between, say, a local group based around a number of volunteers who organise swimming and other leisure activities for children with severe physical disabilities, and a non-statutory project receiving considerable public funding, employing professional workers and whose only volunteers are those who give their time to act on the project's management committee.

This latter type of organisation corresponds to a third category – the quasi-public institution. These organisations are often referred to as non-profit organisations and, following Salamon and Abramson (1982), we can characterise such organisations as 'private in structure' but 'public in purpose'. The most obvious British examples are housing associations and formal 'voluntary' organisations. We would prefer to use the term 'quasi-public' to categorise such organisations. Like welfare institutions, they usually express the public interest in an abstract form. In a sense they hold the interests of the public 'in trust'. Because they are, or have been, in receipt of public monies and because they have to exercise those legal responsibilities entailed by the employment contract they are more formalised organisations. In many respects they also resemble public institutions in terms of the functions that they perform – that is, providing services to users – the difference being that they exist outside the state's organisational boundaries.

They are not, however, collective in nature; in other words, they do not belong to their members. Nor are they accountable to elected representatives of the public. Frequently they are directed by a management body which approximates to an oligarchical clique which is not democratically accountable to either the users of the service or the broader 'general interest'. However, such organisations may have originated from an informal voluntary or membership organisation and for this reason may remain culturally closer to the civil society from which they sprang than, say, state organisations. Because they are not enclosed within larger public bureaucracies many retain an experimental or innovative focus or a lack of standardisation, and hence provide a valuable diversity.

In summary, the public sphere contains four essentially different forms of organisation: (i) state or public institutions, (ii) membership organisations, (iii) informal voluntary groups, and (iv) quasi-public institutions, – but it should not be reduced to these forms. Such organisations constitute only a small part of a sphere of social interaction which is primarily unorganised. The spaces and sites in which people interact – for example, the street, pubs and clubs, parks and open spaces – are also part of the public sphere. Many of these spaces are themselves contested. For example, private shopping malls often discourage 'undesirables'. Meanwhile, women, elderly people and those from ethnic minorities seek to find ways of reclaiming public spaces which are denied to them because of fear of attack or harassment.

A new vision for the public sphere

We might think of the spaces in between public institutions and organisations as a kind of medium upon which they rest or within which they are immersed. Moreover, this should be understood as a kind of primary social medium, one comprising a myriad social networks through which sentiments and opinions are exchanged in a direct and unmediated fashion. Together with quasi-public institutions, state institutions can be thought of as being largely suspended above, rather than immersed in, this social medium, and even where they are in contact with this medium they often tend to be impervious to it. Accountability is strongly 'top-up': that is, upwards towards an elected or non-elected executive body. In contrast, 'bottom-down' accountability – that is, to individual users, groups and communities – is often very weak. In summary, such organisations tend to express an abstracted sense of the 'public good' and the 'general interest', a sense which is often fragile and intangible. It is therefore prone to displacement in a way whereby 'general' becomes 'state' and the 'public good' becomes a mask for the private interests of powerful producer groups and policy communities (Dunleavy, 1980).

Our alternative vision of 'the democratic community' hinges upon the notion of an extended democratic accountability of public institutions at the local level and the progressive re-empowerment of organised civil society as powers and responsibilities are reclaimed both from the public and private sectors. Such a strategy would have several components:

- *The extension of representative democracy* to those many parts of the public sector where it is absent – for example, the national health service; the social security system; the many traditional quangos such as the Countryside Commission, Health and Safety Executive, the Housing Corporation, the BBC and other public corporations, the traditional Universities; the new quangos such as Urban Development Corporations, the Training and Enterprise Councils and so on. One only has to sketch a list such as this to understand how little of the present public sector is in any real sense subject to effective forms of democratic accountability. Such a strategy would require both the development of regionally-based forms of government and a new generation of single-purpose elected bodies. Some of these functions could certainly become the responsibility of local government. For example, local government is responsible for all or part of the health service in several European countries. The extension of these representative forums would have the added advantage of reducing the burden on government ministers who, at present, have to deal with far too much detail.

- *The development of forms of bottom-down accountability* both within the institutions listed above and within local government and quasi-public institutions such as housing associations. As we outlined in our ladder of citizen empowerment in Chapter 6, this may involve the direct transfer of functions to users themselves, the transfer of delegated powers, the creation of joint management bodies for particular bodies or facilities or projects, or more limited forms of involvement and consultation. To reiterate the point we made earlier, the new forms of organisation and management now make it possible for complex tasks to be organised in simple ways. The decentralisation of production provides the necessary conditions for the practical involvement of service users in the day-to-day operation of the organisations which affect their lives.

- *The development of the democratic capacity of civil society itself.* How striking it is that many of our children are now schooled in the art of 'setting up a business' but receive little or no education in organising for democracy – how to set up a club or campaign, to work on a committee, organise a meeting, lobby public or private institutions and so on. How remarkable it is that a vibrant civil society has survived despite the way in which the dominant political parties have underfunded it, taken it for granted or mistrusted it. As Keane (1988, p. 144–5) notes, a truly democratic alternative to either statism or the market requires that such political parties abandon the false assumption that social development is necessarily decided by parties, businesses or states. Specifically, parties would need to explicitly recognise the necessity *and* limits of parties. They would be forced to acknowledge openly that within a democracy the fundamental source of energy and strategic protection lies in the non-party realm of civil society.

- The boundaries between the public and private sectors are contingent political constructions. There can be little doubt that one of the great achievements of Thatcherism was to shift this boundary decisively to the advantage of the private sector. As a consequence a whole number of social issues – transport, energy, and so on – have become commodified in an attempt to remove them from the sphere of public debate and influence. *A genuinely democratic project would seek to reverse this trend by bringing such activities fully back into the public sphere.* Some of these activities could become the responsibility of local or regional government; for others we may look towards the creation of new, single-purpose, elected authorities. In other words, we look forward to the time in which a tier of locally-elected institutions act both as the vehicle for the expansion of social ownership vis-à-vis private ownership and as the midwife for the creation of a whole new generation of democratic, sublocal forms of public provision. As we mentioned earlier the granting to local government of a 'general power of competence' would be a necessary condition for this development. However, a government committed to consumer democracy could establish a national network of locally-elected consumer councils which would combine research, advocacy and watchdog roles. Such councils would be independent of local government and would act as local regulatory bodies championing the rights of the consumer against local government, the national health service, other local public organisations and the local private sector.

Our vision for the future is therefore not one which seeks a public sphere still dominated by an extended but now accountable state. Rather, we seek one which is based upon a much greater plurality of democratic provider organisations, and specifically ones that are collectively accountable or controlled. But, if control and ownership of public services were increasingly collectivised, how could the general interest be maintained, how could particular interest groups such as tenants be deterred from pursuing their own interests to the detriment of others? Again, Keane, in a compelling discussion of

Hegel's theory of civil society, reveals the issue in question. Because the identities, passions and interests around which organised civil society forms are particularistic, because relationships within the organisations of civil society necessarily reflect the inequalities within the family, between generations, between majority and minority ethnic communities and so on, 'the exuberant development of one part of civil society may, and often does, impede or oppress its other parts . . . modern civil society is incapable of overcoming its own fragmentation and resolving its inner conflicts by itself' (Keane, 1988, p. 47).

Strong local democracy therefore requires strong local representative institutions. We have argued consistently that a new paradigm of production is presently emerging which combines extended operational decentralisation with enhanced strategic direction. Conservative governments in the UK have sought to harness such processes by concentrating strategic command within *central* government but a political party committed to a genuinely democratic philosophy could greatly empower *local* government by giving emphasis to its strategic role at the local level. This would involve reversing virtually all of the forms of governmental centralisation which have occurred in the UK in recent years that we listed at the beginning of this chapter. But the restoration of local government's strategic powers should not be confused with a restoration of its monopoly over service provision. In today's circumstances, a democratic project must be pluralistic, one which sees government as just one aspect of an extended democratic public sphere. Because local government and other aspects of the local welfare state could retain a monopoly over the funding and commissioning of services, because they would enjoy devolved strategic powers and because they would derive legitimacy from their role as the focal point for representative politics in the locality, they would have the power to orchestrate the networks of internally devolved service units and non-statutory service-providing organisations which revolve around them.

The 'general good'

As long as our thinking is trapped within the simple opposition between 'majority' and 'minority' interests, we cannot begin to imagine new forms of relationship between representation and participation. Who are 'the minorities'? A moment's reflection would suffice to suggest that the following are all at some time and in some contexts 'minorities' – elderly people, people with disabilities, children, youth, minority ethnic groups, single parents, women, the chronically ill, carers of people with mental health problems, the poor – we could go on. The point surely is that the so called 'minorities' in fact constitute the majority of the population. We are virtually all, at some point in our lives, a part of a minority – that is, part of a group which experiences discrimination and hence is denied the status of full citizenship.

In other words, 'the majority' is always a contingent political force which mobilises around a particular set of identities or interests against a particular 'other'. Far from being universalistic in nature, ' the majority' is always particularistic and sectional. It transcends particular kinds of difference only to the extent that it can constitute and recoil from a greater difference. In this sense 'the majority' gives expression to the flawed character of the civil society in which we live our everyday lives.

From this perspective, it is vital that we are able to distinguish between 'the majority' and the 'general' good. Because, in contrast to the former, the 'general good' as we have used it in this book invokes the image of a benign community, one with the capacity to contain difference without becoming divided upon itself. This provides us with the possibility of giving more meaning to the idea of a community's development. Because, alongside the notion of community development as empowerment for social action, we can place the notion of the development of a community's internal social capacity, of its capacity to contain anxiety, difference and danger.

We can also better understand the contribution that political leadership can make, both in remedying injustice and offering a notion of universality which goes beyond the majority interest. This necessitates a further refinement in the way in which we understand representation and leadership. Within democratic societies, political leaders always have a choice – either to enact their role in a manner which facilitates the development of 'the general good' or to side, opportunistically, with 'the majority' in all its forms and disguises. In other words, they can choose to contribute to the social development of civil society and participative democracy or they can choose to contribute to its disfigurement.

For the issue is not 'either state or civil society' but how to create a situation in which, as Keane puts it, 'the power of civil society and the capacity of state institutions can increase together in a positive-sum interaction' (Keane, 1988, p. 61). An adequate democratic project must centre itself upon a recognition of the need for a plurality of power bases, modes of expression and participatory forms – one in which the power of the political representative, and the potential for opportunism, both checks and is checked by the power of the 'majority community', with its potential for sectionalism and both, in turn, check and are checked by the power of 'minority communities'.

Bibliography

Aglietta, M. (1979) *A Theory of Capitalist Regulation: The US Experience* (London: New Left Books).

Anderson, B. (1983) *Imagined Communities: Reflections on the Origin of Nationalism* (London: Verso).

Aoki, M. (1987) 'Incentives to share knowledge and risk – an aspect of Japanese industrial reorganisation', in S. Hedlund (ed.) *Incentives and Economic Systems* (London: Croom Helm).

Arnstein, S. R. (1971) 'A ladder of participation in the USA', *Journal of the Royal Town Planning Institute*, April, pp. 176–82.

Ashdown, P. (1989) *Citizens' Britain* (London: Fourth Estate).

Association of Metropolitan Authorities (1989) *Community Development: The Local Authority Role* (London: Association of Metropolitan Authorities).

Aucoin, P. (1990) 'Administrative reform in public management: paradigms, principles, paradoxes and pendulums', *Governance*, vol. 2, pp. 115–37.

Audit Commission (1989) *Better Financial Management*, Management Paper 3, May (London: HMSO).

Audit Commission (1991) *Profile of Tower Hamlets 1989/90* (London: Audit Commission).

Baddeley, S. and Dawes, N. (1986) 'Service to the customer', *Local Government Policy Making*, March, pp. 7–11.

Baddeley, S. and Dawes, N. (1987) 'Information technology support for devolution', *Local Government Studies*, July/August, pp. 1–16.

Baranger, M., Baranger, W. and Mon, J. (1988) 'The infantile psychic trauma from Us to Freud: pure trauma, retroactivity and reconstructions', *International Journal of Psycho-Analysis*, vol. 69, pp. 113–28.

Barbalet, J. M. (1988) *Citizenship* (Milton Keynes: Open University Press).

Barnard, H. (1991) 'Neighbourhood environmental action', *Local Government Studies*, March/April, pp. 8–14.

Barrett, S. and Fudge, C. (eds) (1981) *Policy and Action* (London: Methuen).

Barron, J., Crawley, G. and Wood, T. (1991) *Councillors in Crisis: The Public and Private Worlds of Local Councillors* (London: Macmillan).

Beresford, P. and Croft, S. (1986) *Whose Welfare? Private Care or Public Services* (Brighton: Lewis Cohen Urban Studies Centre).

Bion, W. (1961) *Experience in Groups* (London: Tavistock).

Blake, B., Bolan, P., Burns, D. and Gaster, L. (1991) *Local Budgeting in Practice: Learning from Two Case Studies* (School for Advanced Urban Studies, University of Bristol).

Blunkett, D. and Jackson, K. (1987) *Democracy in Crisis: The Town Halls Respond* (London: Hogarth Press).

Boaden, N., Goldsmith, M., Hampton, W. and Stringer, P. (1982) *Public Participation in Local Services* (London: Longman).

Boddy, M. and Fudge, C. (eds), (1984) *Local Socialism? Labour Councils and New Left Alternatives* (London: Macmillan).

Bow Neighbourhood (1989) *Bow Action Plan: Performance Targets/ Standards 1988/89*.

Bramley, G. and Le Grand, J. (1992) *Who Uses Local Services? Striving for Equity*, Belgrave Paper 4 (London: Local Government Management Board).

Branson, N. (1979) *Poplarism, 1919–1925: George Lansbury and the Councillors Revolt* (London: Lawrence and Wishart).

Burns, D. (1984) 'The decentralisation of local authority planning', in J. Montgomery and A. Thornley (eds), *Radical Planning Initiatives* (London: Gower).

Burns, D. (1989) *Decentralisation: A Discussion Document for Trainers and Managers in Housing* (Luton: Local Government Training Board).

Burns, D. (1990a) 'Centres of excellence', *Going Local*, no. 16, p. 5 (School for Advanced Urban Studies, University of Bristol).

Burns, D. (1990b) 'Local democracy in Rochdale', Unpublished report (School for Advanced Urban Studies, University of Bristol).

Burns, D. (1991a) 'Ladders of participation', *Going Local*, no. 18, Summer (School for Advanced Urban Studies, University of Bristol).

Burns, D. (1991b) 'Learning to participate: the Quality Action Group', *Going Local*, no. 18, Summer (School for Advanced Urban Studies, University of Bristol).

Burns, D. (1992) *Poll Tax Rebellion* (London: A. K. Press/Attack International).

Burns, D. and Williams, M. (1989) *Neighbourhood Working: A New Approach to Housing Provision* (School for Advanced Urban Studies, University of Bristol).

Byrne, T. (1992) *Local Government in Britain* (London: Penguin).

Cabinet Office (1988) *Action for Cities*, March (London: HMSO).

Cain, H. and Yuval-Davies, N. (1990) 'The equal opportunities community and the anti-racist struggle', *Critical Social Policy*, vol. 29, pp. 5–26.

Carmon, N. (ed.) (1990) *Neighbourhood Policy and Programmes* (London: Macmillan).

Carter, C. and John, P. (1992) *A New Accord: Promoting Constructive Relations between Central and Local Government* (York: Joseph Rowntree Foundation).

Chanan, G. (1991) *Taken for Granted: Community Activity and the Crisis of the Voluntary Sector* (London: Community Development Foundation).

Chapman, R. (1991) 'Concepts and issues in public sector reform: the experience of the United Kingdom in the 1980s', *Public Policy and Administration*, vol. 6, no. 2, pp. 1–19.

Childs, J. (1987) 'Information technology, organisations and response to strategic challenges', Paper presented to the Eighth EGOS Colloquium, Antwerp, 22–24 July.

Clarke, M. and Stewart J. (1990) *Developing Effective Public Service Management* (Luton: Local Government Training Board).

Clarke, M. and Stewart, J. (1992) *Citizens and Local Democracy: Empowerment – A Theme for the 1990s* (Luton: Local Government Management Board).

Clegg, S. (1990) *Modern Organisations: Organisation Studies in the Modern World* (London: Sage).

Cochrane, A. (1986) 'Community politics and democracy', in D. Held and C. Pollitt (eds), *New Forms of Democracy* (London: Sage).

Cockburn, C. (1977) *The Local State: Management of Cities and People*. (London: Pluto).

Dahl, R. A. (1956) *Preface to Democratic Theory* (Chicago: University of Chicago Press).

Davis, A. *et al.* (1977) *The Management of Deprivation. Final Report of the Southwark Community Development Project* (London: Polytechnic of the South Bank).

Davis, M. (1992) *City of Quartz* (London: Verso).

de Ste. Croix, R. (1992) 'Can quality be assured in an uncertain world?', *Studies in Decentralisation and Quasi-Markets*, 10 (School for Advanced Urban Studies, University of Bristol).

Deakin, N. (1984) 'Decentralisation: panacea or blind alley?', *Local Government Policy Making*, July, pp. 17–24.

Department of the Environment (1973a) *Making Towns Better: Reports on Sunderland, Rotherham and Oldham* (London: HMSO).

Department of the Environment (1973b) *Proposals for Area Management: Liverpool Inner Area Study*, November (London: Department of the Environment).

Department of the Environment (1979) *Central Government Controls over Local Authorities*, Cmnd 7634 (London: HMSO).

Department of the Environment (1991a) *A New Tax for Local Government: A Consultation Paper*, April (London: Department of the Environment).

Department of the Environment (1991b) *The Structure of Local Government in England: A Consultation Paper*, April (London: Department of the Environment).

Department of the Environment (1991c) *The Internal Management of Local Authorities in England: A Consultation Paper*, July (London: Department of the Environment).

Department of the Environment (1993) *Community Leadership and Representation: Unlocking the Potential*, The report of the Working Party on the Internal Management of Local Authorities in England, July (London: HMSO).

Dore, R. (1983) 'Goodwill and the spirit of market capitalism', *British Journal of Sociology*, vol. 34, no. 4, pp. 459–82.

Duncan, S. and Goodwin, M. (1988) *The Local State and Uneven Development* (Cambridge: Polity).

286 *Bibliography*

Duncan, T. (1988) 'Community councils in Glasgow: the first ten years', *Going Local*, no. 9 February, pp. 17–18.

Dunleavy, P. (1980) *Urban Political Analysis* (London: Macmillan).

Durkheim, E. (1984) *The Division of Labour in Society* (De la Division du Travail Sociale) (1893), translated by W. D. Halls, with an introduction by Lewis Coser (London: Macmillan).

Eade, J. (1989) *The Politics of Community: The Bangladeshi Community in East London* (Aldershot: Gower).

Eade, J. (1990) 'Nationalism and the quest for authenticity: the Bangladeshis in Tower Hamlets', *New Community*, vol. 16, no. 4, pp. 493–503.

Elcock, H. (1982) *Local Government: Politicians, Professionals and the Public in Local Authorities* (London: Methuen).

Foucault, M. (1979) *Discipline and Punish: The Birth of the Prison* (Harmondsworth: Penguin).

Fox, A. (1974) *Beyond Contract: Work, Power and Trust Relations* (London: Faber).

Fuller, L. and Smith, V. (1991) 'Consumers' reports: management by customers in a changing economy', *Work, Employment and Society*, vol. 5, no. 1, pp. 1–16.

Gaster, L. (1991) *Quality at the Front Line* (School for Advanced Urban Studies, University of Bristol).

Gaster, L. (1992) 'Quality in service delivery', *Local Government Policy Making*, vol. 19, no. 1, July.

Goss, S. (1988) *Local Labour and Local Government* (Edinburgh University Press).

Gottdiener, M. (1987) *The Decline of Urban Politics* (London: Sage).

Gower Davies, J. (1974) *The Evangelistic Bureaucrat* (London: Tavistock).

Green, D. G. (1987) *The New Right: The Counter-revolution in Political, Economic and Social Thought* (London: Harvester Wheatsheaf).

Gutch, R. (1992) *Contracting Lessons from the US* (London: National Council of Voluntary Organisations).

Gyford, J. (1985) *The Politics of Local Socialism* (London: George Allen and Unwin).

Gyford, J. (1986) 'Diversity, sectionalism and local democracy', in *The Conduct of Local Authority Business* (Widdicombe Committee), Research Volume 4, Cmnd 9801, June (London: HMSO).

Gyford, J. (1991a) *Does Place Matter? – Locality and Local Democracy*, Belgrave Paper no. 3 (Luton: Local Government Management Board).

Gyford, J. (1991b) *Citizens, Consumers and Councils* (London: Macmillan).

Gyford, J., Leach, S. and Game, C. (1989) *The Changing Politics of Local Government* (London: Unwin Hyman).

Hadley, R. and Young, K. (1990) *Creating a Responsive Public Service* (London: Harvester Wheatsheaf).

Hain, P. (ed.) (1976) *Community Politics* (London: John Calder).

Hambleton, R. (1975) 'Preferences for policies', *Municipal Journal*, 25 July, pp. 979–83.

Hambleton, R. (1978) *Policy Planning and Local Government* (London: Hutchinson).

Hambleton, R. (1986) *Rethinking Policy Planning: A Study of Planning Systems Linking Central and Local Government* (School for Advanced Urban Studies, University of Bristol).

Hambleton, R. (1988) 'Consumerism, decentralisation and local democracy', *Public Administration*, vol. 66, Summer, pp. 125–47.

Hambleton, R. (1989) 'Room in the small print', *Local Government Chronicle*, 27 October, pp. 16–17.

Hambleton, R. (1990) *Urban Government in the 1990s: Lessons from the USA* (School for Advanced Urban Studies, University of Bristol).

Hambleton, R. (1991) 'American dreams, urban realities', *The Planner*, 28 June, pp. 6–9.

Hambleton, R. (1993) 'Reflections on urban government in the USA', *Policy and Politics*, vol. 21, no. 4, pp. 245–57.

Hambleton, R. and Hoggett, P. (eds) (1984) *The Politics of Decentralisation: Theory and Practice of a Radical Local Government Initiative*, Working Paper no. 46 (School for Advanced Urban Studies, University of Bristol).

Hambleton, R. and Hoggett, P. (1987) 'The democratisation of public services', in P. Hoggett and R. Hambleton (eds), *Decentralisation and Democracy: Localising Public Services* (School for Advanced Urban Studies, University of Bristol).

Hambleton, R. and Hoggett, P. and Tolan, F. (1989) 'The decentralisation of public services: a research agenda', *Local Government Studies*, January/February, pp. 39–56.

Hambleton, R. and Hoggett, P. (1990) *Beyond Excellence: Quality Local Government in the 1990s*, Working Paper no. 85 (School for Advanced Urban Studies, University of Bristol).

Hambleton, R. and Mills, L. (1993) 'Local government reform in Wales', *Local Government Policy Making*, vol. 19, no. 4, March, pp. 45–53.

Hambleton, R. and Warburton, M. (1991a) 'Left with absent words', *Local Government Chronicle*, 1 November.

Hambleton, R. and Warburton, M. (1991b) 'In search of a system which serves', *Local Government Chronicle*, 8 November.

Hambleton, R., Stewart, M. and Taylor, M. (1991) 'The strategic role of local government in the community' (Unpublished).

Hampton, W. (1987) *Local Government and Urban Politics* (London: Longman).

Handy, C. (1990) *The Age of Unreason* (London: Arrow Books).

Harlow Council (1990) *A Charter for Citizen's Rights*, Harlow Council, Information Services.

Harrop, K. J., Mason, T., Vielba, C. A. and Webster, B. A. (1978) *The Implementation and Development of Area Management* (Institute of Local Government Studies, University of Birmingham).

Havel, V. (1992) *Summer Meditations on Politics, Morality and Civility in a Time of Transition* (London: Faber and Faber).

Heater, D. (1990) *Citizenship: The Civic Ideal in World History, Politics and Education* (London: Longman).

Heery, E. (1984) 'Decentralisation in Islington', in R. Hambleton and P. Hoggett (eds), *The Politics of Decentralisation: Theory and Practice of a Radical Local Government Initiative*, Working Paper No. 46 (School for Advanced Urban Studies, University of Bristol).

Held, D. (1986) 'Introduction: new forms of democracy?', in D. Held and C. Pollitt (eds), *New Forms of Democracy* (London: Sage).

Held, D. (1987) *Models of Democracy* (Cambridge: Polity Press).

Held, D. and Pollitt, C. (eds), (1986) *New Forms of Democracy* (London: Sage).

Herbert, Sir E. (Chairman) (1960) *Report of the Royal Commission on Local Government in London*, Cmnd 1164 (London: HMSO).

Hinshelwood, R. (1987) *What Happens in Groups?* (London: Free Association Books).

Hirschman, A.O. (1970) *Exit, Voice and Loyalty* (Cambridge, Mass.: Harvard University Press).

Hirst, P. (1992) 'There is an alternative', *Chartist*, no. 137, pp. 30–1.

HM Government (1991) *The Citizen's Charter*, Cm 1599 (London: HMSO).

HM Treasury (1991) *Competing for Quality: Buying Better Public Services*, CM 1730 (London: HMSO).

Hodge, M. (1987) 'Central/local conflicts: the view from Islington', in P. Hoggett and R. Hambleton (eds), *Decentralisation and Democracy: Localising Public Services* (School for Advanced Urban Studies, University of Bristol).

Hodgson, G. (1988) *Economics and Institutions: A Manifesto for a Modern Institutional Economics* (Cambridge: Polity Press).

Hoggett, P. (1987) 'Going beyond a rearrangement of the deckchairs', in P. Hoggett and R. Hambleton (eds), *Decentralisation and Democracy: Localising Public Services* (School for Advanced Urban Studies University of Bristol).

Hoggett, P. (1990a) 'Modernisation, political strategy and the welfare state: an organisational perspective', *Studies in Decentralisation and Quasi-Markets*, no. 2 (School for Advanced Urban Studies, University of Bristol).

Hoggett, P. (1990b) *The Future of Central Services* (Luton: Local Government Management Board).

Hoggett, P. (1991) 'A new management in the public sector?', *Policy and Politics*, vol. 19, no. 4, pp. 143–56.

Hoggett, P. (1992a) *Partisans in an Uncertain World: The Psychoanalysis of Engagement* (London: Free Association Books).

Hoggett, P. (1992b) 'A place for experience: a psychoanalytic perspective on boundary, identity and culture', *Environment and Planning D: Society and Space*, vol. 10, pp. 345–56.

Hoggett, P. and Bramley, G. (1989) 'Devolution of local budgets', *Public Money and Management*, Winter, pp. 9–13.

Hoggett, P. and Burns, D. (1991) 'The revenge of the poor: the anti-poll tax campaign in Scotland and England', *Critical Social Policy*, vol. 33, pp. 95–110.

Hoggett, P. and Hambleton, R. (1987) (eds) *Decentralisation and Democracy: Localising Public Services* (School for Advanced Urban Studies, University of Bristol).

Hoggett, P. and McGill, I. (1988) 'Labourism: means and ends', *Critical Social Policy*, vol. 23, pp. 22–33.

Hoggett, P., Lawrence, S. and Fudge, C. (1984) 'The politics of decentralisation in Hackney', in R. Hambleton and P. Hoggett (eds), *The Politics of Decentralisation: Theory and Practice of a Radical Local Government Initiative*, Working Paper 46 (School for Advanced Urban Studies, University of Bristol).

Holmes, A. (1992) *Limbering Up: Community Empowerment on Peripheral Estates* (Brighton: Delta Press).

Holmes, C. (1976) 'Self-help housing', in P. Hain (ed), *Community Politics* (London: John Calder).

Hood, C. (1990) *Beyond the Public Bureaucracy State? Public Administration in the 1990s* (Inaugural Lecture: London School of Economics).

Hood, C. (1991) 'A public management for all seasons?', *Public Administration*, vol. 69, Spring, pp. 3–19.

Husbands, C. (1982) 'East End racism 1900–1980', *London Journal*, vol. 8, no. 1, pp. 3–26.

Insight (1989) 'Cleaning up the Tower', 8 November, p. 3.

International City Management Association (1989) *The Citizen as Customer* (Washington, DC: International City Management Association).

Islington Labour Party (1982) *A Socialist Programme for Islington*.

Islington Labour Party Working Group on Decentralisation (1981) *Decentralising Social Services in Islington*, Discussion paper.

Islington Labour Party (1986) *Council Manifesto 1986*.

Islington Labour Party (1990) *Islington Labour's Manifesto 1990–94*.

Jones, D. and Mayo, M. (eds), (1974) *Community Work One* (London: Routledge and Kegan Paul).

Jones, G. and Stewart, J. (1983) *The Case for Local Government* (London: George Allen and Unwin).

Judd, D. and Parkinson, M. (eds), (1990) *Leadership and Urban Regeneration* (London: Sage).

Kanter, R. (1984) *The Change Masters: Corporate Entrepreneurs at Work* (London: Unwin).

Keane, J. (1988) *Democracy and Civil Society* (London: Verso).

Keating, M. (1991) *Comparative Urban Politics* (Aldershot: Edward Elgar).

Khan, U. (1989) 'Neighbourhood forums: the Islington experience', *Local Government Policy Making*, vol. 16, no. 2, September, pp. 27–33.

Labour Party (1991) *Citizen's Charter: Labour's Better Deal for Consumers and Citizens* (London: The Labour Party).

Lane, C. (1988) 'Industrial change in Europe: the pursuit of flexible specialization in Britain and West Germany', *Work, Employment and Society*, vol. 2, no. 2.

Lansley, S., Goss, S. and Wolmar, C. (1989) *Councils in Conflict: The Rise and Fall of the Municipal Left* (London: Macmillan).

Lawson, E., Goodman, L. and Mowat, S. (1989) *Liam Johnson Review: Report of Panel of Inquiry* (London Borough of Islington).

Layfield Committee (1976) *Report of the Committee of Enquiry into Local Government Finance*, Cmnd 6453 (London: HMSO).

Le Grand, J. (1990) *Quasi-markets and Social Policy*, July (School for Advanced Urban Studies, University of Bristol).

Leborgne, D. and Lipietz, A. (1987) New technologies, new modes of regulation: some spatial implications', Paper given to the International Conference on technology, Restructuring and Urban/Regional Development, Dubrovnik.

Local Government Management Board (1988) *Learning from the Public* (Luton: Local Government Management Board) (previously known as the Local Government Training Board).

Local Government Training Board (1987) *Getting Closer to the Public* (Luton, LGTB).

Logan, J. R. and Molotch, H. (1987) *Urban Fortunes: The Political Economy of Place* (Berkeley, Calif.: University of California Press).

Logan, J. R. and Swanstrom, T. (eds), (1990) *Beyond the City Limits* (Philadelphia, Pa.: Temple University Press).

London Borough of Islington (1984) *Setting up Advisory Councils in Decentralised Neighbourhood Areas*, Paper for consultation, June.

London Borough of Islington (1985) *Neighbourhood Forums: Public Guidelines. Have Your Say on Your Neighbourhood.*

London Borough of Islington (1986) *Going Local: Decentralisation in Practice*, December.

London Borough of Islington (1989) *Review of Neighbourhood Forums*, Report by Chief Executive to the Neighbourhood Services Sub-Committee, 11 September.

London Borough of Islington (1990) *Gillespie Neighbourhood Action Action Plan*.

London Borough of Islington (1991) *The Composition of Neighbourhood Forums: Findings of a Survey Conducted in June 1990.*

London Borough of Tower Hamlets (1986) *Power to the Hamlets: Decentralisation – What this Will Mean for You* (Publicity leaflet for residents).

London Research Centre (1990) *Comparative Housing Statistics.*

Loney, M. (1983) *Community Against Government: The British Community Development Project 1968–78* (London: Heinemann).

Loney, M. *et al.* (eds) (1987) *The State or the Market: Politics and Welfare in Contemporary Britain* (London: Sage).

Lowndes, V. and Stoker, G. (1992a) 'An evaluation of neighbourhood decentralisation – Part 1', *Policy and Politics*, vol. 20, no. 1, pp. 47–61.

Lowndes, V. and Stoker, G. (1992b) 'An evaluation of neighbourhood decentralisation – Part 2', *Policy and Politics*, vol. 20, no. 2, pp. 143–52.

Mackintosh, M. and Wainwright, H. (eds), (1987) *A Taste of Power: The Politics of Local Economics* (London: Verso).

Marquand, D. (1989) 'Subversive language of citizenship', *Guardian*, 2 January.

Marris, P. and Rein, M. (1974) *Dilemmas of Social Reform: Poverty and Community Action in the United States* (Harmondsworth: Penguin).

Marshall, T. H. (1950) *Citizenship and Social Class* (Cambridge University Press).

Mather, G. (1990) 'Radical steps?', *Public Money and Management*, Autumn, pp. 18–19.

McCafferty, P. and Riley, D. (1989) *A Study of Co-operative Housing* (London: HMSO).

McLean, I. (1986) 'Mechanisms for democracy', in D. Held and C. Pollitt (eds), *New Forms of Democracy* (London: Sage).

Menzies Lyth, I. (1988) *Containing Anxiety in Institutions: Selected Essays*, vol. 1 (London: Free Association Books).

Michels, R. (1959) *Political Parties: A Sociological Study of the Oligarchical Tendences of Modern Democracy* (New York: Dover).

Miller, C. (1992) 'Public service trade unionism and the decentralisation of the local state', Unpublished PhD thesis (School for Advanced Urban Studies, University of Bristol).

Miller, C. and Bryant, D. (1990) 'Community Work in the UK: reflections on the 1980s', *Community Development Journal*, vol. 25, no. 4, pp. 316–25.

Milner, L., Ash, A. and Ritchie, P. (1991) *Quality in Action: A Resource Pack for Improving Services for People with Learning Difficulties* (University of Bristol, Norah Fry Research Centre).

Mintzberg, H. (1979) *The Structuring of Organisations* (Englewood Cliffs, NJ: Prentice Hall).

Morgan, G. (1986) *Images of Organisation* (London: Sage).

MORI (1987) *Service Provision and Living Standards in Islington* (London: MORI).

MORI (1990) *Tower Hamlets Residents' Attitudes Survey* (London: MORI).

Morphet, J. (1987) 'Local authority decentralisation – Tower Hamlets goes all the way', *Policy and Politics*, vol. 15, no. 2, pp. 119–26.

Murray, F. (1983) 'The decentralisation of production – the decline of the mass collective worker', *Capital and Class*, vol. 19.

National Economic Development Office (NEDO) (1986) *Changing Working Patterns: How Companies Achieve Flexibility to Meet New Needs* (London: NEDO).

Nozick, R. (1974) *Anarchy, State and Utopia* (London: Basil Blackwell).

O'Connor, J. (1973) *The Fiscal Crisis of the State* (New York: St Martin's Press).

Offe, C. (1975) 'The theory of the capitalist state and the problem of policy formation', in Lindberg, L. *et al.* (eds), *Stress and Contradiction in Modern Capitalism* (New York: Lexington Books).

Offe, C. (1984) *Contradictions of the Welfare State* (London: Hutchinson).

Osborne, D. and Gaebler, T. (1992) *Reinventing Government* (New York: Plume).

Ouchi, W. (1980) 'Markets, bureaucracies and clans', *Administrative Science Quarterly*, vol. 25, pp. 120–42.

Pascale, R. (1991) *Managing on the Edge* (Harmondsworth: Penguin).

Pateman, C. (1970) *Participation and Democratic Theory* (Cambridge: University Press).

Perrin, J. (1986) *Democratically Elected Councils at Neighbourhood Level in Urban Areas* (Association of Neighbourhood Councils).

Peters, T. (1988) *Thriving on Chaos: Handbook for a Management Revolution* (London: Pan).

Peters, T. J. and Waterman, R. H. (1982) *In Search of Excellence* (New York: Harper & Row).

Peterson, P. E. (1981) *City Limits* (Chicago: University of Chicago Press).

Pfeffer, N. and Coote, A. (1991) *Is Quality Good for You?*, Social Policy Paper no. 5 (London: Institute for Public Policy Research).

Pickvance, C. (1985) 'The rise and fall of urban movements and the role of comparative analysis', *Environment and Planning D: Society and Space*, vol. 3, pp. 31–53.

Pickvance, C. and Preteceille, E. (1991) *State Restructuring and Local Power* (London: Pinter).

Pilkington, E. and Kendrick, T. (1987) 'Area repairs: a new deal for tenants or papering over the cracks?', in P. Hoggett and R. Hambleton (eds), *Decentralisation and Democracy: Localising Public Services* (School for Advanced Urban Studies, University of Bristol).

Piore, M. and Sabel, C. (1984) *The Second Industrial Divide* (New York: Basic Books).

Piratin, P. (1980) *Our Flag Stays Red* (London: Lawrence and Wishart).

Platt, S. (1987) 'The Liberals in power', *New Society*, 11 September, pp. 8–10.

Pollitt, C. (1990) *Managerialism and the Public Services: The Anglo-American Experience* (Oxford: Basil Blackwell).

Potter, J. (1988) 'Consumerism and the public sector: how well does the coat fit?', *Public Administration*, vol.66, Summer, pp. 149–64.

Powell, W. (1990) 'Neither market nor hierarchy: network forms of organisation', *Research in Organisational Behaviour*, vol. 12, pp. 295–336.

Power, A. (1984) *Local Housing Management: A Priority Estates Project Survey* (London: Department of the Environment).

Rao, N. (1993) *Managing Change: Councillors and the New Local Government* (York: Joseph Rowntree Foundation).

Rawls, J. (1972) *A Theory of Justice* (Oxford: Clarendon Press).

Redcliffe-Maud, Lord (Chairman) (1969) *Royal Commission on Local Government in England*, vol. 1, Report, Cmnd 4040 (London: HMSO).

Rhodes, R. (1987) 'Developing the public service orientation', *Local Government Studies*, May/June, pp. 63–73.

Ridley, N. (1988) *The Local Right: Enabling not Providing*, Policy Study no. 92 (London, Centre for Policy Studies).

Rowe, A. (1975) *Democracy Renewed: The Community Council in Practice* (London: Sheldon Press).

Salamon, L. and Abramson, A. (1982) *The Federal Budget and the Non-Profit Sector* (Washington, DC: Urban Institute Press).

Schattschneider, E. (1960) *The Semi-Sovereign People* (New York: Holt Rinehart).

Schein, E. (1985) *Organisational Culture and Leadership* (San Francisco: Jossey-Bass).

Schon, D. A. (1971) *Beyond the Stable State* (London: Maurice Temple Smith).

Schumacher, E. F. (1974) *Small is Beautiful* (London: Abacus).

Schumpeter, J. A. (1943) *Capitalism, Socialism and Democracy* (London: George Allen and Unwin).

Scott, A. J. (1988) 'Flexible production systems and regional development: the rise of new industrial spaces in North America and Western Europe', *International Journal of Urban and Regional Research*, vol. 12, no. 2, pp. 171–86.

Seabrook, J. (1984) *The Idea of Neighbourhood: What Local Politics Should be About* (London: Pluto Press).

Shiers, J. (1989) 'Information, decentralisation and customer care', *Going Local*, no. 14, November, pp. 13–15.

Smith, J. (1985) *Public Involvement in Local Government: A Survey in England and Wales* (London: Community Development Foundation).

Smith, L. (1981) 'Public participation in Islington – a case study', in L. Smith and D. Jones (eds), *Deprivation, Participation and Community Action* (London: Macmillan).

Stedman Jones, G. (1976) *Outcast London: A Study in the Relationship between Classes in Victorian Society* (Harmondsworth: Penguin).

Stewart, J. D. (1971) *Management in Local Government: A Viewpoint* (London: Charles Knight).

Stewart, J. (1974) *The Responsive Local Authority* (London: Charles Knight).

Stewart, J. (1986) *The New Management of Local Government* (London: George Allen and Unwin).

Stewart, J. (1992) *The Rebuilding of Public Accountability* (London: European Policy Forum).

Stewart, J. (1993) 'The limitations of government by contract', *Public Money and Management*, July, pp. 1–6.

Stewart, J. and Clarke, M. (1987) 'The public service orientation: issues and dilemmas', *Public Administration*, vol. 65, Summer, pp. 161–77.

Stewart, M. and Taylor M. (1993) *Local Government: The Community Leadership Role* (Luton: Local Government Management Board).

Stewart, M. and Whitting, G. (1983) *Ethnic Minorities and the Urban Programme*, Occasional Paper 9 (School for Advanced Urban Studies, University of Bristol).

Stoker, G. (1991) *The Politics of Local Government* (London: Macmillan).

Suttles, G. (1972) *The Social Construction of Communities* (Chicago: University of Chicago Press).

Taylor, M. (1992) *Signposts to Community Development* (London: Community Development Foundation).

294   *Bibliography*

Taylor, M. and Hoggett, P. (1993) 'Quasi-markets and the transformation of the independent sector', paper presented at 'Quasi-Markets: the Emerging Issues', a conference held at the University of Bristol, March 1993.

Taylor, M., Hoyes, L., Lart, R. and Means, R. (1991) 'User empowerment in community care: unravelling the issues', *Studies in Decentralisation and Quasi-Markets*, no. 11 (School for Advanced Urban Studies: University of Bristol).

Thatcher, M. (1987) Interview, *Woman's Own*, 31 October.

Thomas, C. (1987) 'Staff security in housing offices', *Going Local*, no. 7, March, pp. 14–15.

Thompson, J. (1967) *Organizations in Action* (New York: McGraw-Hill).

Thomson, W. (1990) 'Neighbourhood planning', Presentation to the Local Service Management course, School for Advanced Urban Studies, University of Bristol, 2 March.

Tomlinson, M. (1989) 'Restructuring Tower Hamlets: local authority, decentralisation as a response to crisis and change', MA thesis (Polytechnic of Central London).

Tower Hamlets Liberal Association (1986) *Handing Power to the Hamlets*.

Vickers, G. (1972) *Freedom in a Rocking Boat* (London: Pelican).

Wallman, S. (1982) *Living in South London* (London: Gower).

Walsall Labour Party (1980) *Walsall's Haul to Democracy – the Neighbourhood Concept* (Walsall: Labour Party).

Warren, R., Rosentraub, M. S., Weschler, L. F. (1992) 'Building urban governance: an agenda for the 1990s', *Urban Affairs Quarterly*, vol. 14, no. 3/4, pp. 399–422.

Weber, M. (1948) *From Max Weber: Essays in Sociology*, translated, edited and with an introduction by H. H. Gerth and C. W. Mills (London: Routledge and Kegan Paul).

Wheatley, Lord (Chairman) (1969) *Royal Commission on the Local Government in Scotland*, Report, Cmnd 4150 (Edinburgh: HMSO).

Whitfield, D. (1992) *The Welfare State: Privatisation, Deregulation and Commercialisation of Public Services: Alternative Strategies for the 1990s* (London: Pluto Press).

Widdicombe Report (1986) *The Conduct of Local Authority Business*, Report of the Committee of Inquiry. Cmnd 9797 (London: HMSO).

Williamson, O. (1985) *The Economic Institutions of Capitalism* (New York: Free Press).

Willmott, P. (1989) *Community Initiatives: Patterns and Prospects* (London: Policy Studies Institute).

Willmott, P. and Hutchinson, R. (eds), (1992) *Urban Trends 1* (London: Policy Studies Institute).

Willmott, P. and Young, M. (1957) *Family and Kinship in East London* (London: Penguin).

Wills, J. (1991) 'Chartered streets', *Local Government Chronicle*, 17 May, pp. 15–16.

Winnicott, D. (1974) *Playing and Reality* (Harmondsworth: Penguin).

Wood, S. (1989) 'New wave management?', *Work, Employment and Society*, vol. 3, no. 3, pp. 379–403.

Woolley, T. (ed) (1986) *The Characteristics of Community Architecture and Community Technical Aid*, Occasional Paper 85 (Department of Architecture and Building Science, University of Strathclyde).

Young, M. (1970) 'Parish councils for cities?', *New Society*, 29 January, pp. 178–9.

Index

access
  to benefits   43
  physical, to services   89;
    Islington   112–14
accountability
  bottom-down   277, 278
  democratic   277–8
  Islington neighbourhood
    forums   195
  staff   94
  top-up   277
  Tower Hamlets neighbourhood
    committees   203, 213–14
action plans   130–2
age composition
  Islington neighbourhood
    forums   191
  tenants' associations'
    leaders   236
Anti-Poll Tax Unions   38, 269
area committee systems   14–15, 36
  citizen participation   168–9
Ashdown, Paddy
  citizenship   49
  Tower Hamlets   217
autonomy of local
    authorities   10–12, 74, 148
  Tower Hamlets   136–40

back-line/front-line
    concept   106–7
Bangladeshi population, Tower
    Hamlets   53, 55, 207–8,
    216–17, 234
Barnes, Maurice   60
Basildon
  commitment to change   108
  decentralised services   91, 92
  devolved management   102
  generic working   96, 108–9

multiservice neighbourhood
    offices   99
openness of neighbourhood
    offices   90
Beackon, Derek   139
Birmingham
  one-stop service   92
  participation, citizen   168–9;
    parish councils   173
block elections   205
Bow
  Action Plan   130, 131
  consultative forum   205–6
  neighbourhood committee   206
  'neighbourhood
    inspection'   212–13
Bradford
  devolved management   102
  matrix management   100
  participation, citizen   169
British National Party (BNP)   139,
    217, 218
bureaucracy, democracy
    without   270–3

Cairns, John   167
Camden   37
capital mobility   8
Capital Programme Teams   126
child abuse   97
choice of services   43–5
  and participation, public   155–6
citizens' charters   167–8
  Citizen's Charter   5, 260
citizenship   46–50, 51
  operational   265
civil rights   47, 49
civil society   242–5
  democratic capability   278–9
clients   39–41, 51

Cloverhall Tenants'
Association 173
Co-operative Retail Society 274
co-operatives, tenant
management 173
co-option 36
collaborative working 144
collective choice 155
Collins, Brenda 129
Commission of Racial Equality
(CRE) 137–8
community
constructions of 224–34;
Islington 71–3; Tower
Hamlets 71–3;
Walsall 69
development: participatory
democracy 37, 38;
political
innovations 15–16
politicisation of 210–13
community action groups 19–20
community care 267–8
Community Care Act (1990) 97
community charge (poll tax) 17
abolition 259
capping 17, 254
opposition 38, 269
community councils 169
see also parish councils
Community Development
Projects 16
Community Health Services 87
competition
capital mobility 8
introduction 22–3
new right 33
comprehensiveness of
services 91–3
Conservative Party
Heath government
(1970–74) 13–14, 259
Major government
(1990–) 258–62
new public management 84–5
Thatcher government (1979–90):
change in public
services 4–5, 32–3; civic

marketing 165; local
government battles 16–17;
local government
finance 253–5;
policies 61
consistency throughout
organisations 94
consultation 167–9
cynical 165
neighbourhood forums,
Islington 183
consultative forums, Tower
Hamlets 205–8
consumer democracy 264, 265,
266–8
consumers 43–6, 51
and citizenship 48–9
consumption, community as basis
of 225
contractual control 82–3, 175–6
control
delegated 172–6, 178–9
and participation,
public 155–6, 162–3,
174–9
core–periphery model 271, 273
corporate management,
local 98–101
Tower Hamlets 128
corporate plans 130
costs of decentralisation 142–3
council tax 259
capping 17, 254
cultural change 104–7, 112, 147–8
Islington 143–5
Tower Hamlets 143–5
customer care programmes 41–2
participation, citizen 166
customers 41–3, 51
and clients 40
cynical consultation 165
Czechoslovakia 153

decentralisation, definitions 6
decentralised management 147–9
decision-making,
decentralised 169–72
delegate democracy 19

delegated control, citizen
    participation   172–6, 178–9
delivery, service   124–6
democratisation   7
'dented shield' strategy   61
Department of the
    Environment   15
deprivation, social   55
design of neighbourhood
    offices   90–1
    Islington   114, 119
deskilling   98
development, community
    participatory democracy   37, 38
    political innovations   15–16
devolved management   101–4,
    111–12, 147
    empowerment, citizen   159
    Islington   132–6;
        efficiency   140–2
    Tower Hamlets   132–6;
        efficiency   140–2
direct democracy   264, 265–6
disabled people, Islington
    neighbourhood forums   191
discontinuity, representative
    democracy   263–5
discrimination
    equal opportunities objectives,
        Islington   144–5
    racism: Tower Hamlets   137–9;
        and Liberalism   216–18;
        Stepney   229–35, 241–2
District Health Authorities   87
docks, Tower Hamlets   65
dual labour markets   9
Dunfermline   92

economic restructuring   7–9
education
    central government policy   255
    political, and neighbourhood
        forums   196–7
    school governing bodies   161
Education Reform Act (1988)   23
efficiency, service   140–2
elections, county councils   34
    voter turnout   34, 210–13

empowerment
    of citizens   31–4, 157–79,
        269–70; fragmented
        communities   250–1;
        importance   154;
        neighbourhood forums,
        Islington   186, 198–200
    of local government   256–8
entrusted control   176, 178–9
equal opportunities   144–5
Estate Management
    Boards   172–3
ethnic minorities
    Islington   55; neighbourhood
        forums   191
    Tower Hamlets   53, 55, 70;
        Bangladeshi
        population   53, 55, 207–8,
        216–17, 234
exit   24–5
    empowerment   31–2, 33
    loyalty   42–3
expenditure decisions   *see* financial
    management
external decentralisation   82–3

Fife   92
financial management
    devolved   103, 106–7;
        Islington   132–3; Tower
        Hamlets   133–4
    empowerment, citizen   160–1
    Islington neighbourhood
        forums   184
    public expenditure restraints   16
Finsbury
    community   73
    neighbourhood forum   193–4,
        197; land-use
        planning   185–6
flexibility of services   94–101, 109,
    111, 147
    Islington   124–32
    Tower Hamlets   124–32
flexible specialisation   8
Flounders, Eric   65, 67, 70, 73
    representative democracy   203
'Fordist' regime   8

fragmented communities 223
  empowerment, citizen 250–1
  Stepney 228–35

gender balance, neighbourhood
    forums 190
'general good' 280–2
general practitioners 98
generic working 95–8, 108–9, 118,
  124
  efficiency 142
  Islington 125–6
  Tower Hamlets 125
Gillespie Neighbourhood Action
    Plan 131–2
Glasgow
  community councils 169
  multiple service shops 92
Globe Town
  Bangladeshi community 209
  consultative forum 205–6
Greater London Council
  creation 13
  participatory democracy 37, 154

Hackney 109
Haringey
  multidisciplinary project
    teams 97
  participation, citizen 168
  staff accountability 94
Harlow
  citizens' charter 167
  decentralised services 91
  devolved management 102
Havel, Václav 153
Heath government
    (1970–74) 13–14, 259
Herbert Commission 13
heritage, community as 225
Hertfordshire 92
Heseltine, Michael 255, 258
Higgins, Martin 62
Hodge, Margaret 60–1
home care services
  Islington 123; cultural
    change 144
  Tower Hamlets 123–4

horizontal integration 271
housing
  decentralisation 86
  generic working 96
  Islington: characteristics 53;
    flexibility 124;
    localisation 117; rent
    arrears 140–2; tenants'
    associations 188
  Lambeth 109
  participation, citizen 169, 173
  Tower Hamlets:
    characteristics 55, 65;
    devolved
    management 135–6;
    flexibility 125;
    localisation 117;
    racism 137–9; rent
    arrears 140–2; tenants'
    associations 205–6, 209,
    228–35
Housing Act (1988) 23
Housing and Planning Act
    (1986) 173
Hughes, Peter 71
hype, civic 165

imagined communities 227–8,
  236–40
income tax, local 256–7
individual choice 155
industrial democracy 264, 265
information 44
  and participation,
    citizen 165–6, 167–9
  services 92–3
information technology, and
    bureaucracy 271
interdependent control 176–7,
  178–9
interest, communities of 227,
  240–2
internal decentralisation 82–3
Islington 52–6, 146–8
  commitment to change 108
  community, constructions
    of 71–3

Islington (*cont.*)
  costs of decentralisation   142
  decentralisation strategy   60–4
  decentralised services   91,
      109–10
  devolved management   132–6;
      efficiency   140–2
  flexibility   124–32
  localisation   114–24
  NALGO   97–8
  neighbourhood forums   174,
      200–1, 218–20, 245–6;
      composition   189–91;
      empowerment   198–200;
      membership and
      organisation   186–9;
      operation   192–4;
      organisational
      responsiveness   194–6;
      political education   196–7;
      proposals   180–2; scope
      and purpose   182–6
  neighbourhood repair teams   93
  participatory democracy   37
  politics   56–60; innovation   73–
      4, 76–7; and organisational
      structure   112–14

Kinnock, Neil   61

Labour Party
  citizens' charter   5
  Islington   57–9, 62, 76;
      participatory
      democracy   180, 182, 219
  Tower Hamlets   65, 66–7, 71,
      77; housing   136;
      neighbourhood
      committees   204–5;
      neighbourhood
      loyalties   128; rent
      arrears   142;
      Stepney   215–16, 231–2
  welfare state   75
Lambeth
  change, process of   109
  housing   109
land-use planning   184–6

Lewisham   90
Liam Johnson Review   122
Liberal Democrats   5
Liberal Party
  politicisation of local
      government   18
  Tower Hamlets   65–71, 72–3,
      76–7; Advanced Leasing
      Scheme   242; devolved
      management   135;
      neighbourhood
      committees   202–5, 212,
      219; 'principle of
      neighbourhood
      autonomy'   128, 137; and
      racism   138–9, 216–18,
      231; rent arrears   141–2;
      Stepney   214–16
Liverpool   90
local corporate
      management   98–101
  Tower Hamlets   128
Local Government (Access to
      Information) Act (1985)   167
Local Government Act (1972)
  neighbourhood forums   183
  parish councils   173
  two-tier structure   13
Local Government Act (1980)   23
Local Government Act (1988)   23
Local Government and Housing
      Act (1989)   254
  co-option   36
Local Government Finance Act
      (1992)   259
Local Government (Scotland) Act
      (1973)   14
localisation of services   89–94, 109,
      111, 147
  Islington   114–24
  support   146
  Tower Hamlets   114–24
locality, importance of   10–12, 74
London Government Act
      (1963)   13
Los Angeles
  community   226
  marketing   165

loyalty, customer 42–3

Major, John 5, 167
Major government
      (1990–) 258–62
management
   of change 145
   changes in 20–1
   by customers 120
   decentralised 147–9
   devolved 101–4, 111–12, 147;
         empowerment,
         citizen 159;
         Islington 132–6, 140–2;
         Tower Hamlets 132–6,
         140–2; local
         corporate 98–101; Tower
         Hamlets 128
   matrix 99–101
   neighbourhood 85–9;
         offices 61–3, 114–16
   'new public' 83–5
   operational 127–9
   strategic 129–32
Manchester
   change, process of 109
   information service 92–3
manufacturing sector
   dual labour markets 9
   and service sector 8
market models 5–7
marketing of cities 165
mass production 8
matrix management 99–101
McBride, John 137
membership
   neighbourhood forums 186–7,
      188
   organisations 275
Middlesbrough
   area committee system 168
   community councils 169
   matrix management 101
multidisciplinary teams 96–7
   Islington 124–5
   Tower Hamlets 125
multiple service shops 92

National Association of Local
      Government Officers
      (NALGO) 97, 126
National Health Service 87
need, unmet 94
needs-based budget
      allocation 133–4
Neighbourhood Action
      Plans 130–2
neighbourhood committees, Tower
      Hamlets 202–6
   participation 206–9
   politicisation of
         community 210–13
   power 183
neighbourhood
      decentralisation 6–7
neighbourhood forums,
      Islington 200–1
   composition 189–91
   empowerment 198–200
   membership and
         organisation 186–9
   operation 192–4
   organisational
         responsiveness 194–6
   political education 196–7
   proposals 180–2
   scope and purpose 182–6
Neighbourhood Government Act
      (1975) 164
neighbourhood management 85–9
Neighbourhood Managers,
      Islington 133, 184
neighbourhood repair teams 97
   Islington 93
Neighbourhood Services
      Department, Islington 62,
      133
'new public management' 83–5
'new' regime 8
'new right' 32–3
Newcastle
   area committee system 168
   participation, citizen 171
nominal devolution 101–2
non-participation, citizen 162,
      164–6

North Staffordshire Health
    Authority   100
North Tyneside   92
Norwich
    generic working   96
    neighbourhood offices   90

objectives of decentralisation   87,
    88
O'Halloran, Michael   58
oil shocks   8
one-stop services   92
    citizen participation   167
    Tower Hamlets   125
openness of neighbourhood
    offices   90–1
    Islington   114, 119
operational decisions
    empowerment, citizen   160–1
    flexibility   127–9
opportunism   246–8
'overspending' penalties   17

parish councils
    empowerment, citizen   161
    participation, citizen   173–4
    see also community councils
participation, public   153–8,
    166–74
    empowerment strategies   160–4
    Islington   57, 59–60
    political innovations   15–16
    spheres of power   158–60
participatory democracy   19, 264,
    265–8
    neighbourhood forums,
        Islington   200–1;
        composition   189–91;
        empowerment   198–200;
        membership and
        organisation   186–9;
        operation   192–4;
        organisational
        responsiveness   194–6;
        political education   196–7;
        proposals   180–2; scope
        and purpose   182–6

non-materialisation   15–16
    voice   34, 35–8
partnership, citizen
    participation   172–4
Performance Review
    Committee   135
peripatetic workers   118–19
physical accessibility of services   89
    Islington   112–14
place
    communities of   227–8
    marketing   165
planning, strategic   130–2
pluralistic public sphere   273–7
polarisation, social   9, 56
polarised communities   223
    empowerment, citizen   250–1
    Stepney   228–35
policy-making   160–1
political citizenship   47–8
political democracy   264, 265
political education   196–7
politicisation
    of community   210–13
    of local government   18–19
politics of local
    communities   19–20
poll tax   17
    abolition   259
    capping   17, 254
    opposition   38, 269
Poplar   204, 205
population characteristics
    Islington   53, 55, 72
    Tower Hamlets   53, 55, 72
'post-Fordism' debate   81–2
power, community as   225
primary labour market   9
professionalised departments   91–2
provision, community as basis
    of   225
public expenditure, restraints   16
    see also financial management
public participation   *see*
    participation, public
public relations   167
publicity
    cities   165

neighbourhood forums,
  Islington 192
purchasing points, local 92

quality
  culture 107
  service 120
Quality Action Groups 170–1
quasi-public institutions 276

racism, Tower Hamlets 137–9
  and Liberalism 216–18
  Stepney 229–35, 241–2
radical devolution 101
rate capping 17, 254
ratepayer democracy 19
Rates Act (1984) 254
redress, consumer 44
reliability of services 118
Renfrew 91
rent arrears 140–2
representation, consumer 44
representative democracy 263–7
  extension 277–8
  Tower Hamlets 202–6, 213–16;
    participation 206–9;
    politicisation of
    community 210–13;
    racism 216–18
  voice 34, 35–7
responsiveness,
  organisational 194–6
revenue support grant 17
riots, urban 9
risk-taking 107
  Tower Hamlets 145
Rochdale
  change, process of 108
  community development 37
  information service 92–3
  participation, citizen 171–2;
    Cloverhall Co-
    operative 173
  staff accountability 84
Royal Commission on Local
  Government in England 13
Royal Commission on Local
  Government in Scotland 13

safety, staff 90–1
school governing bodies 161
Schumacher, E.F. 14
secondary labour market 9
self-improvement 27
service sector 8
Shipley 100
social citizenship 47–8
Social Democratic Party (SDP)
  defections to 58, 76
  Islington 58
  politicisation of local
    government 18
social exchange principle 262
social polarisation 9, 56
social relationships, community
  as 225
social work
  community development 38
  Islington 121–4
South Somerset
  matrix management 100–1
  participation, citizen 169
specialisation, flexible 8
specialist posts
  Islington 124–5
  Tower Hamlets 125
stability and localisation 120
staff
  accountability 94
  attitudes to localisation 120,
    121
  collaboration 144
  cover 118–19
  loyalty 128
  safety 90–1
  skills 93
  training 106
Standard Spending Assessments
  (SSAs) 134
Stepney
  Bangladeshi community 209
  consultative forums 205–6
  neighbourhood committee 206
  polarised communities 228–35,
    241–2
  problems 214–16
Stockport 14–15, 168

strategic management 129–32
subsidiarity principle 257

taxation, local 256–7
  council tax 259; capping 17,
    254
  poll tax 17; abolition 259;
    capping 17, 254;
    opposition 38, 269
  rate capping 17, 254
tenant management
  co-operatives 173
tenants' associations
  age profile of leaders 236
  Islington 188
  Tower Hamlets 205–6, 209;
    Stepney 228–35
Thatcher, Margaret 49
Thatcher government (1979–90)
  change in public services 4–5,
    32–3
  civic marketing 165
  local government battles 16–17
  local government finance 253–5
  policies 61
Thurrock 92
Tower Hamlets 52–6, 149–50
  autonomy, local 128, 136–40
  change, process of 108, 109
  community, constructions
    of 71–3
  costs of decentralisation 142–3
  decentralisation strategy 67–71
  decentralised services 91, 92
  devolved management 102,
    132–6; efficiency 140–2
  flexibility 124–32
  generic working 96, 98
  Liberalism and racism 216–18
  localisation 114–21, 123–4
  multiservice neighbourhood
    offices 99
  opportunism 247–8
  participation, citizen 174,
    202–9, 218–20, 245–6
  polarised communities 228–35,
    241–2
  politicisation of
    community 210–13

politics 64–7;
  innovation 73–4, 76–7;
  and organisational
    structure 112–14
  problems 213–16
turnout, voter 34, 210–13
Tyneside, North 92

United States of America
  influence in British local
    government 260
  Los Angeles: community 226;
    marketing 165;
  Neighbourhood Government Act
    (1975) 164
unrest, urban 9
urban parish councils 36
user groups
  participatory democracy 38
  success 170–1

vertical integration 271
violence against staff 90–1
virement 99
  Tower Hamlets 135
voice 24, 26
  empowerment 31–2, 33–8
  loyalty 42–3
  Tower Hamlets 207
voluntary organisations 275–6

Walker, Neil 129, 137
Walsall
  change, process of 108, 109
  community 69
  customer loyalty 43
  generic working 96, 98
  Labour Party 18
  openness, neighbourhood
    offices 90
  politicisation of local
    government 18
  staff training 106
welfare state 74–5
Williams, Bryn 65
women, Islington neighbourhood
  forums 190

York 167